Turkey and the EU in an Energy Security Society

Dicle Korkmaz

Turkey and the EU in an Energy Security Society

The Case of Natural Gas

palgrave
macmillan

Dicle Korkmaz
Department of Political Science and International Relations
Antalya Bilim University
Antalya, Turkey

ISBN 978-3-030-45773-0 ISBN 978-3-030-45774-7 (eBook)
https://doi.org/10.1007/978-3-030-45774-7

Cover illustration: Vladislav Mitic/Alamy Stock Photo

This Palgrave Macmillan imprint is published by the registered company Springer Nature Switzerland AG.
The registered company address is: Gewerbestrasse 11, 6330 Cham, Switzerland

In loving memory of my father…

Acknowledgements

The journey of this book has been a long one, with many ups and downs. The book has its origins in my PhD thesis and is continued as a book. I am grateful for the support of many people and institutions during this long process each of which helped me to overcome difficult times and share happy moments.

I am indebted above all to my supervisor, Pami Aalto. Without his support and supervision, I would not have been able to reach this stage. His insightful comments and criticism always came at the right time and made me question my thoughts and writing. He did this in such a professional way so as not to deprive me of my independence. I was honoured to have Mert Bilgin and Pekka Korhonen as my external examiners, and Eero Palmujoki as my internal examiner. I am grateful to them and the valuable comments and feedback I received that allowed me to question my approaches and improve the text.

I received funding during and after my PhD from various institutions. I would like to thank Tuomas Forsberg, the Director of the National Graduate School of Political Studies (POLITU), and the administrative staff of the POLITU, which funded me between 2010 and 2014. In addition to POLITU, I received funding from the Centre for International Mobility (Finland) and travel funding from the POLITU, Tampere University, the Finland Peace Research Association and the Scientific and Technological Research Council of Turkey (TUBITAK). I had the opportunity to complete a post-doc to update my data and revise the thesis to be published as a book. Adapting the PhD thesis into a book would not have been possible without TUBITAK's post-doc scholarship, which I was awarded for the period of January to June 2019.

I am grateful to the academic and administrative staff of the Tampere University, Faculty of Management and Business for their support in my doctoral studies. It was an incredibly friendly and professional environment that I always felt very lucky to be a part of. Among the academic and administrative staff, I would like to thank in particular Tapani Turkka, who also provided me feedback to improve the text, Minna Höijer, Riitta Lehtimäki, Sirke Mäkinen, Maija Mattila, Hanna Ojanen and Sanna Tuurnas. During my doctoral studies, I had the opportunity to be a visiting scholar at The George Washington University, Elliott School of International Affairs, Institute for European, Russian and Eurasian Studies between January and June 2012. I am grateful to my supervisor Robert Orttung for his support. Furthermore, I completed two Erasmus work placements, one at the Middle East Technical University, European Research Centre and one at the Ankara University European Research Centre. I would like to particularly thank Serif Onur Bahcecik, Sanem Baykal, Erdem Denk, Atila Eralp, and Özgehan Şenyuva for their belief in my studies.

My post-doc studies would not have been accomplished without the support of Antalya Bilim University. I'd like to thank my colleagues at the Department of Politics and International Relations for the invaluable friendship and their contribution to our academic environment, which is a perfect combination of amateur spirit and professional attitude. During the process of adapting the PhD thesis into a book, I had the opportunity to be a visiting fellow at The Oxford Institute for Energy Studies for six months in 2019. I had the privilege to get feedback from Patrick Heather, James Henderson, Anouk Honoré, David Ledesma, Simon Pirani, Gulmira Rzayeva, Jack Sharples and Katja Yafimava. I am grateful for their constructive comments on how to improve the related sections. Furthermore, I'd like to thank Kate Teasdale for her administrative support and Andrew Hudson for his help in obtaining access to the Institute's rich database. Moreover, I appreciate the support of Erisa Senerdem, Deputy Editor of Argus Media, for finding the recent data.

I conducted interviews with policy makers, representatives of the private sector, non-governmental organisations and think-tanks in Turkey in 2011, 2012 and 2018. I am grateful to all my interviewees whose names need to be kept anonymous. I participated in many doctoral seminars and international conferences during and after my doctoral studies where I was faced with many critical questions and constructive comments which contributed a lot to my thinking. I would like to particularly thank Andrei Belyi, Milja Kurki, Heikki Patomäki and Evgeny Roshchin within this context. I would like to thank Ambassador Cagatay Erciyes for his support. I owe special thanks to Virginia Mattila and Ariel Surface for proofreading and improving the language of the text.

I am indebted to my friends in Finland and Turkey for all their help, support and friendship and for the enjoyable times we spent together. I am grateful to Johanna Muukkonen, Achillefs Papageorgiou, Mikko Perkiö and Tarja Seppä for the wonderful years we had during my stay in Finland. I am lucky to have the friendship of Burak Toygar Halistoprak, who also read some of the chapters and provided feedback to improve the text, Isil Cerem Cenker Ozek and Ozlem Badak. I have felt the support of Emre Temel in different periods of my life. I'd like to thank him for his patience, tolerance and encouraging attitude.

The research process and this book not only contributed to my efforts to be a part of academia but also afforded me an opportunity to gain new friends, colleagues and strengthen my relationships.

I am grateful to my family… I feel their support in my heart for all my decisions. I'd like to thank my sister, Deniz Korkmaz, my brother-in-law, Suhan Cumhur Guler, my nephew and niece, Alp and Mina, for all the trust and joy they bring to my life. I am indebted to my mum and dad, Ayten Korkmaz and Tevfik Korkmaz (RIP). Words are insufficient for how much I appreciate their continuous faith and infinite support.

Antalya
February 2020

Contents

Abbreviations

AKP	Justice and Development Party
BO	Build-Operate
BOT	Build-Operate-Transfer
BOTAS	Petroleum Pipeline Company
CEO	Chief Executive Officer
CHP	Republican People's Party
CS	Copenhagen School
EMRA	Energy Market Regulatory Authority
ES	English School
EU	European Union
GDP	Gross Domestic Product
HDP	People's Democratic Party
ICJ	International Court of Justice
IEA	International Energy Agency
IMF	International Monetary Fund
IP	Good Party
ITE	Iran-Turkey-Europe
LNG	Liquefied natural gas
MEP	Member of European Parliament
MHP	Nationalist Movement Party
MP	Member of Parliament
MUSIAD	Independent Industrialists' and Businessmen's Association
OPEC	Organisation of the Petroleum Exporting Countries
PETFORM	Petroleum Platform Association
SCO	Shanghai Cooperation Organisation
SOCAR	State Oil Company of Azerbaijan Republic
TANAP	Trans Anatolian Pipeline

TEIAS	Turkish Electricity Transmission Corporation
THY	Turkish Airlines
TMMOB	Union of Chambers of Turkish Engineers and Architects
TPAO	Turkish Petroleum Corporation
TRNC	Turkish Republic of Northern Cyprus
TUSIAD	Turkish Industry and Business Association
UNCITRAL	United Nations Commission on International Trade Law
UNCLOS	United Nations Convention on the Law of the Sea
WTO	World Trade Organization

List of Figures

List of Tables

CHAPTER 1

Introduction

In their letter of congratulations to President Recep Tayyip Erdogan following Turkey's June 2018 presidential elections, Donald Tusk, the President of the European Council, and Jean-Claude Juncker, the President of the European Commission, highlighted energy as one of the areas of common interest in Turkey-European Union (EU) relations. Three months prior, before flying to Brussels to meet with Tusk and Juncker, Erdogan included energy among the topics for co-operation with the EU (Cumhurbaskani Erdogan 2018). Given Turkey's long wait for membership since 1959, deteriorating relations between Turkey and the EU in recent years and Turkey's intensifying relations with Russia, energy plays a significant role in the relations between Turkey and the EU.

The concept of a book[1] on Turkey-EU energy relations in the sphere of natural gas began with the EU's inclusion of Turkey within the framework of the pan-European energy community in the 2006 Green Paper. The term referred to a "common regulatory space around Europe" (European Commission 2006, p. 16) which included all energy producers, consumers and transit states in Europe, Eurasia, the Middle East and the Mediterranean coast. Within this scope, Turkey was also mentioned by name along with Ukraine, Norway, Algeria, Caspian and Mediterranean countries, the EU-Maghreb electricity market and the EU-Mashrek gas market. It was expected that the pan-European energy community would serve as a tool for the EU and all other countries and regions within the Community to achieve energy security. EU terminology defines energy security as the

D. Korkmaz, *Turkey and the EU in an Energy Security Society*,
https://doi.org/10.1007/978-3-030-45774-7_1

secure, competitive and sustainable supply of energy (European Commission 2006, p. 16). Furthermore, underlying the fact that energy policy is often considered to be a tool in the foreign policies of energy producers and transit countries, the Commission stated in its Energy Union Package dated 2015 that the EU would use all foreign policy instruments to establish strategic energy partnerships with producers and transit countries, including Turkey (European Commission 2015, pp. 2, 6).

These efforts arose from EU concerns on energy security. Energy security in natural gas is important considering the significant share of natural gas in the EU's energy mix, accounting for 23.8 per cent in 2017, as well as declining indigenous reserves. Overall EU energy import dependency in 2017 was 55.1 per cent, well-below the corresponding figure of 74.3 per cent for gas (European Commission 2019, pp. 22, 24). The EU seeks to achieve energy security through internal and external integration. For the EU, internal integration means the establishment of an internal energy market within the EU, while external integration refers to energy relations and the development of a pan-European energy community with non-EU nations. The development of common trade, transit and environmental rules in order to harmonise and integrate markets "would create a predictable and transparent market to stimulate investment and growth, as well as security of supply, for the EU and its neighbors" (European Commission 2006, p. 16). Thus, concerns on energy security necessitate initiatives, of which Turkey is deemed a part.

Of equal significance is the manner in which Turkey perceives itself in the pan-European energy community in general and its energy security and relations with the EU in the sphere of natural gas in particular. Turkey's relations with the EU are exceptional considering the history of its decades-long membership process. The Association Agreement signed in 1963 envisaged three phases of the accession: preparation, transitional and final phases. It was foreseen that the final stage would be based on a customs union, which was established in 1996, and would include closer co-ordination of economic policies. Turkey's candidacy to the EU was declared in 1999 and membership negotiations began in 2005. However, relations have deteriorated since 2008 due to domestic dynamics in Turkey and the EU as well as changes in global politics. Turkey has pursued a foreign policy that seeks greater autonomy and aims to intensify its relations with Russia and other non-Western countries (Oguzlu 2018; Keyman

2017; Unay 2016). Therefore, the positions of Turkish and European actors on energy security deserve attention, bearing in mind the regional and global developments and their repercussions on Turkish foreign policy.

This book thus aims to understand the extent to which the positions of Turkish actors on energy security in the sphere of natural gas constrain and/or enable integration with the EU. This will allow us to better comprehend the position in which the various Turkish actors aim to locate Turkey within the pan-European energy community in the sphere of natural gas, and to what extent this position overlaps with that desired by the EU. To achieve this goal, the book utilises two tools: the English School (ES) theory of International Relations (IR) and narrative policy analysis. The ES theory of IR, particularly Barry Buzan's approach, is used to identify the type of integration sought by the actors and the main motivations behind their preferences. In the book, integration does not necessarily mean full membership to the EU; there are different types of integrations, as elaborated on in Chap. 2. Narrative policy analysis, the second tool, is used here to comprehend and compare the positions of EU and Turkish actors. A narrative is "a kind of story told by someone (a "narrator") with a beginning, middle and end" (Esterberg 2002, p. 182) and thus represents a cognitive map of narrators. Utilisation of these tools provides identification of the main dynamics in the narratives of the EU actors on Turkey's role in the European energy security and the narratives of the Turkish actors on natural gas pipelines and the liberalisation of the Turkish natural gas market. Turkish actors` narratives on pipelines and the market serve as answers to the EU actors` narratives, as the latter have both geopolitical and market-oriented focuses. An examination of these narratives provides an understanding of the type of integration sought by both EU and Turkish actors in the sphere of natural gas.

The book offers two main contributions to the literature, one theoretical and one empirical. From a theoretical perspective, matters related to energy are often examined within the scope of geopolitics (Klare 2008 among others), economics (Bhattacharyya 2011; Bohi and Toman 1993 among others) or environmental studies (Luft et al. 2011; Brown and Dworkin 2011, among others). The geopolitical literature focuses on pipeline politics, energy shortages and crises through the lens of states, regional blocs, state-bound companies and political leaders. Dependencies and vulnerabilities of suppliers, consumers and transit countries command a central role in this type of literature. In contrast, energy economics focuses on trade, transportation, investments and finance. The economic viability of actors, including not only states and regional blocs but also companies and international financial institutions, is central in the study of energy economics. On the other hand, environmental studies examine energy security from the perspective of sustainability and ecological awareness and criticise the short-term perspectives of foreign policies based on geopolitics and economics (Aalto and Westphal 2007, pp. 3–5; Aalto and Korkmaz-Temel 2012, pp. 79–82).

The book attempts to use a different theoretical framework than the more commonly used geopolitical, environmental or energy economics perspectives. This is owing to the fact that energy is an inherently multi-faceted field and necessitates a broader and more inclusive perspective. It is crucial for industrial production, transportation and heating and is equally significant for the financial sector due to benefits delivered especially by the oil trade, and knowledge production in energy and environment related technology (Belyi 2003, p. 353; Strange 1994, pp. 190–210). Furthermore, energy is directly related to politics owing to its strategic implications for a country. Globalisation further consolidates the complex character of energy by blurring "the once sharp dividing line between foreign, domestic and economic policies" (Umbach 2010, p. 1238). Bearing in mind the multi-faceted character of energy and the impact of globalisation on energy matters, the book applies the ES theory of IR to examine several perspectives at the same time. Indeed, applying the ES to natural resources is not new, given the work of Wubbeke (2011) on natural resources and power. Wubbeke uses the classical ES division of the three traditions of world politics of realism, rationalism and revolutionism to explore possible scenarios for interlinkages between natural gas and power in world politics. However, the dividing line between this book and Wubbeke's work is the inclusion of Buzan's (2004) structural interpretation of the ES. Drawing from Buzan's approach, the book uses the concept of energy security society, which is sketched by Aalto (2009). This concept is used by Aalto and Korkmaz-Temel (2012) to examine European energy security in the wider Eurasian context, and natural gas and the integration process in the EU (Aalto and Korkmaz-Temel 2014). What differentiates this book from earlier works on energy security society is that the book applies the concept of energy security society to Turkey-EU relations in the sphere of natural gas and aims to enhance our understanding of society by utilising the concept of primary institutions, which are elaborated on below, and their interlinkages. Accordingly, the book aims to ascertain the positions of Turkish actors regarding energy security in the sphere of natural gas and examine how their positions contribute to Turkey-EU energy relations, and thereby determine Turkey's place in the pan-European energy community.

The application of the English School, which includes the theories of realism, rationalism and revolutionism, makes it possible to analyse different types of energy relations within the same framework. Furthermore, a theoretical framework such as that provided by the ES is called for considering the European Commission's suggestion of the creation of a pan-European energy community, which specifically referenced Turkey. Additionally, Buzan's approach best allows us to consider the EU's relations with energy suppliers and transit states in light of its external dependency (Aalto and Korkmaz-Temel 2014). This provides a broader perspective, such as the international society perspective, that includes different actors with varying motivations and interests. Moreover, the English School's concept of primary institutions, which "define both the basic character and purpose of any ... society" (Buzan 2004, p. xviii), provides grounds for the consideration of the relevant economic, geopolitical and environmental literature within the same framework. As mentioned above, the multi-faceted nature of energy demands a theoretical framework broad enough to embrace these different literatures. Furthermore, the concept of primary institutions offers an opportunity to locate the institutional structures in what will be called energy security societies. Different perspectives, such as geopolitics or energy economics, and institutions determine the character and purpose of society and require analysis. Last but not least, Buzan's revision of the classical ES and his opinion on different types of integration provide an opportunity to include non-state actors in the analysis and to scrutinise the positions of different EU and Turkish actors on the type of integration between Turkey and the EU in the sphere of natural gas.

The book's second contribution to the literature comes from its examination of the positions of various Turkish actors on energy security in the sphere of natural gas vis-à-vis EU integration. The book aims to ascertain the grounds on which these actors build their positions. Understanding the main starting points of their arguments makes it possible to identify the institutional structure of the Turkish actors in natural gas policy. If we assume that the state and non-state actors directly/indirectly active in the formulation of Turkish natural gas policy form a sort of 'domestic society in the field of energy', then questions on the foundations of this society and how it functions are crucial to the understanding of Turkish energy policy and the potentials/limitations in Turkey-EU natural gas relations. A parallel can be made to social institutions in sociology. As Schaefer aptly puts it, "social institutions are organized patterns of beliefs and behaviour that are centred on basic social needs" (2008). The family, religion, education and the economy are examples of social institutions. Likewise, this book aims to identify the institutions in Turkish energy society and understand how they constitute the positions of Turkish actors on energy security vis-à-vis integration with the EU in the field of natural gas. Such an analysis elaborates the scope of energy integration between the EU and Turkey and answers the question on the extent to which the positions of Turkish actors constrain/enable integration with the EU. Therefore, the added value of the book is its examination of the institutional structure of Turkish domestic energy society and the building blocks of different arguments on energy security in natural gas and the analysis of their implications on Turkey-EU relations.

Before delving into more detail on Turkey, the book analyses EU views on Turkey's role in its energy security in order to understand the type of integration the EU seeks to have with Turkey in the sphere of natural gas. The positions of the EU institutions and Member States involved in the discussions of Turkey's role in the EU's energy policy provide a significant background against which to discuss the Turkish positions. Given the fact that the EU is not a homogeneous body and consists of different institutions and member states with varying attitudes to Turkey, it is necessary to differentiate among the EU actors and analyse the positions of each institution and member states involved. Accordingly, this book aims to examine how Turkey is perceived within the scope of Turkey-EU energy relations in the sphere of natural gas in the EU narrative(s) and the extent to which these narratives differ from each other.

The next chapter sets out the book's overall theoretical and methodological frameworks. It begins with an introduction of Buzan's structural interpretation and continues with its application to energy. The chapter defines the main concepts such as *energy security in the sphere of natural gas* and *energy security society* and presents different types of integration within this society. Furthermore, the chapter introduces the primary institutions and attempts to establish the institutional structure of the energy security society. Accordingly, the chapter defines the primary institutions of sovereignty, energy diplomacy, balance of power, great power management, the market, state capitalism and security of supply/demand. It also elaborates on the manner in which these primary institutions function in energy security societies using examples from the EU and Turkey. Moreover, Chapter Two defines the concept of narrative and provides a very brief explanation on how the analysis is conducted and inferences are made. The relationship between narratives and primary institutions and the methodological and theoretical frameworks are visualised using figures.

Chapter Three aims to explore the type of integration the EU seeks to establish with Turkey in the sphere of natural gas and understand how Turkey is perceived within the scope of European energy security. Analysis is based on the narratives of the European Commission, the European Council, the Parliament, the Council of the European Union and those Member States involved in the discussions on Turkey and energy security. The analysis shows that all EU narrators agree that Turkey plays a significant role in the EU's efforts to diversify energy suppliers and routes and on the necessity of extending EU values, such as a competitive market, in the field of energy. Although different actors disagree on the means by which to extend EU values, all EU actors prefer a converging integration between the EU and Turkey in the sphere of natural gas. This chapter serves as a background for the comprehension of the main problems in EU energy policy and their solutions and linkages with Turkey. Furthermore, analysis of the EU's views on Turkey within European energy security allows us to compare them with the views of Turkey on the EU.

Based on the background in Chap. 3, Chaps. 4 and 5 examine Turkish responses to the EU narratives on the diversification of suppliers and routes and the extension of EU values to Turkey. These chapters consider state and non-state actors, including the Justice and Development Party (AKP), which has been the governing party since 2002, public authorities concerned with energy matters, opposition parties, think-tanks, representatives of the private sector and unions. Chapter 4 begins by scrutinising the concept of energy security in various Turkish narratives and examines the positions of various Turkish actors on natural gas pipelines. Accordingly, it examines Turkish narratives on its role as an energy hub/energy terminal and discusses their positions regarding pipeline projects, such as the Trans Anatolian Pipeline (hereinafter TANAP) and Turk Stream, and the developments in the Eastern Mediterranean. From a theoretical perspective, the chapter analyses the functioning of the primary institutions of security of supply, balance of power, great power management and modern sovereignty. Within this context, the AKP's foreign policy and its linkage with energy policy and relations with Russia are also scrutinised.

Chapter 5 examines the Turkish actors' positions on the liberalisation of the natural gas market. This provides an understanding of their views of the EU's narratives on extending liberal values. The domestic discussions in Turkey on the market revolve around the question of the extent to which the market should be liberalised and the state's role in the market. Accordingly, the chapter scrutinises the functioning of the primary institutions of the market and the state capitalism. Actors differ on their understandings of the scope of public service, the role and the structure of the state company in the market and the Transit Law. Examination of the narratives based on these differences provides an understanding of the main dividing lines not only between market-oriented and the state capitalist narratives but also within market-oriented narratives. Furthermore, the chapter examines modern sovereignty as a primary institution functioning in the narratives on the Energy Community, which is an initiative of the EU to export its market values. Analysis of the Turkish narratives on the liberalisation of the market enables us to complete the picture and identify the nature of the integration between the EU and Turkey in the sphere of natural gas.

The concluding chapter presents the theoretical and empirical findings. The examination of the fundamental character and the starting points of Turkish actors' arguments affords an insight into the institutional structure of Turkish domestic energy society, the extent of co-operation and contrast among institutions and how the Turkish domestic energy society functions internally and in regard to EU-Turkey relations. Identification of the functioning of institutions in the positions of the Turkish actors provides an opportunity to determine the current nature of integration between the EU and Turkey in the sphere of natural gas, as well as the type of integration Turkish actors would like to achieve. The analyses of the Turkish and the EU views enable a comparison of the two actors' positions on integration and their institutional structures. Within this context, the comparisons of the EU and Turkish narratives and primary institutions constituting those narratives, where those narratives are situated in the theoretical framework, and Turkey in the European energy security society are visualised in tables and figures.

Note

1. I'd like to thank Burak Toygar Halistoprak for his comments on the earlier version of this chapter.

Bibliography

Aalto, P. (2009). European perspectives for managing dependence. In J. Perovic, R. Orttung, & A. Wenger (Eds.), *Russian energy power and foreign relations: Implications to conflict and cooperation* (pp. 157–180). London and New York: Routledge.

Aalto, P., & Korkmaz-Temel, D. (2012). Towards a European/Eurasian energy security society: From vulnerability and viability to sustainability. In P. Aalto, V. Harle, & S. Moisio (Eds.), *Towards the interdisciplinary study of global and regional policy problems* (pp. 79–104). Aldershot: Ashgate.

Aalto, P., & Korkmaz-Temel, D. (2014). European energy security: Natural gas and the integration process. *Journal of Common Market Studies, 52*(4), 758–774.

Aalto, P., & Westphal, K. (2007). Introduction. In P. Aalto (Ed.), *The EU-Russian energy dialogue: Europe's future energy security* (pp. 1–21). Aldershot: Ashgate.

Belyi, A. (2003). New dimensions of energy security of the enlarging EU and their impact on relations with Russia. *European Integration, 25*(4), 351–369.

Bhattacharyya, S. (2011). *Energy economics concepts, issues, markets and governance.* London: Springer.

Bohi, D., & Toman, M. (1993). Energy security: Externalities and policies. *Energy Policy, 21*(11), 1093–1109.

Brown, M., & Dworkin, M. (2011). The environmental dimension of energy security. In B. Sovacool (Ed.), *The Routledge handbook of energy security* (pp. 43–55). New York and Oxon: Routledge.

Buzan, B. (2004). *From international to world society.* Cambridge: Cambridge University Press.

Cumhurbaskani Erdogan: Avrupa Birligi ile Gorusmelerimizi Surdurecegiz. (2018, March 26). *Sabah.* Retrieved from https://www.sabah.com.tr.

Esterberg, K. (2002). *Qualitative methods in social research.* Boston: McGraw Hill.

European Commission. (2006). *Green paper—A European strategy for sustainable, competitive and secure energy* (COM (2006) 105 final). Retrieved from http://europa.eu/documents/comm/green_papers/pdf/com2006_105_en.pdf.

European Commission. (2015). *Energy Union package—A framework strategy for a resilient energy union with a forward-looking climate change policy* (COM(2015) 80 final). Retrieved from https://eur-lex.europa.eu/resource.html?uri=cellar:1bd46c90-bdd4-11e4-bbe1-01aa75ed71a1.0001.03/DOC_1&format=PDF.

European Commission. (2019). *EU energy in figures.* Retrieved from https://op.europa.eu/en/publication-detail/-/publication/e0544b72-db53-11e9-9c4e-01aa75ed71a1/language-en.

Keyman, F. (2017). A new Turkish foreign policy: Towards proactive moral realism. *Insight Turkey, 19*(1), 55–69.

Klare, M. (2008). *Rising powers, shrinking planet.* Oxford: OneWorld Publications.

Luft, G., Korin, A., & Gupta, E. (2011). Energy security and climate change: A tenuous link. In B. Sovacool (Ed.), *The Routledge handbook of energy security* (pp. 43–55). New York and Oxon: Routledge.

Oguzlu, T. (2018). Turkish foreign policy in a changing world order. *All Azimuth, 0*(0), 1–13. https://doi.org/10.20991/allazimuth.464076.

Schaefer, R. (2008). Social institutions. In V. Parrillo (Ed.), *Encyclopedia of social problems* (pp. 874–876). Thousand Oaks, CA: SAGE Publications. https://doi.org/10.4135/9781412963930.n531.

Strange, S. (1994). *States and markets* (2nd ed.). London and New York: Pinter.

Umbach, F. (2010). Global energy security and the implications for the EU. *Energy Policy, 38*(3), 1229–1240.

Unay, S. (2016). Turkiye-Rusya Yakinlasmasi: Jeo-Ekonomik Boyut. *Kriter, 1*(5) Retrieved from https://kriterdergi.com/suriye-idlib/turkiye-rusya-yakinlasmasi-jeo-ekonomik-boyut.

Wubbeke, J. (2011). Three worlds of natural resources and power. In E. Fels, J. Kremer, & K. Kronenberg (Eds.), *Power in the 21st century international security and international political economy in a changing world* (pp. 97–115). Berlin Heidelberg: Springer.

CHAPTER 2

Theoretical and Methodological Frameworks: The English School and Narrative Policy Analysis

The theoretically pluralist approach of the English School provides a good basis for the examination of a number of energy relations within the same framework. Classical ES theory attempts to reconcile the various theoretical IR approaches to realism, rationalism and revolutionism and defines the international system, international society and world society as the three spheres of IR that exist simultaneously. While the international system element refers to international anarchy and power politics among states, international society addresses shared interests, norms, rules and institutions. The focus of world society rests on global societal identities and arrangements (Buzan 2004a, pp. 6–9). ES theory assumes states to be a part of international society similar to human beings' presence as individuals in societies. Both states in international society and individuals shape their societies and are in turn shaped by them. The history and further development of international society is related to the concepts of international system and world society (Buzan 2004a, p. 8). This pluralist approach provides a relevant framework for the examination of different types of relations within the pan-European energy community and the various considerations of different Turkish actors with regards to Turkey-EU relations in the sphere of energy security.

Critical of classical ES, Buzan (2004a) proposes a structural interpretation of the English School, upon which this book draws. Structural studies are one of the three orientations in the English School's understanding of world politics. While structural studies analyse the institutional structure

D. Korkmaz, *Turkey and the EU in an Energy Security Society*,
https://doi.org/10.1007/978-3-030-45774-7_2

of international society, functional studies examine the functioning of the institutional structure of international society and therefore focuses on the concept of "order". Historical studies scrutinise the historical evolution of the institutional structure (Linklater and Suganami 2006, pp. 43–75). With the help of Buzan's approach, this book aims to comprehend the institutional structure of energy issues in Turkey and how those institutions function to achieve energy security. This recognition aids in the understanding of what constitutes the Turkish actors' arguments on energy security vis-à-vis integration with the EU.

To achieve this aim, this book applies the method of narrative policy analysis. A narrative is "a kind of story told by someone (a "narrator") with a beginning, middle, and an end" (Esterberg 2002, p. 182). Narratives are more than mere reports as they are sources on how to understand the way in which people think and knowledge is produced. They represent the cognitive map of the narrator. Therefore, narrative policy analysis allows for the comprehension of different actors` arguments and an understanding of the institutional structure of societies. Following in large part Emery Roe's (1994) approach to narrative policy analysis, this book examines the Turkish and EU narratives on natural gas and energy security. Additionally, narrative policy analysis is convenient for the analysis of highly complex, polarised and uncertain issues. In this context, complexity refers to an issue's interdependent and interrelated features whereas polarisation refers to extreme opinions. Both complexity and polarisation cause uncertainty, which means a lack of knowledge on how things are related (Roe 1994, pp. 2–3, 9). Accordingly, the multifaceted nature of energy and discussions on energy security vis-à-vis integration necessitate the use of narrative policy analysis, bearing in mind the complex and polarised character of these issues. Furthermore, to understand the structure of the narratives, this study draws upon Pertti Alasuutari's (1995) approach to coding goals, means, obstacles and reasons within narratives.

This chapter[1] begins with an explanation of Buzan's criticisms of classical ES theory and briefly introduces his structural interpretation. Thereafter, the book applies Buzan's structural interpretation to the field of energy. Within this framework, the chapter defines the notion of "energy security in the sphere of natural gas" and "energy security society" and introduces different integration types in energy affairs. Furthermore, the chapter defines the primary institutions existing in energy security societies and exemplifies their functioning in the EU and/or Turkey. Additionally, it sets out the methodological framework, establishing the inclusion criteria for data and the analysis. Overall, the chapter aims to contribute to the theorisation of the concept of energy security, establish a theoretical framework to examine energy issues in Turkey-EU relations and elaborate on the methodological choices and processes to analyse the data.

2.1 Buzan and the English School

Buzan argued that classical English School theory has weaknesses regarding levels, sectors, boundaries, normative conflicts and methodology. By developing a social structural interpretation of the theory, he aimed to address these weaknesses and establish a structural interpretation as a complement to the normative interpretation.

Buzan reformulated the concepts and structure of classical ES theory. First, he removed the concept of the international system on the grounds that all human interaction is social and presupposes physical interaction of some kind. Thus, while no distinction between system and society is needed, societies must be classified as either poorly developed or well-developed. Second, he abandoned the distinction of the international system and international society at the state level and of the world society at the non-state level. Accordingly, Buzan set out a framework of inter-human, transnational and interstate domains engaging in interaction with each other. The states system determines the structure of international societies while the states draw the lines of the inter-human and transnational domains. Conversely, states are not dominant in world societies in which the three domains are in play together. Third, leaving aside the classical thinking of pluralism[2] and solidarism,[3] he proposed the use of these two concepts for benchmarking integration types within interstate society. Accordingly, he argued that asocial, power political and coexistence societies are pluralist, whereas co-operative, convergence and confederative societies are solidarist. Fourth, he used the ES concept of primary institutions, which will be elaborated on further below, to define the character and aim of any international society. By introducing "the market" as a primary institution, he brought international political economy into the theory. Fifth, he created an opportunity to discuss why and how values are shared via the concept of binding forces, which are coercion, calculation and belief. Sixth, Buzan introduced the sub-global level by pointing out the existence of different regional international societies. Seventh, and not used in this research, he succeeded in moving from one type of integration into another by introducing the concept of driving forces (Buzan 2004a, pp. 2, 16–24, 91, 92, 100, 158, 166, 202, 228, 229).

This book applies Buzan's structural interpretation of ES to the field of energy. He used the concept of international society when "political and legal frames of international social structure is set by the states-system, with individuals and TNAs [transnational actors] being given rights by states" (Buzan 2004a, xvii). The application of this concept to a different field (such as energy) and a sub-global region (such as the EU) follows Buzan's argument on the ability of different regional international societies to "build on common global international society foundations, as they have done in Europe, the Islamic world and Southeast Asia (and earlier amongst the communist states)" (Buzan 2004a, p. 18). Arguing that the classical ES "tells only a liberal story, either because it is looking at European history becoming global history, or because it is specifically concerned with promoting liberal values" (Buzan 2004a, p. 226), Buzan asserted that "other stories are perfectly possible" (Buzan 2004a, p. 226). Accordingly, the application of ES theory to regional international societies can be found in the context of the European Union (Diez and Whitman 2002; Diez et al. 2011; Czaputowicz 2003; Stivachtis 2002), the Middle East (Buzan and Gonzalez-Pelaez 2009) and the Nordic region (Schouenborg 2013). However, application of the ES theory to the field of natural gas demonstrates that Buzan's argument is not only applicable to different types of societies (such as liberal, Islamic or communist) and different regions but also to different fields, such as energy.

2.2 Energy Security Society

Why do we need to think of a society when dealing with energy issues? Increasing levels of demand and limited energy sources, coupled with technological and financial restraints, require a strong relationship between suppliers and consumers. As long as the need for energy remains, energy actors will be in co-operation and conflict with each other, necessitating the consideration of a society. For the aims of this book, the energy security society[4] addressed will be that of the prospects of the pan-European energy community, which is an EU concept referring to a "common regulatory space around Europe" (European Commission 2006, p. 16). However, the theoretical framework introduced in this section is applicable for any energy security society.

The section begins with a definition of the concept of energy security in the sphere of natural gas and explanation of how it is contextualised in the empirical case. The section also introduces different types of integration in energy security societies and outlines their institutional structure. The institutional structure enables an analysis of the different dynamics within the different types of integration and understanding "the basic character and purpose" (Buzan 2004a, p. xviii) of societies. The section also defines and conceptualises each institution existing in the pan-European energy community with regard to Turkey-EU relations. Furthermore, it exemplifies each institution through specific empirical examples from the EU and Turkey to underline the ways in which they function and finally elaborates on the interactions between primary institutions.

2.2.1 *The Concept of Energy Security in the Sphere of Natural Gas*

To understand the meaning of the concept of energy security in the sphere of natural gas, we must first define the concept of energy security. The EU defines energy security as the secure, competitive and sustainable supply of energy (European Commission 2006, p. 16). This represents only one side of the coin, the liberal perspective of the consumer. For the aims of this book, it is significant to consider all perceptions, actors, fields and levels in the discussion of "energy security". The book thus draws upon the Copenhagen School (CS) for its definition of energy security. The CS is a school of thought on the concept of security represented by scholars including Buzan. It is significant to underline that neither the CS nor ES focuses on "energy" as such. However, whereas the theoretically pluralist approach of the ES makes it possible to cover all types of relations in the pan-European energy community and different perceptions of Turkey-EU relations in the sphere of natural gas, the CS is valuable in the conceptualisation of energy security. Accordingly, this section begins with the introduction of the CS' concepts of "security sectors", "existential threat" and "multi-level", and establishes the linkage with the concept of energy security. Each component of the EU's definition of energy security is examined to achieve a broader definition. Additionally, the definition and concept are contextualised in the empirical case. Finally, the decision to narrow the concept of energy security to address only natural gas is discussed.

One must recall the multi-faceted character of energy when defining energy security. A suitable framework for considering this aspect of energy security can be found in the security sectors of the CS. As part of its aim to develop a theoretical framework on security from a constructivist perspective (Mcdonald 2008, p. 68), the CS uses the concept of "security sectors" to refer to military, political, societal, economic and environmental fields (Buzan et al. 1998) which have "particular forms of security interactions and particular definitions of referent objects" (Mcdonald 2008, p. 73). Energy security can be considered within the scope of the political, military, economic and environmental sectors of the School. For example, states' interest in secure energy supply or demand can be considered within the sector of political security. A lack of energy resources can affect military and economic security by increasing the likelihood of war or economic uncertainty. Similarly, the consumption of fossil fuels impedes environmental security (Belyi 2003, p. 354; Natorski and Surrallés 2008, p. 74). Therefore, the multi-faceted nature of energy issues requires energy security to be linked with different security sectors. This has been exemplified in the Turkish case. Illustrations of this could be found in concerns about the security of supply following the Russia-Ukraine dispute or the terrorist bombing of natural gas pipelines, and when the share of energy imports exceeded half of Turkey's trade deficit or a considerable number of licences were issued for imported coal fired power plants.

The multifaceted nature of energy and the fact that energy issues intersect with many different security sectors necessitate a broader perception of "threat" which requires the inclusion of all energy actors in the discussion. The CS uses the term "securitisation" to conceptualise the link between "security" and "threat". This refers to a process in which an actor "defines a particular issue or actor as an 'existential threat' to a particular referent object and this move is accepted by a relevant audience" (Mcdonald 2008, p. 73). Here it is significant to underline the strong linkage between identity and energy security owing to the fact that the perception of threat, the decisions of actors and the debates within the energy security change according to the identity of the actor (Godzimirski 2009, pp. 173–177). This also demonstrates, as supposed by the ES' understanding of security, that energy security is also "socially constructed". A good example of this is increasing concerns about energy security after the Russian-Ukrainian gas crises of 2006 and 2009, despite no change in material factors. Threat can come from (a) state(s), region(s), company(ies) or nature. Furthermore, as Godzimirski (2009, p. 175) argued, threat can manifest in different forms, such as legal, technological, environmental, political, economic and resource. The concept not only changes according to whether it concerns a state, company, non-governmental organisation or an individual, but also differs as to whether the security of a producer/consumer/transit state is in question or whether the concept is perceived by a buyer/seller/investing company/individual. The latter is significant as Buzan et al. (1998, p. 21) argued that threat exists in relation to a referent object which is not necessarily always a state. Therefore, energy security is a significant concept for all kinds of actors, ranging from states to individuals and from producer states to transit states. Accordingly, this book examines the definitions of the concept of energy security according to different Turkish actors, including those of governmental bodies, companies, unions and political parties and their arguments on energy security vis-à-vis integration with the EU. It also examines the opinions of different EU institutions on Turkey's role in European energy security.

In line with the application of the CS' (Buzan et al. 1998, pp. 5–6) "multi-level" analysis to energy, energy security exists on several levels: international (systemic level such as global energy markets), regional (sub-systems such as the EU), national (unit level) and internal (sub-unit level such as consumers) (Belyi 2003, p. 354; Natorski and Surrallés 2008, p. 74). The fact that energy security exists at different levels does not necessitate the prioritisation of any level to achieve security. This may be one of the aspects that differ between the concept of energy security and the conceptualisation of security in classical ES thinking.[5] According to the classical ES, priority is given to states' security in pluralist international societies "with a relatively low degree of shared norms" (Buzan 2004a, p. xvii). Conversely, the security of individuals is prioritised in solidarist/cosmopolitan societies since states are considered the means to security rather than ends (Bellamy and Mcdonald 2004, pp. 317–318; Makinda 2005, pp. 275–288). However, such prioritisation does not work in energy security societies since it is the states' energy security that is prioritised in any case. Furthermore, states' energy security does not automatically ensure energy security for individuals. There may be cases in which the state has obtained secure supplies due to its own rich indigenous resources but lacks sufficient infrastructure to supply its own citizens. Bearing in mind these different levels, energy security in the EU is usually perceived at regional, national (for the member states) and consumer levels, whereas Turkish actors consider energy security to function at the national and consumer levels.

To arrive at a broad understanding of the concept of energy security, we can begin by thinking about how to reformulate the EU's definition to cover all perceptions. Secure energy supply in the EU's definition refers to the continuity and reliability of supply. However, this security dimension of the definition of energy security must also include security of energy demand, depending on whether the actor under question is a buyer, a seller or a transit country. While a reliable supply is crucial for consumers, uninterrupted demand and security in indigenous supply are also crucial for producers. For transit states or countries with an energy hub, both the security of demand and of supply are significant since producers are reluctant to supply without the former whereas consumers are reluctant to buy in the absence of the latter. Briefly, to understand the security dimension within energy security, one has to recall the changing perception of security according to the character of the actor in the energy chain. High external dependencies of both the EU and Turkey necessitate the consideration of energy security from the supply point of view.

Regarding this component, it is highly important to underline that tools to remove threats change depending on the cause. Threats to a secure energy supply/demand can appear in different ways ranging from legal, technological and political to economic, resource related and environmental, as mentioned earlier (Godzimirski 2009, p. 175). For example, sanctions may decrease energy imports, thus demand, whereas environmental concerns and technological problems in exploring the European shale energy resources affect secure indigenous supply. Terrorist attacks, wars and economic crises can be cited as examples of threats that endanger the security of energy demand and supply. Similarly, Russian disputes with Ukraine raised concerns about energy security both in the EU and Turkey, while terrorist attacks on pipelines threatened the security of energy supply in Turkey. Therefore, consideration of the broad scope of possible threats is crucial in ensuring secure energy.

The second component in the EU definition of energy security concerns competitive energy supply. However, this definition shows a preference for a liberal market, and thus represents only one viewpoint. Although prices are significant for all actors, how prices are considered differs depending on whether the subject is a consumer or a supplier. Whereas the EU seeks competitive prices, "a steady income … [and] a fair return on capital" (OPEC 2006) are also crucial for suppliers. Since neither the EU nor Turkey are suppliers, this dimension will not be included in the definition. However, not all consumers seek competitive prices. There are cases where consumers prefer an illiberal market for securing energy. Therefore, "competitive/low-cost prices"[6] in the definition of energy security has a broader scope and represents the interests of all consumers. This kind of definition also meets the needs of Turkish actors since some are opposed to a liberal energy market, as will be analysed in the empirical chapter. Therefore, we do not refer to competitiveness in their definition of energy security.

The third component in the EU's definition of energy security is sustainability, which is related to minimising the environmental and climatic impacts of energy related segments ranging from exploration to consumption. This is a significant component of energy security for all sides. Any harm to the environment in any of these segments has negative consequences for all living beings. Therefore, no matter whether the subject is a producer/consumer or a state/company, sustainability matters to everyone. As will be elaborated in the empirical chapters, both the EU and Turkish actors refer to sustainability in their definitions of energy security.

In light of the need to highlight all dimensions of energy and include all sectors, actors and levels, energy security can be defined in the broadest sense as the security of supply/demand at competitive/low prices in a sustainable manner. It is important to consider that different actors may have different understandings of the definition and that energy security is realised in different sectors and at different levels. Both EU and Turkish actors refer to the political, economic and environmental aspects in their definitions of the concept of energy security, thus referring to "security", "competitiveness/low-cost" and "sustainability". As shown by an elaboration on the definitions of the Turkish actors (see Chap. 4), EU and Turkish actors agree on security of supply, due to external dependency and sustainability, while some Turkish actors differ with the EU in regard to competitiveness.

One significant question at this point may be the trade-off among these components of energy security. It should be underlined that energy security is achieved when energy is received in secure, competitive/low-cost and sustainable ways. Fulfilment of just one of these aspects does not bring energy security. For example, secure energy does not automatically mean low-cost/competitive energy. It is possible to receive natural gas continuously but at high prices. Likewise, affordable energy does not always guarantee sustainable energy, as shown in the low coal prices in the EU as a result of developments in shale gas production in the USA. However, the choice to prioritise security, competitiveness or sustainability in achieving energy security is a significant point similar to the discussion within the ES to prioritise the security of states or individuals. In energy issues, this usually depends on whether the state is an exporter or an importer.

In order to be able to contextualise the empirical case, we must first define what energy security in the sphere of natural gas means in Turkey-EU relations. Although both EU and Turkish actors refer to political, economic and environmental aspects within the context of energy security, they focus only on the political and economic components in discussions of energy security in natural gas within Turkey-EU relations. This is because the sustainability component of energy security in EU-Turkey relations is related mainly to renewables and energy efficiency. As the environmental component is not a topic of this book, it will not address stories of actors working on environmental issues. Moreover, the EU considers natural gas a complementary source for renewable energy (European Commission 2011a, p. 11; 2010b, p. 6). Natural gas is considered to create sustainability more than other fossil fuels. Accordingly, energy security in the sphere of natural gas refers to the "security of supply/demand at competitive/low-cost prices". The understanding of the definition of different actors, such as governments, companies, non-governmental organisations, institutions, political parties and think-tanks will be examined in the empirical chapters. Additionally, the book considers energy security to be realised in different sectors such as the political, military, economic and environmental sectors, and at different levels (regional and national). Accordingly, definitions of the concept of energy security will refer to different sectors whereas the regional level manifests itself in the EU and the national level in both the member states and Turkey. From this perspective, the book questions the extent to which Turkish actors are willing to adopt a regional level via a pan-European energy community.

2.2.2 *Types of Energy Security Society*

We can conceptualise energy security society at this stage as "a society of state and non-state actors conducting their energy relations". A final definition will be made at the end of the next sub-section after the primary institutions have been defined. It is necessary to include states and other actors in international society owing to the constant interplay between states, transnational actors and individuals (Buzan 2004a, pp. 119, 134, 231). Accordingly, energy security society consists of three domains, namely the interstate,[7] transnational and interhuman domains. The transnational domain is comprised of intergovernmental organisations, energy companies, international financial institutions and other transnational actors and the interhuman domain large-scale communities. The interstate domain refers to the "institutionalization of shared interest and identity amongst states" (Buzan 2004a, p. xvii). To show that each domain is a constitutive unit in society, clear boundaries are drawn between different domains (Fig. 2.1) (Buzan 2004a, p. 133). This book does not include the interhuman domain in the theoretical framework as the role of citizens/individuals is limited in the Turkish natural gas market. Within the scope of the transnational domain, non-state actors such as energy companies, unions, think-tanks and political parties are considered.

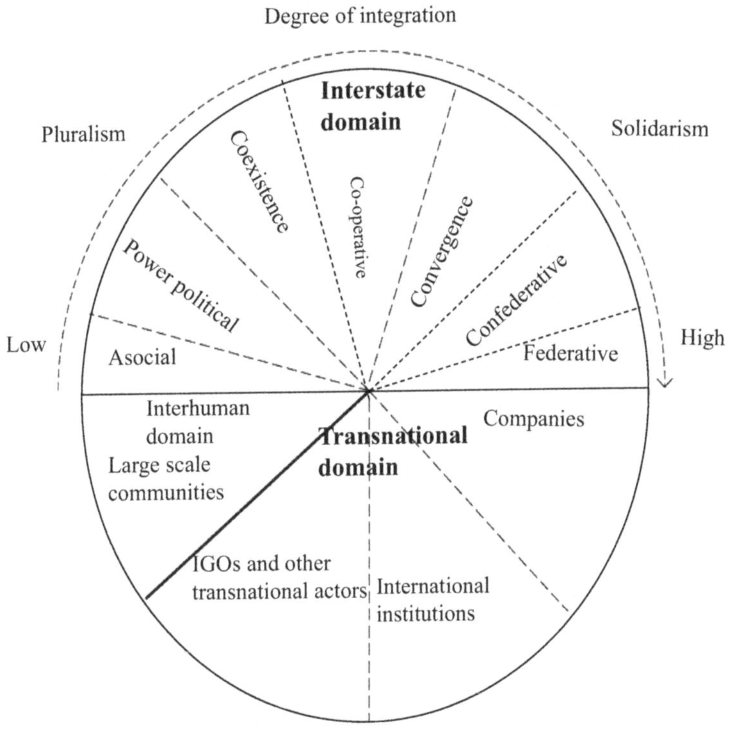

Fig. 2.1 Energy security society. (Source: Adapted from Buzan 2004a, p. 159; Aalto and Korkmaz-Temel 2012, p. 88)

Drawing on Buzan's typology based on pluralism and solidarism, there are different integration types of energy security societies, including asocial, power political, coexistence, co-operative, converging, confederative and federative types of integration. In contrast to the classical ES approach, pluralism and solidarism no longer define the boundaries of international society in Buzan's work but instead different types of integration within that society. Pluralist types of societies are based on the self-interest of states and survival is the main concern. On the other hand, solidarist types of societies are based on the idea of co-operation and shared values that go beyond survival and coexistence (Buzan 2004a, pp. 106–108). Accordingly, asocial, power political and coexistence types of energy security societies represent a pluralist type, whereas co-operative, converging, confederative and federative societies are solidarist. Utilising this theoretical framework, the book considers the pan-European energy community an "energy security society" and determines what type of an energy security society the pan-European energy community is and discusses the type of energy security society Turkish actors want to build with the EU in the sphere of natural gas.

Questions of "what values are shared" and "why and how values are shared" remain central. Whereas the first question deals with the type of social structure, the second considers the depth of internalisation of values. Here, Buzan referred to Wendt's idea of the internalisation of values by coercion, calculation or belief. Solidarism is not necessarily based on belief. It is also possible that shared values are adopted coercively or due to their calculated advantages. Thus, the depth of internalisation is important in the understanding of the durability of shared values and solidarism, which means that values internalised by coercion are less stable than those internalised by calculation or belief (Buzan 2004a, pp. 106–108, 152–154, 157).

There are several levels of international societies, all of which can be applied to the context of energy security societies. The lowest level of international society is the asocial energy security society. As in asocial societies "the only contact between states is wars of extermination unaccompanied by diplomacy or any other form of social contact" (Buzan 2004a, p. 159), they are quite rare in practice and generally do not exist except in science fiction. The next level of international society is the power political energy security society in which survival is the main concern of states (Buzan 2004a, pp. 159–160). Energy trade takes place not in terms of co-operation and integration but to the extent that trade brings in money. Concerns for energy nationalism and modern sovereignty, which refers to self-help based on non-interventions and reciprocity, dominate the relations among actors. Despite diplomacy, the formation of energy blocs and coalitions does not take place due to enmity among actors, which even has the potential to result in war (Aalto and Korkmaz-Temel 2012, p. 86; Buzan 2004a, pp. 159–160).

Coexistent energy security societies represent a kind of society in which "energy problems are resolved primarily by relying on the established practice of diplomacy, international law, when any such regulation is available but ultimately major energy producers and other great powers define the patterns of regional energy exchange through their mutual management" (Aalto and Korkmaz-Temel 2012, p. 87). Trade can take place in a protectionist manner and/or in a way mainly dominated by the state as an actor. Energy nationalism can manifest itself in states' decisions. Modern sovereignty is present in this type of society although a struggle between contemporary and modern sovereignty occurs when international law is applicable. While modern sovereignty refers to non-intervention and reciprocity, contemporary sovereignty allows for legitimate intervention, as will be further elaborated on in the next section. Energy sources are often used for political leverage (Aalto and Korkmaz-Temel 2012, p. 87). In power political and coexistence energy security societies there are no shared values beyond survival and coexistence.

Moving one step further, in a co-operative energy security society states are still the main actors in energy policy although they share the principles of energy policy such as security, competitiveness and sustainability in the pan-European energy community. Therefore, we can speak of shared values and solidarism in this type of integration. There is no transfer of competence to any authority; however, states are willing to co-operate (Aalto 2009, p. 161). While states move beyond coexistence, domestic convergence remains lacking (Buzan 2004a, p. 160). States prefer bilateral deals in external energy policy and exercise an energy policy within their own polity, which is still perceived as a national concern. The struggle between modern and contemporary sovereignties continues in co-operative energy security societies. If we apply this theoretical framework to a different group of countries, co-operation may exist among gas exporters, such as the Russian attempt to create a Gas OPEC which aims to support the sovereign rights of energy producing countries (Gas Exporting Countries Forum n.d.). However, since this book aims to understand Turkey's position in the pan-European energy community, which is the energy security society under examination, the co-operative energy security society discussed in this research is based on shared values such as competitiveness and security of supply.

Converging energy security society has a higher degree of integration, which would mean the convergence of internal markets. Buzan understood convergence as

> …the development of a substantial enough range of shared values within a set of states to make them adopt similar political, legal and economic forms. The range of shared values has to be wide enough and substantial enough to generate similar forms of government and legal systems based on similar values in respect of such basic issues… (Buzan 2004a, p. 160)

Shared values in converging energy security societies may occur in all kinds of societies. On one hand, convergence refers to internal market principles and a commitment to the liberalisation of energy sectors without rejecting the state's inclusion as a player in the market. A competitive internal energy market with a reliable energy network is one possible outcome of this type of integration. Contemporary sovereignty exists in converging energy security societies. On the other hand, convergence can take place among other types of countries not aiming at a competitive energy market. For example, the Russian proposal to create a customs union among Belarus, Kazakhstan and Russia is a type of integration in which shared values lead to some kind of convergence. However, transfer of competence to any superior authority in external energy issues does not happen in converging energy security societies. As for Turkey's position in the pan-European energy community, convergence refers to the EU's liberal values because this community foresees common rules on trade, transit and the environment.

Confederative energy security societies are a more solidarist type of integration in which there is a transfer of competence to a superior authority in both internal and external affairs. The difference between converging and confederative integration is that external energy policies are conducted by a supranational authority in the latter. Federative energy security society, in which a single unity is established and member states become provinces of a federal structure, is the most solidarist of the integration types. Just as asocial energy security societies are found in science fiction, federative energy security societies are utopian.

Different types of integration are distinguished by the practices based on different values[8] that characterise the various primary institutions. The next section defines the concept of primary institutions and attempts to establish the institutional structure of energy security societies in general. The following sub-sections then define the primary institutions in the pan-European energy community and exemplify their functioning in Turkey and the EU.

2.3 Primary Institutions

Borrowing from Buzan, primary institutions in an energy security society mean "durable and recognized practices rooted in values held commonly by the members ..., ...embodying a mix of norms, rules and principles" (Buzan 2004a, p. 181).[9] Although Buzan (2004a, p. 181) argued that primary institutions are held by members of interstate society and may be extended to non-state actors in some cases, primary institutions in an energy security society are accepted not only in the interstate domain but also in the transnational and individual domains. Therefore, the different primary institutions in non-state actors' arguments are also examined in the empirical chapters. The primary institutions of energy security societies explain the "basic character and purpose of [the] society" (Buzan 2004a, p. xviii), represent all practices shared by each member of the society and play "a constitutive role in relation to both the pieces/players and the rules of the game" (Buzan 2004a, p. 181). As Fig. 2.2 shows, every

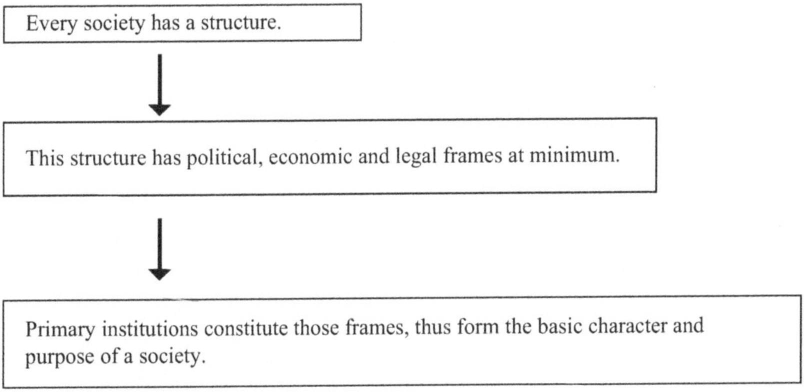

Fig. 2.2 Relationship between primary institutions and societies

society has a structure involving at least the political, economic and legal frames, made up of the involved primary institutions. These frames constitute the minimum requirements for the structure of a society.

How is the concept of primary institutions applied in this book? First, primary institutions allow us to distinguish the borders between different types of integration (see previous sub-section). As Buzan (2004a, p. 181) and Holsti (2004) argued, although they are durable, they can develop, evolve and decline. For example, it can be argued that although war, as a primary institution, is prevalent in pluralist societies such as power political and coexistent societies, it does not occur in more integrated types such as confederative security societies. Similarly, as elaborated below, the primary institution of sovereignty exists differently in different integration types of energy security society, demonstrating the transformation of the primary institutions. Second, as will be explained in the next chapter, primary institutions are constructed through the arguments and practices of actors, thus forming the institutional structure of the society. Therefore, we must first define the type of energy security society the pan-European energy community is by identifying the primary institutions functioning in EU narratives on Turkey's role in European energy security. Then we need to determine the institutional structure of the Turkish domestic energy society to be able to discuss the extent to which the positions of Turkish actors constrain/enable a convergence with the EU (Fig. 2.3).

It is necessary to re-define energy security society bearing in mind that primary institutions are the distinguishing element for energy security societies drawing the borders between different integration types. Primary institutions reveal "what the pieces are and how the game is played" (Buzan 2004a, p. 162) in different types of energy security societies and determine the political, legal and economic frames of the international structure. Accordingly, drawing on Buzan (2004a, p. xvii), Bull (2002, pp. 9–13) and Aalto (2009, p. 162), energy security society can be defined as a society of states and non-state actors acting in line with political, legal and economic frames of that society for conducting their energy relations. The goal of actors in each society is to achieve energy security.

Sovereignty, energy diplomacy, balance of power, great power management, the market and state capitalism (Table 2.1) appear as the main primary institutions in the pan-European energy security society regarding Turkey-EU relations in the sphere of natural gas. Furthermore, although it is not considered a primary institution in the ES, the book analyses the security of supply/demand. It is crucial to recall that there is no agreed set

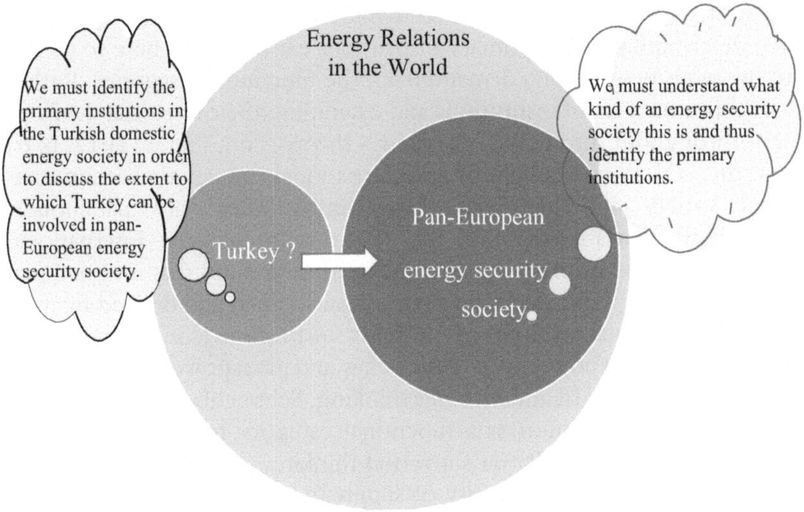

Fig. 2.3 The link between theoretical framework and the aim of the book

Table 2.1 Primary institutions and functional categories in an energy security society

Functional category	*Primary institutions*
Membership	Modern sovereignty, contemporary sovereignty, post-modern sovereignty
Authoritative communication	Energy diplomacy (bilateral, multilateral)
Limits to the use of force	Balance of power Great power management
Allocation of property rights	The market, state capitalism
International organisations	Security of supply/demand

of primary institutions for international societies in the ES (Buzan 2004a, p. 174) and the question of how primary institutions are classified is treated in different ways by different authors.[10] This book draws mainly on the functional categories set out by Buzan (2004a, pp. 188–189), Donnelly 2006, pp. 6–12) and Navari (2013, p. 1) to generate an idea of the primary institutions.[11]

Parrat's (2012) approach of studying international society first and then determining which primary institutions exist helps us here to generate the security of supply/demand from the functional categories. Rather than choosing a set of institutions and examining their historical development throughout the centuries as the ES theorists do, Parrat (2012, p. 6) took the UN as an example of an international organisation in international society and identified which institutions[12] are paramount. Accordingly, Navari examined the relationship between international organisations and primary institutions, bearing in mind that international organisations are "shoved, shaped, bent, constrained and defined by master or fundamental institutions [primary institutions], including sovereignty, a balance of power, international law and great power management" (Navari 2013, p. 1). In line with this thinking, Schouenborg (2013) added international organisation as a functional category to generate primary institutions. Therefore, Parrat's inverted thinking on institutions makes it possible to consider the security of supply/demand within the scope of primary institutions. Security of supply/demand is one of the significant policy issues underpinning the establishment of energy related international organisations.

States gather to co-operate in securing supply/demand. For example, the securing of supply was the main goal at the time of the establishment of the International Energy Agency (IEA). It was a response to the 1973/1974 oil crisis "in order to help countries to co- ordinate a collective response to major disruptions in oil supply through the release of emergency oil stocks to the markets" (IEA n.d.). On the other hand, "the strong link between the security of supply and the security and transparency of world oil demand" (OPEC 2009, p. 14) was emphasised by Organisation of the Petroleum Exporting Countries (OPEC) in its Second Solemn Declaration of 2000. Accordingly, Mr. Barkindo, the then Acting Secretary General of OPEC, clearly highlighted the significance of security of demand for producers: "..., for OPEC and all producing countries, there is another equally important parameter- the assurance of steady, predictable demand. This is often overlooked by consumers; but for producers, it is as important and as basic as security of supply" (OPEC 2006). The reference to "a steady income to producers" (OPEC 2006) in OPEC's mission is also related to the security of demand. In terms of natural gas, Russian President Putin's response to the idea of creating a gas-OPEC among producers also highlights the need for secure supply: "... I think it would be a good idea to coordinate our activities, especially in the context of achieving our main aim of ensuring certain and reliable supply of energy resources for our main consumers" (President of Russia 2007). Therefore, bearing in mind that the security of supply/demand underpins the establishment of energy related international organisations, it is relevant to consider the security of supply/demand as an important aspect to be examined in the context of energy security society. In this research, each reference to primary institutions in energy security society also includes the notion of security of supply/demand.

Buzan differentiated between "master" and "derivative" to construct the hierarchy among primary institutions. As he clearly explained, "the idea of two layers of primary institutions implies that some are 'deeper' than others" (Buzan 2004a, p. 176). Since it is not in our interest to determine which primary institution shapes or generates others, this distinction will not be used. However, another kind of division is needed to differentiate primary institutions. Although all primary institutions constitute narratives, some have the role of determining the main character of a narrative whereas others exist as a supplementary institution. Therefore, those which identify a narrative are called foundational primary institutions while those which serve as auxiliaries are deemed supportive primary institutions. For example, the market institution and state capitalism underpin Turkish narratives on the market, while modern sovereignty and great power management play a supportive role in these narratives, as elaborated on in the coming chapters.

Having set out the theoretical framework of the energy security society and the primary institutions, the next sub-sections define each primary institution and illustrate their functioning using examples. Furthermore, the interaction between different primary institutions is also examined in order to understand the co-operation and contradictions between them.

2.3.1 Sovereignty

There are three different notions of sovereignty utilised in this analysis: modern, contemporary and post-modern. This classification is based on Sørensen's conceptualisation of sovereignty, which is a synthesis of the discussion of continuity[13] vs. change.[14] Arguing that this discussion is incorrect and useless since the parties of the discussion are not addressing the same thing,[15] Sørensen (1999) suggested accepting that both continuity and change exist concurrently.[16] Accordingly, regulative rules and the statehood change in different integration types of the energy security society, which requires sovereignty to adapt itself to those changes. Here, globalisation is regarded as the differentiating feature among different types of sovereignties and the reason for the changes in regulative rules and statehood. For example, the content of the rule of non-intervention is different in coexistent and converging energy security societies. Whereas the rule includes non-intervention in energy legislation in the former, the scope of the rule changes to legitimate intervention owing to the harmonisation of energy legislation in the latter. Furthermore, the structure of the economy and polity as well as nationhood are different in coexistent and confederative energy security societies. Introverted economic structures and national identity exist in the former while supranational identity, interdependencies and multilevel governance manifest in confederative energy security societies. Therefore, while the sovereignty institution is present in all types of energy security societies, modern sovereignty evolves into contemporary and postmodern sovereignty in certain types of integration in that society. This interpretation is also in line with Buzan's argument on the possibility for primary institutions to develop, evolve or decline due to their non-permanent character (Buzan 2004a, p. 181).

"Modern sovereignty"[17] used here refers to the modern state, or the nation state. States have well-developed statehoods based on national concerns in modern sovereignty. Accordingly, identity in this type of sovereignty means belonging to a nation with territorially defined borders. The effects of globalisation are minimal. Integration with foreign powers is limited to co-operation. Regarding regulative rules, modern sovereignty is a game of self-help based on non-intervention and reciprocity. Without any outside interference, states decide on their own when conducting domestic and foreign affairs, including whether any external assistance is needed. Reciprocity is the symmetrical part of the game which provides equal opportunities for players based on giving and taking to benefit mutually from bi/multilateral transactions (Sørensen 1999, pp. 599–600).

From the perspective of energy security, modern sovereignty can be witnessed not only in pluralist energy security societies such as power political and coexistent ones, but also in co-operative societies. There may also be cases where modern sovereignty operates in a specific field. For example, as will be examined in detail in forthcoming chapters, modern sovereignty manifests itself in some Turkish actors' arguments on the transit issue owing to their understanding that the state is the sole body able to decide transit issues. A lack of harmonisation of the legislation on this specific segment demonstrates the functioning of non-intervention as the main regulative rule.

In contemporary sovereignty,[18] the economy is extroverted rather than introverted, and interdependency and status as a part of the global economy are significant (Sørensen 1999, p. 602). Within this scope, contemporary sovereignty meets the needs of the global world and overcomes "the fear that the WTO regime degrades sovereignty by imposing rules and restrictions on states" (Buzan 2004a, p. 185). Furthermore, openness not only to economic but also political external factors in the decision-making processes of state and non-state actors are issues differentiating contemporary sovereignty from modern sovereignty. However, it is noteworthy that "contemporary sovereignty" consists of a range of different polities and identities. A nation-based structure of polity as well as a network of international, national and regional governance can work. This may manifest as multilevel governance in the EU or national governance affected by globalisation and regionalisation in some other individual countries such as Turkey. Accordingly, nationhood is quite a vague concept in contemporary sovereignty. Identity no longer refers to a nation owing to the emergence of local, regional and/or supranational identities. Furthermore, there is a rising interaction among all actors, which necessitates consideration of the actions of others.[19] This change in the structure and content of economy and polity also has implications for regulative rules. Legitimate intervention in domestic affairs replaces the rule of non-intervention. Arbitration mechanisms such as the International Centre for the Settlement of Investment Disputes and the United Nations Commission on International Trade Law in case of disputes in energy contracts can be given as examples. Reciprocity in contemporary sovereignty is based on co-operation rather than competition (Sørensen 1999, pp. 602–603). Therefore, contemporary sovereignty meets the needs for different regulative rules while it also demonstrates the necessity for the transformation of some primary institutions. This type of sovereignty manifests itself in co-operative and converging energy security societies, although on different levels.

The concept of "contemporary sovereignty" in the EU is used in this book when the EU shares and/or supports competence.[20] According to EU Law, energy is one of the fields in which the EU and EU Member States have shared competence (European Union 2012b, p. 51). Therefore, the Member States may take legally binding decisions when the EU does not exercise its competence (European Commission 2019).

Contemporary sovereignty exists in the EU in energy matters bearing in mind the EU Member States' willingness to retain their sovereignty in energy matters. This was very well exemplified in the wording below:

> ...with this in mind, the Energy Policy for Europe will pursue ... three objectives, fully respecting Member States' choice of energy mix and sovereignty over primary energy sources and underpinned by a spirit of solidarity amongst Member States... (European Council 2007, p. 11)

Furthermore, contemporary sovereignty was also observed in Member States' opposition to the Commission's liberalisation packages. The Commission's proposal for "ownership unbundling"[21] that would break up big energy companies and provide market access to newcomers encountered opposition, notably from France and Germany, which have national energy champions, and thus would face problems in case of ownership unbundling. They even managed to gain the right to retain ownership of the gas and electricity grids of former state monopolies such as EDF and GDF in France and E.ON and RWE in Germany, on condition that they would be supervised (Euractiv 2009). For Turkey, the concept is used in the context of the harmonisation of legislation with the EU *acquis communautaire*. Adoption of external legislation, which can be considered to be within the scope of legitimate intervention as the regulative rule, is an example of contemporary sovereignty.

Post-modern sovereignty refers to cases in which the EU has exclusive competence such as the customs union and/or competition policy, therefore in the fields where the Member States transferred their competence to the EU. Applying Sørensen's framework, it can be argued that, although the structure and content of economy in post-modern sovereignty may be similar to contemporary sovereignty, there is a difference vis-à-vis the type of polity, owing to the transfer of competence affecting nationhood and regulative rules like intervention. Accordingly, while postmodern sovereignty exists for example in common commercial policy, contemporary sovereignty still persists in other areas such as energy. Thus, different types of integration necessitate different sovereignty games in energy security societies.

2.3.2 *Energy Diplomacy*

Applying Watson's (1992, p. 172) definition of diplomacy to energy specifically, energy diplomacy refers to the process of managing energy security society and the relations of state and transnational actors with one another in energy security society. Although diplomacy is traditionally perceived as an official relationship between sovereign states, Bull included non-state actors, which is also relevant in the case of the energy security society, and defines diplomacy as "*official relations of not only states but also other political entities*" (Bull 2002, p. 157, emphases in original). He argued that "entities other than states have standing as actors in world politics, and that they are engaged in diplomacy vis-à-vis states and one another" (Bull 2002, p. 158). Accordingly, non-state actors such as non-governmental organisations, international organisations and energy companies can be regarded as actors in energy diplomacy. This interpretation is also in line with Strange's (2000, pp. 60, 63, 66) argument that new forms of diplomacy, as state-firm and firm-firm diplomacy, have developed owing to changes in international political economy. While competition among states pushes them to negotiate with foreign and/or national firms, which eventually creates partnerships and alliances, negotiations among companies also result in strategic or tactical alliances in the same or different sectors. As long as those companies are state-linked or owned, we can think about energy diplomacy alongside trade.

In fact, the traditional definition of diplomacy as a relationship between two sovereign actors refers to one form of diplomacy called bilateralism. The relationship between Germany and Russia is a good example of bilateralism in energy security society. This bilateral relationship has produced the Nord Stream pipeline project, which links Russia and Northern Germany across the Baltic Sea bypassing a number of countries (Estonia, Latvia, Lithuania and Poland), and therefore raised concerns especially in those Member States on the grounds that the project threatens their energy security (Westphal 2006, p. 57). The rising concerns found a voice in the Polish Foreign Minister Sikorski's speech in which he, as a defence minister in 2006, equated the project and the Molotov-Ribbentrop Pact of the Second World War (Euractiv 2010).

Bilateralism in Turkish energy policy manifests itself, probably best, in the case of the TANAP, which transports Azeri gas to Turkey for its own energy needs and to be further transported to Europe. The project is presented to the public as the fruit of relations between the two countries and the consolidation of their historical brotherhood ties with the mission of "one nation, two states" (TANAP n.d.). Similarly, the Blue Stream Pipeline, which delivers 16 bcm of Russian natural gas to Turkey across the Black Sea bypassing the third countries, is an example of bilateral relations between Turkey and Russia.

The other form of diplomacy, multilateralism, refers to relations between more than two actors. The same concept is used to explain the economic world order. Therefore, when multilateralism is defined as a type of diplomatic relations between more than two actors, this does not necessarily involve a market-based approach. Multilateral diplomacy can also be adopted vis-à-vis specific issues among states which do not share the vision of market liberalisation, for example the Russian initiative to build a gas-OPEC. On the other hand, multilateralism within the context of the economic world order does necessitate a multilateral type of diplomacy. Therefore, while multilateralism does not require multilateral economic order, a multilateral economic order necessitates a multilateral type of diplomacy.

Multilateralism as an economic order and as a type of diplomacy can be witnessed in the Union's efforts towards the Energy Charter Treaty, of which Turkey is also a member, to export liberal values to energy producing as well as transit countries. Furthermore, any politically bilateral pipeline can be considered multilateral from an economic point of view due to the existence of multilateral consortiums. This shows the complexity of energy issues. For example, BP became a shareholder in TANAP in 2015, transforming the bilateral structure of the pipeline into a multilateral one. Similarly, the bilateralism in the Blue Stream Pipeline shifted to multilateralism by involving the Italian ENI in the construction and management of the pipeline. This multilateral dimension was pictured very well at the official inauguration ceremony of the pipeline, where Berlusconi attended as the then Italian Prime Minister alongside Russian President Putin and then Turkish Prime Minister Erdogan (Gazprom 2005).

The primary institution of energy diplomacy is introduced in this subsection as it is by nature a primary institution in the energy security society and functions in Turkey-EU energy relations. However, the empirical chapters will not examine this primary institution as they analyse the primary institutions existing in the Turkish and EU narratives. The next subsection examines the primary institutions of great power management and balance of power.

2.3.3 Great Power Management and Balance of Power

The distinctive elements of a great power are its material capabilities, self-declared status and acceptance of this status by others and being part of the calculations of others. This understanding is based on Buzan's (2004b) classification of superpowers, great powers and regional powers.[22] It is difficult to consider any country a superpower in energy affairs, bearing in mind that securitisation or de-securitisation processes in natural gas do not take place similarly in all regions because of the regional nature of natural gas markets. Although the natural gas market has gradually become more global owing to the impact of unconventional gas and new linkages between regional markets with expanding sales of LNG, we are far from able to consider the natural gas markets fully global. Furthermore, none of the actors has the power to establish universal values taking into account the limited success of the Energy Charter Treaty and gas-OPEC. Therefore, while Europe lacks a superpower in energy issues, it is possible to examine the great powers based on the above-mentioned distinctive elements.

Russia is a great power in energy affairs, with material capabilities including 18.4 per cent of world natural gas production (IEA 2018, p. 6) and 18.1 per cent of global proved natural gas reserves (BP 2018, p. 26). Additionally, Russia's self-declared great power status has been accepted by third parties. It is active in EU securitisation and de-securitisation processes such as in the gas crises with Ukraine and Belarus and in the Nord Stream I and II pipelines connecting Russia and Germany, which created a division among EU Member States. Therefore, Russia's behaviour and choices are part of the calculations of other actors on issues such as security of supplies or investments in the upstream sector. The impact of Russia as a great power on Turkish energy security can best be seen in its dependence on Russian natural gas imports, which account for approximately 47 per cent of Turkey's total gas imports (Enerji Piyasasi Duzenleme Kurumu 2019, p. 9). Russia is often criticised by some actors on the grounds that it designed the Turkish natural gas market, as will be elaborated on in the empirical chapter (Chap. 5). As Russia has the power to influence the processes of securitisation and de-securitisation in Turkey, it is part of the calculations made by Turkish actors.

Balance of power is another primary institution generated from the same functional category, along with great power management. Balance of power[23] exists in both pluralist and solidarist types of international societies, albeit in different ways. Therefore, the definition of balance of power changes depending on whether it is present in pluralist or solidarist international societies. This conceptualisation is based on the understandings of Little (2006) and Buzan et al. (Rengger 2000).[24] However, in this research, the concept is used within the scope of solidarist international societies. On the definition of balance of power, Wight (1966, p. 156) made a distinction depending on who maintains the balance of power. The definition changes if the power is evenly distributed among all partners (actors),[25] by a particular power[26] or by laws.[27] Accordingly, this book considers that all partners (actors) are involved in the distribution of power[28] in solidarist international societies in general and balance of power refers to "the existing distribution of power" (Wight 1966, p. 156). As balance in this meaning does not refer to an equilibrium, the concept here does not mean the even distribution of power. Rather, it is more related to change than stability, and thus describes "the relationship of power prevailing at a given time" (Wight 1966, p. 155). For example, in an energy security society, the balance of power may be in favour of sellers or buyers. Furthermore, bearing in mind that order refers to energy security and balance of power refers to 'the existing distribution of power' in solidarist international societies, balance of power can bring order for some members but endanger it for others.

Balance of power is examined in this book within the context of Turkish arguments. A strong link between Turkey's significance in the region and the pipelines crossing Turkey was established in the governments` arguments (see Chap. 4). Although Turkey lacks indigenous fossil fuels, it is expected that the transit pipelines crossing its borders contribute to Turkey's role in the existing distribution of power, help others to accept Turkey's significance, allow Turkey to securitise/de-securitise and be included in the calculations of others. Accordingly, Turkey's power in the region is expected to increase according to this narrative.

2.3.4 *The Market and State Capitalism*

Abundance of natural gas in some regions and scarcity in others make trade inevitable in all types of energy security societies. Among trade related primary institutions, the market institution refers to a structure in which resources are allocated by the interplay of supply and demand rather than by the state (Seyidoglu 1992, p. 691; Oatley 2011, pp. 8–9; O'Brien and Williams 2004, p. 18). Interdependence is key in the market institution; thus it exists in extroverted economics, in which foreign trade plays a big role. The presence of the market as a primary institution in an energy security society requires several elements: interplay between supply and demand, "effective (in law and practice) and non-discriminatory access for competitors" (Talus 2013, p. 68) (third party access), the existence of eligible customers who can "choose their supplier and have access to the transport networks" (Talus 2013, pp. 68–69) (market openness), the existence of a regulatory authority and separate transmission activities from production and supply (unbundling) (Akcollu 2006, p. 37).

Energy markets, as well as other public service markets such as telecommunications and postal services, were formerly not open to competition in Europe and were covered by European Commission competition rules for state enterprises as public services. Nonetheless, the Commission adopted a new approach at the end of the 1980s driven by the primary institution of the market and based on the assumption that a larger, competitive, integrated and well-interconnected single gas market receiving gas from different producers would be more secure than individual markets (Behrens 2009, p. 2). Therefore, in order to liberalise energy markets, the Commission initiated a policy based on a differentiation between infrastructure and commercial activities related to that infrastructure. It is assumed that a vertically integrated company is not interested in increasing the capacity of its network. Thus, a separation between management of infrastructure and production or sales brings new entries into the market by introducing competition and encouraging companies to invest more in networks (European Union 2007). By separating transmission from production and supply, unbundling aims to prevent companies active in both transmission and production/supply of energy from using their position to impede the access of their competitors to the network and commercial information (European Commission 2010a, p. 4). Although a network can be owned by a monopolist, third party access to the network should be ensured (Tradacete 2000). Third party access and market openness are expected to bring benefits for consumers by increasing efficiency, decreasing prices and developing innovation.

At this point it is crucial to elaborate on the linkage between the primary institution of the market and other primary institutions. The interrelationship between different primary institutions is significant for the manner in which the energy security society functions and the EU constructs its narratives. The first example is the interrelationship between the market institution and great power management. In the EU it is expected that the market institution helps the EU deal with the great power. For example, in order to prevent any non-EU company from developing vertical integration in EU territories, the EU introduced the "third country clause" in its Third Energy Package on improving the functioning of the internal energy and gas market. This clause aims to prevent individuals or companies of third countries from gaining control over a transmission system unless permitted by an agreement between the EU and the third country. The third country clause obliges non-EU companies to comply with the same unbundling rules as EU companies (Talus 2013, pp. 83–84). Underlying the belief that the Third Energy Package does not discriminate against anyone, the European Commission (2007b) stated that the package was to ensure that all actors taking part in energy markets are subject to the same rules. However, provisions in favour of establishing an internal market impose limits and draw borders for a great power, no matter which country. The rule for unbundling and third-party access automatically threatens Gazprom's activities in Europe since it operates in the production, transportation and transmission of gas in European countries (Euractiv 2011).

The interrelationship between the market and contemporary sovereignty is another example of the interrelationship between primary institutions. The market is related to how states constitute themselves and how they interpret sovereignty (Buzan 2005, p. 126). Bearing in mind the "continuous intensification of the social, cultural and economic internationalization or globalization of markets" (Correljé and Van der Linde 2006, p. 535), the existence of the market in its current form best corresponds to contemporary and post-modern sovereignties. As will be elaborated in Chap. 5, the market primary institution was introduced by the International Monetary Fund (IMF) in Turkey and is followed by the EU, showing the impact of globalisation and the existence of contemporary sovereignty. Furthermore, as seen in the EU example, by sharing the competence with the Commission in the field of energy, EU Member States are obliged to implement regulations on liberalisation.

As for the functioning of the market institution in Turkey, it is significant to emphasise that domestic discussions in Turkey on the market are dominated by the main question of the extent to which and in what form the state should be involved in the market (see Chap. 5). This question arises from the dilemma of the state vs. the market in the literature. As Soysal et al. (2012, p. 8) established, when the state dominates the market as a whole, arguments for the state leaving the market in favour of the private sector due to government failures in the long term become stronger. Conversely, when the energy sector is left totally to private actors and market mechanisms, state interference is advisable due to the behaviour of market actors regarding investments and risk management and market failures in the long term. Therefore, as neither the state nor the market is sufficient to ensure competitive, sustainable and secure energy by itself, Soysal et al. (2012, p. 8) underlined the significance of the role of the state and the level and timing of interference in the markets. Accordingly, this book uses the concept of "the market in its purest form" when the state is only a regulator and/or an actor responsible for only the transmission of gas, whereas "the market" is used when there are private companies in the market along with a state company/companies. When the market operates as a primary institution, the establishment of a competitive market is still the main focus but there may be state companies in the economy. The book thus aims to underline the distinction in competitive markets based on the roles of the state.

The concept of state capitalism is applied to cases where the state functions as the leading economic actor in an economy and considers not only economic but also political gains. In state capitalism there is a perception of energy resources as strategic tools which strengthen the interplay between politics and economics. This contextualisation is derived from Vivien Schmidt's (2002) classification of capitalism, which included market capitalism, managed capitalism and state capitalism. While the first refers to a liberal state allowing autonomous operation of economic actors, in managed capitalism an enabling state encourages actors to operate in co-operation and co-ordination with each other and the state. In state capitalism the state intervenes in the organisation of co-operation among autonomous economic actors and leading their activities. Schmidt's classification is based on the differentiation of three components of capitalism, which include interaction among firms and between industry and finance, management of labour relations, and interaction between state and firms, and state and labour. Regarding these components, there is a reliance on market and arms` length relations with the government in market capitalism while there is coordination and negotiation outside the market in managed capitalism and direction, organisation and control of the state in state capitalism. While Britain and the USA are examples of market capitalism, Germany and the Netherlands represent managed capitalism and France and Italy have the characteristics of state capitalism. Schmidt (2002) argued that developments in the global political economy have caused some changes in each type of capitalism and transformed traditional state capitalism into state-enhanced capitalism in which the state continues to play a significant but less direct influence in the economy.

Schmidt's classification provides a broad framework and a more balanced assessment of relations among state, labour and economic actors. For the aims of this book, Musacchio et al.'s (2015, pp. 115–118) broad definition of state capitalism, which refers to the majority and minority shares of the state in private undertakings or privileges and subsidised credits to private actors, is not applicable. As Wooldridge underlined, the state's involvement in private companies or the presence of sovereign wealth funds do not necessarily cause state capitalism. This is very well exemplified by the case of Norway, which has a sovereign wealth fund and an energy company, Equinor, largely owned by the Norwegian state. On the other hand, Bremmer's narrow definition designating state capitalism only to authoritarian states and his linkage with the consolidation of the political elite's power (The Economist 2012; Bremmer 2009) do not provide a sufficient ground for this book, as it attributes a negative meaning to the concept. The book's aim of retaining objectivity towards energy actors in Turkey necessitates a broader perspective without ascribing any negative meaning to their motivations. Therefore, this book does not consider state capitalism a consequence of political motivations and the rent-seeking of politicians. Instead, government intervention to solve market failures, pursue societal goals and keep out foreign investors are regarded as causes for the emergence of the concept. Complex historical processes coupled with institutional conditions also play a role (Musacchio and Lazzarini 2014, pp. 57–58). For the purposes of this study, state capitalism is limited to situations in which the state is the leading actor in the market, which in turn is centrally conducted. As discussed further in Chap. 5, the state capitalist narrative in Turkey does not include references to consolidation of the power of the political elite. Rather, the motivation derives from the necessity of introducing a new model in energy governance, which has an ideological perspective, and questioning the benefits of a liberal system and adopting the perception of energy as having a strategic character with geopolitical considerations.

2.3.5 Security of Supply/Demand

The English School does not discuss all the relevant features of energy security despite the fact that the security of supply/demand is a crucial component of energy security. None of the primary institutions mentioned above concern the security of supply/demand. Furthermore, the presence of other primary institutions does not automatically imply security of supply/demand. Energy security is achieved as long as the three components of reliable/continuous, competitive/low-cost and sustainable energy supply and demand are realised together. There is only partial energy security if the price of energy is acceptable for both suppliers and consumers and energy resources are sustainable but the supply/demand is not reliable and is interrupted. However, it is equally important to underline that energy security is not ensured when there is security of supply, but prices are high for consumers and the energy is not sustainable. Therefore, we must consider security of supply/demand separately from the other primary institutions. As mentioned previously, this book adopts Parrat's approach to generate security of supply/demand from functional categories.

For the aims of this book, the interrelationship between security of supply and the market institution must be explained. Security of supply is related to not only secure energy sources from producers and their secure transportation to Europe via transit states, but also to methods to prevent gas supply disruptions, respond to such crises and ensure proper and continuous functioning of the internal market (European Union 2011). In other words, the security of supply is not only a geopolitical concept but is also related to the liberalisation of markets according to the EU's understanding. In 2006, then Competition Commissioner Kroes highlighted the interconnection between the two primary institutions by stating that the liberalisation of the European internal energy market sought "to reinforce security of supply and the competitiveness" (Kroes 2006, p. 2). It is expected that the opening of energy markets to competition increases efficiency, improves technology, promotes investments, decreases prices, produces high quality services and provides secure and sustainable energy (European Commission 2012).

There are three ways in which the efficient operation of a single market is able to secure supply. First of all, an integrated internal market necessitates a well-interconnected system which improves both competitiveness and security of supply. Interconnection among pipelines enhances the security of supply by increasing the ability to meet demand in case of a shortage and competitiveness due to the scale of markets. The significance of interconnection was underlined by the Commission: "...a fully interconnected and bidirectional gas network, where appropriate, within the

EU [is] needed" (European Commission 2010c, p. 7). By giving the Russian-Ukrainian gas crisis and its impact on the EU's energy security as an example, the Commission argued that deficiencies in the internal market during the crisis made the EU more vulnerable to a supply crisis: "...as was demonstrated during the gas dispute between the Russian Federation and Ukraine in January 2009, when the internal market is not functioning properly, the EU is more vulnerable to security of supply risks" (European Commission 2011b, p. 2). Similarly, then Energy Commissioner Oettinger argued that "a fully functioning market is able to take adequate corrective measures in case of a disruption" (2011, p. 8) and underlined market anomalies and lack of interconnections as the main reason why the Ukrainian-Russian gas crisis affected the EU supply: "Our experience is that during the gas crisis in January 2009 there was enough gas on the European market. But because of market anomalies and lack of interconnections it could not flow to those places where demand for it was the highest" (Oettinger 2011, p. 8).

Second, a competitive and integrated market is expected to ensure the security of supply by producing the right signals for investments and offering fair network access for all potential investors (European Commission 2007b, p. 2; 2006, p. 8). The presence of more market players searching for supply from different sources and routes increase the likelihood of diversification,[29] as the then Director at DG Competition Ungerer explained:

> A competitive market is by far the best proven platform for diversifying risks. Competition leads to: More market actors looking for more opportunities outside established supply areas, diversification of infrastructures and new investment, correct investment and price signals. Europe's security of energy supply will therefore depend to a large extent on the creation of effective pro-competitive market structures. (2007, p. 4)

Diversification strengthens competition by providing an opportunity to receive gas from different sources and transit countries, therefore increasing choice. As noted by the Commission, the internal market can function as long as customers have access to more than one supplier, which requires a well-developed interconnection between different pipelines:

> ...if customers in Member States have access to gas from only one of these sources [supplier countries] then the internal market cannot function. The

> objective must therefore be that individual customers in the EU should all have the potential access to buy from a portfolio of the various primary sources of natural gas that are available. This clearly requires a well-developed network and consistent rules at EU level. (European Commission 2003, p. 15)

Similarly, the European Council underlined the interconnection between security of supply and the market by stating that security of supply should be achieved via "effective diversification of energy sources and transport routes, which will also contribute to a more competitive internal energy market..." (European Council 2007, p. 18).

Third, an integrated market is also expected to be attractive to exporters due to its large number of customers with better access and its interconnected system, thereby ensuring the security of demand for exporters. The European Commission referred to the interrelationship between the market and security of demand by mentioning that integrated market without any national boundaries and with necessary infrastructure ensures the "security of demand by providing for more choice and a bigger market for gas producers to sell their products" (European Commission 2010b, p. 11) and increases the attractiveness of the market (Lowe 2006, p. 5). Furthermore, an integrated market is expected to increase the bargaining power of the EU "since there is a larger range of options available as regards supply routes and better access to customers" (European Commission 2007a, p. 15).

Having defined the types of energy security societies and the concept of primary institutions and explored the ways in which those primary institutions function in different societies and interact with each other, the next section introduces the methodological framework and the relation between the theory and the methodology in the book.

2.4 Methodological Framework

This book aims to understand the positions of Turkish actors on energy security in the sphere of natural gas vis-à-vis integration with the EU and the positions of the EU actors on Turkey's role in European energy security. The time period for the data begins in 2001, when the Turkish legislation on liberalisation of the natural gas market was enacted, and continues until July 2019. Turkey is analysed in this book as a case study of the pan-European energy community, rather than in respect to its role in the EU enlargement process. Accordingly, this study aims to understand where Turkey is located in the EU's energy framework and the extent to which Turkish actors agree with this position.

Data on Turkey was first collected via face-to-face interviews done in Turkish with Turkish state and non-state actors[30] in 2011, 2012 and 2018. The goal of the interviews was to understand the main arguments and views of Turkish actors and to comprehend their tacit knowledge. To achieve these goals, a "semi-structured" interview technique was preferred to understand "how case study interviewees construct reality and think about situations, not just giving answers to specific questions" (Yin 2009, p. 264). Within this method, the author asked "major questions the same way each time, but [was] free to alter their sequence and probe for more information" (Gilbert 2008, p. 246). After understanding the main dynamics in the Turkish views, more data was collected in the form of policy papers, reports of different state and non-state actors, views of representatives of these actors and news and/or interviews published in newspapers. Moreover, the minutes of sessions in the Turkish Grand National Assembly were searched via keywords (e.g. Energy Community) and specific discussions on developments related to natural gas (e.g. discussions on intergovernmental agreements on the TANAP, Nabucco and Turk Stream pipelines).

For data on the EU, policy papers of different EU institutions were analysed due to increased efforts for energy security by the beginning of the new millennium. The EU documents were limited to documents related to energy security vis-à-vis relations with Turkey. The Commission's task of proposing legislation justifies starting the analysis from the Commission's policy papers and then continuing with discussions on those papers in the Council of the European Union and the Parliament. To include Member States' perspectives, the views of Member States in the Council of the European Union on the Commission's policy papers on energy security including Turkey, if available, were examined, in addition to the European Council conclusions.

The data was examined by utilising narrative policy analysis. Using narratives, people explain how they assess their social presence and interpret the world. Narratives provide an understanding of how the narrator makes sense of the events/persons/ideas/objects that he/she tells about (Esterberg 2002, p. 181; Fischer 2003, p. 179; Patterson and Monroe 1998, p. 330). Three features of narratives are crucial for the purposes of this book. First, narratives reflect the narrator's interpretation, which means that narratives change according to the narrator. People tell different narratives accentuating different parts of the story, since individuals perceive the same world or events differently depending on their backgrounds (Bridgman and Barry 2002, p. 141). Hence, the research aims to understand different narratives told by different narrators. Second, as Patterson and Monroe (1998, pp. 315–316) stated, not only real people but also nations or groups have narratives in which they understand and interpret the world. Therefore, official documents are also considered as narratives, including interpretations of events in addition to the events themselves. Accordingly, the official documents of both Turkey and the EU were considered as narratives and examined as part of the data. Third, it is also crucial to keep in mind that while the narrator tells narratives according to their perception of the world and event, what is told by the narrator gives indications of how they will behave. Thus, narratives play a prominent role in the construction of policies (Patterson and Monroe 1998, pp. 315–316). Figure 2.4 shows what a narrative is and how it is related with policies/practices of different actors.

The relationship between narratives and primary institutions needs to be established to justify the choice of methodology. Primary institutions constitute the actors' cognitive map, underpin the narratives they tell on that basis and determine the resulting policies of the narrator. Different primary institutions constitute different narratives. In addition, the thoughts of narrators, the stories they tell and their practices/policies constitute primary institutions. Thus, they are mutually constitutive. Accordingly, analysis of the narratives of different narrators sheds light on the primary institutions and the institutional structure of a society. Figure 2.5 explains this relationship.

The question as to what extent the positions of Turkish actors in energy security in the sphere of natural gas constrain and/or enable integration with the EU can be best answered by comparing the energy security societies that actors in the EU and Turkey desire to have with each other. Accordingly, we must identify the primary institutions in the Turkish and EU narratives. This can best be achieved by examining different narratives. As Fig. 2.6 shows, analysis of the narratives of EU actors on Turkey's role in European energy security in the sphere of natural gas is necessary. This enables us to identify the primary institutions and ascertain the type of energy security society(ies) the EU narrators prefer to have with Turkey. Second, we must analyse the Turkish narratives on energy security in the sphere of natural gas. This type of analysis sheds light on the primary

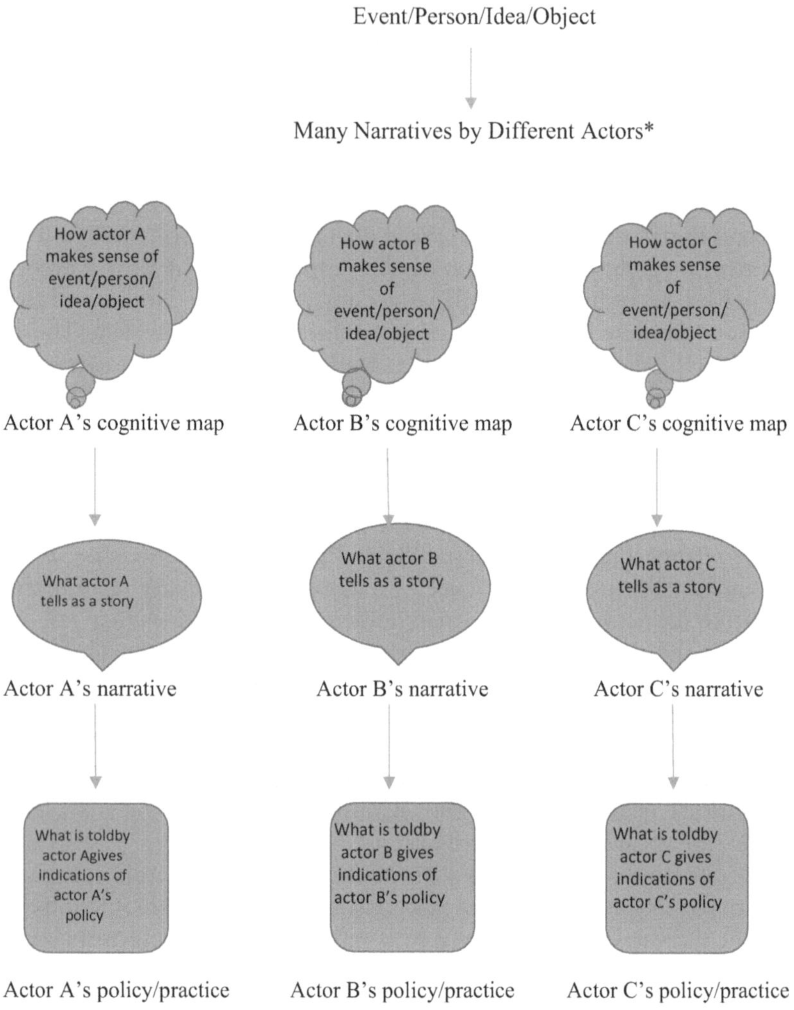

*These actors may be people, political parties, governments, institutions, companies, think tanks, unions etc.

Fig. 2.4 What is a narrative?

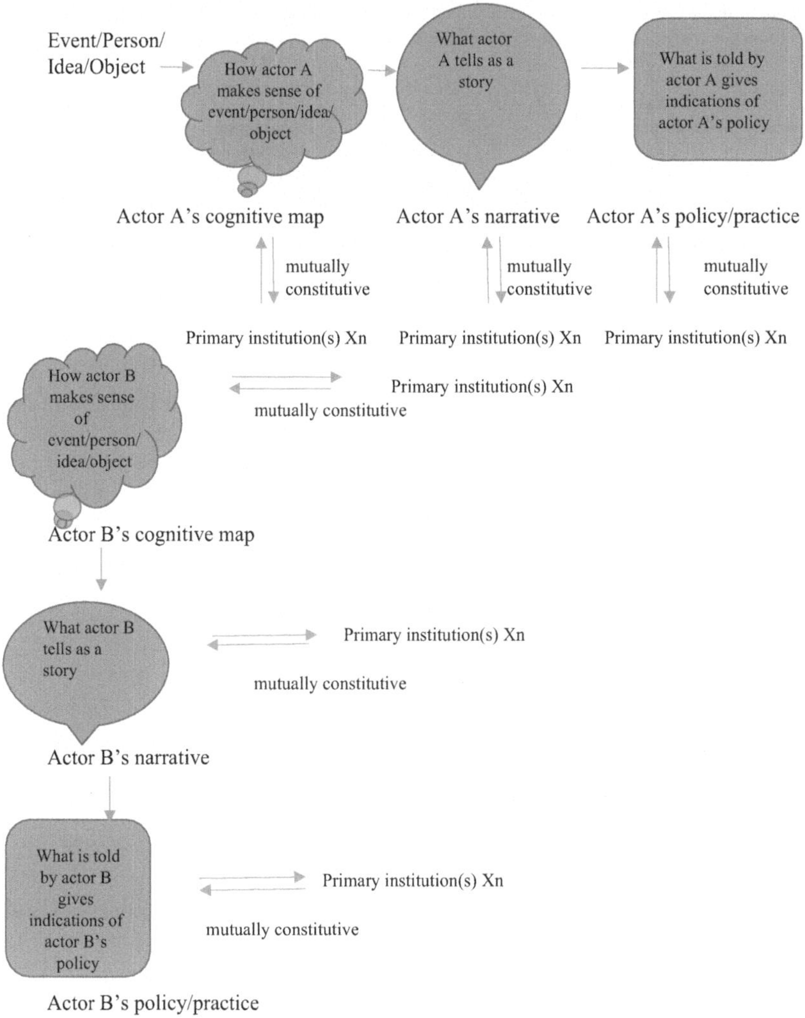

Fig. 2.5 The relationship between narratives and primary institutions

institutions and determination of energy security society Turkish narrators prefer. Classifying the EU and Turkish narratives and identifying the primary institutions within them form the main part of the analysis. Third, primary institutions enable us to understand the positions of Turkish

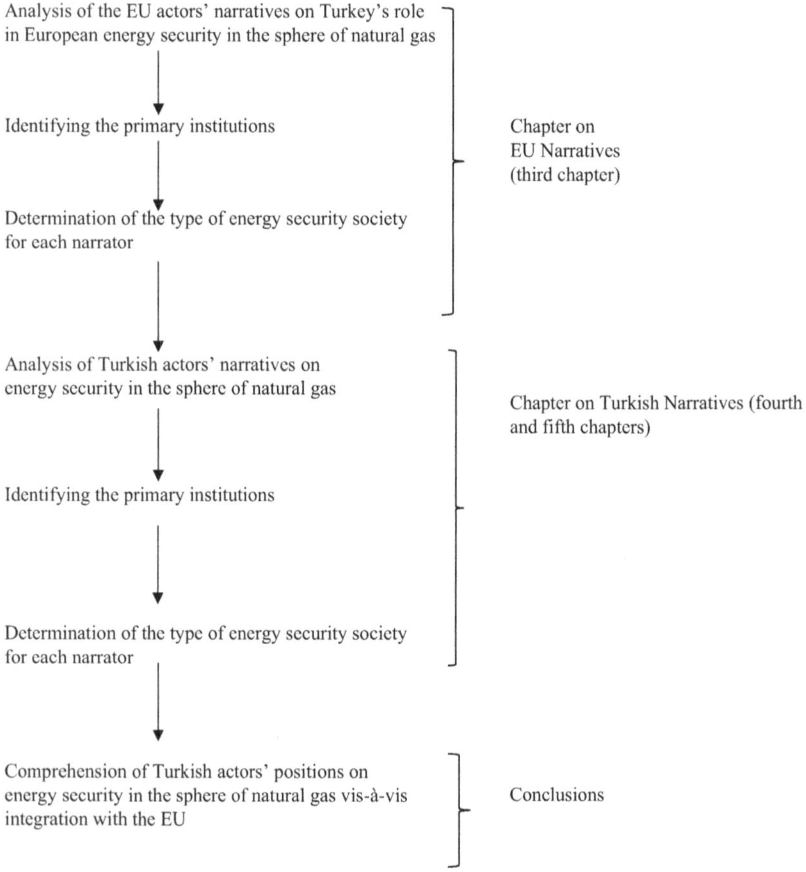

Fig. 2.6 The relationship between the methodology, theoretical framework and the aim of the book

actors on energy security in the sphere of natural gas vis-à-vis integration with the EU. Comprehension of the EU actors' choice(s) for the type(s) of energy security society vis-à-vis Turkey provides background for us to understand to what extent the type(s) of energy security society the Turkish actors prefer converges with the EU's choice(s).

Although the book chapters are organised based on the primary institutions in the narratives, the methodological process in the research included three phases: coding the data according to Alasuutari's (1995) approach of analysing goals, means, obstacles and reasons; classifying the narratives by adopting Roe's (1994) approach; and identifying the primary institutions constituting narratives (Fig. 2.7). Although Alasuutari used his method for stories without a plot, it is used in this study for all narratives with and without plot. Alasuutari's method is a good start if a researcher lacks background in the subject and faces difficulties in identifying beginnings, middles and ends, which form the structure of a narrative. Following Roe's approach, the book analyses different policymakers' narratives, which are classified as uncertain, complex and polarised. These policy narratives are stories with a beginning, middle and end, or arguments with premises and conclusions. Roe defined policy narratives as "stories—scenarios and arguments—that are taken by one or more parties to the controversy as underwriting (that is, establishing or certifying) and stabilizing (that is, fixing or making steady) the assumptions for policymaking in the face of the issue's uncertainty, complexity or polarization" (Roe 1994,

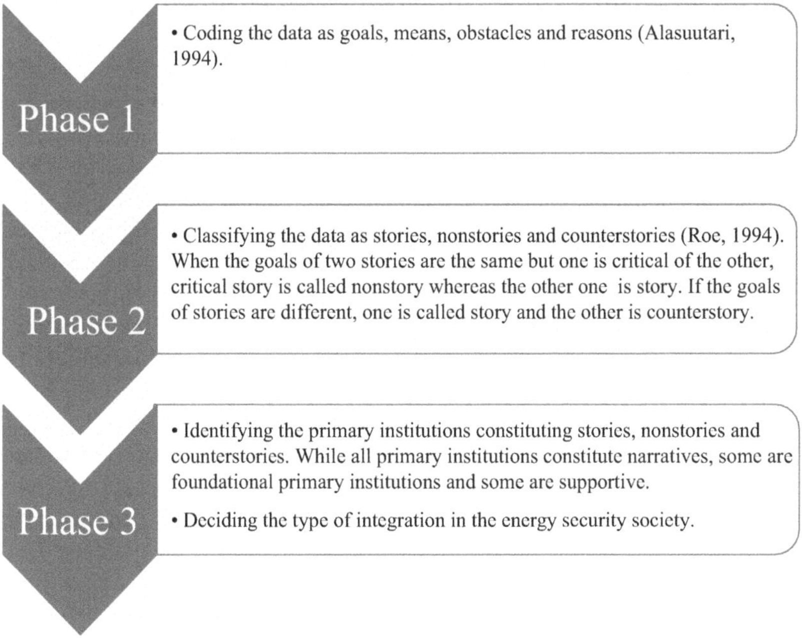

Fig. 2.7 Methodological process

p. 3). Furthermore, the "policy narratives of interest are those that dominate the issue in question" (Roe 1994, p. 3). Second, the book analyses nonstories, which lack a proper structure of beginning, middle and ends (e.g. critiques), and counterstories as alternatives to dominant policy narratives (Roe 1994, p. 3). Narratives in the book refer to policy narratives (stories), critiques (nonstories) and alternative narratives (counterstories). Accordingly, narratives of not only the Turkish government but also those of different actors (opposition parties, unions, the private sector etc.) criticising the government's narrative and/or explaining an alternative narrative on energy security vis-à-vis integration with the EU are analysed in the empirical chapters.

2.5 Conclusion

Energy security is a broad concept referring to both state and non-state actors on different levels and sectors. Since sources are not distributed equally and energy needs are paramount, producers, consumers and transit states must interact with each other, necessitating the notion of an energy society. Like other societies, energy security societies have institutional structures established by different primary institutions. Constituting the political, legal and economic frames of the society, primary institutions determine the grounds for state and non-state actors' policies and practices and borders between different integration types in the energy security society. Therefore, using the theoretical framework presented, this book aims to understand the extent to which Turkey can be involved in the pan-European energy security society. To achieve this aim, we need first to identify the primary institutions in the EU regarding Turkey's role in its energy security and comprehend what kind of a society the EU wants to have with Turkey in the sphere of natural gas. Second, we must identify the primary institutions existing in Turkish domestic energy society in order to discuss the extent to which they converge with those of the EU. Accordingly, this chapter examined the primary institutions of sovereignty, energy diplomacy, great power management, balance of power, the market, state capitalism and security of supply/demand and exemplified briefly how these primary institutions function in the EU and Turkey. The empirical chapters aim to analyse those primary institutions further within the context of Turkey-EU relations in the sphere of natural gas. At the stage of identifying the primary institutions, the book utilises the narrative policy analysis to examine the data collected in the form of interviews and sources from the EU and Turkey. Narratives play an important role in the construction of policies considering that the narratives told show the cognitive map of the narrator and gives an indication of the narrator's policy.

One significant contribution of this book to the literature on energy security society is its analysis of the interrelationship between different primary institutions, which helps us to understand the functioning of energy security societies. One example of the mutual dependencies of primary institutions is the interrelationship between the market and contemporary sovereignty. In the existence of the market institution, the aim is to improve efficiency and technology, promote investments, decrease prices, produce high quality services and provide secure and sustainable energy (European Commission 2012). Therefore, the European Commission's regulations which the Member States are expected to implement aim to establish a single integrated energy market. This demonstrates the shared competence between the Commission and the Member States, which proves the presence of contemporary sovereignty. Similarly, IMF preconditions of the liberalisation of energy markets in Turkey, as discussed further in the empirical chapter, reveal contemporary sovereignty. Furthermore, the EU establishes a linkage between the market and security of supply where the market brings security of supply via intensified competition, improved efficiency and increased investments. Accordingly, the EU expects to secure supply via the establishment of a single energy market. A well-functioning market improves security of supply by giving investors the right signals and increasing competition. Similarly, an integrated market necessitates a well-interconnected system which also contributes to the security of supply. Moreover, there is an interaction between great power management and the security of supply as exemplified in the Russian case and its implications for the EU and Turkey. The operation of great power management creates a risk to the establishment of a functioning single energy market, and thus necessitates diversification. Furthermore, the market is expected to promote diversification while diversification is considered to enhance competitiveness. It is crucial to keep these mutual relations in mind while dealing with empirical facts.

Notes

1. I'd like to thank Burak Toygar Halistoprak for his comments on the earlier version of this chapter.

2. Discussion of pluralism and solidarism is based on the character of international society and the extent to which norms, rules and institutions are shared in state systems (Buzan 2004a, p. 45). Whereas pluralists "lean towards the realist side of rationalism" (Buzan 2004a, pp. 46–47), solidarists "lean towards the Kantian side of rationalism" (Buzan 2004a, pp. 46–47) in classical ES thinking. In pluralism, "international society is limited to the creation of a framework that will allow them to coexist in relative harmony" (Mayall 2000, p. 14). In Buzan's thinking, pluralism defines "second order societies of states with a relatively low degree of shared norms, rules and institutions amongst the states" (Buzan 2004a, p. xvii).
3. In contrast to pluralists, solidarists believe in convergence and assert that "humanity is one, and …the task of diplomacy is to translate this latent or immanent solidarity of interests and values into reality" (Mayall 2000, p. 14). Therefore, solidarism refers to cosmopolitanism according to classical ES thinking. However, in Buzan's usage, the term defines "international societies with a relatively high degree of shared norms, rules and institutions among states, where the focus is not only on ordering coexistence and competition, but also on co-operation over a wider range of issues" (2004a, p. xviii).
4. The difference between society (*gesellschaft*) and community (*gemeinschaft*) was not adopted in the research.
5. One of the main discussions on security in ES focus on whether ES theorists are explicitly (Makinda 2005, pp. 275–288) or implicitly (Bellamy and Mcdonald 2004, pp. 307–330) interested in "security". Further discussion can also be found on which traditions form the basis for the ES' security perspective. In other words, Bellamy and McDonald (2004, pp. 311–319) argued that the security concept of ES is divided between "pluralism" and "solidarism" and the security of individuals are prioritised in solidarism. Makinda (2005, pp. 275–288) added "cosmopolitanism" to this picture as the third stream and argued that the state is an end in pluralism whereas it is a means for achieving individual security in cosmopolitanism.
6. The book deliberately avoids using the term affordability. The terminology in the definition was chosen based on the actors' preferences. As will be elaborated in the empirical chapter on Turkey, some Turkish actors were reluctant to establish a competitive market and did not use this term, instead preferring the term "low prices".
7. To examine Turkish and EU views on energy security and integration within the context of the pan-European energy community, the EU is considered to be within the "domain of interstate/state-like actors". There are two reasons behind this choice. First, although the EU is not a state, it has institutions with executive, legislative and judicial tasks. Second, the EU

consists of Member States and the intergovernmental institutions have considerable power.

8. Values refer to "the moral principles and beliefs or accepted standards of a person or a social group" (Buzan 2004a, p. 164).
9. Buzan referred to Krasner when defining the terms "norm", "principle" and "rule". Accordingly, he used Krasner's distinction between norm and rule: "norms feel more like the customs of a society, with rules occupying the more formal, written, possibly legal end of the spectrum" (Buzan 2004a, p. 164). Krasner stated that "principles are beliefs of fact, causation, and rectitude. Norms are standards of behaviour defined in terms of rights and obligations. Rules are specific prescriptions or proscriptions for actions" (Buzan 2004a, p. 163).
10. Regarding functional categories, which generate primary institutions, Buzan considered membership, authoritative communication, limits to the use of force, allocation of property rights and sanctity of agreements. While Bull used limits to the use of force, allocation of property rights and sanctity of agreements and Schouenborg included legitimacy and membership, authoritative communication, trade, international organisation, regulating conflicts (Schouenborg 2013, p. 17). Donnelly (2006) preferred a different classification which consists of foundational regulative practices, hegemonic cultural values, and principles and practices of domestic and international legitimacies. Within the scope of foundational regulative practices, he took into account making rules, regulating conflicts, regulating the use of force, regulating ownership and exchange, communicating and interacting and aggregating interests and power. Last but not least, Navari and other members of her research team argued that international organisations "are shoved, shaved, bent, constrained and defined by master and functional institutions" (Navari 2013, p. 1), demonstrating the strong link between international organisations and primary institutions.
11. Accordingly, sovereignty emerges from the category of membership whereas energy diplomacy evolves from the category of authoritative communication. While great power management and balance of power are driven by the category of limits to the use of force, trade and territoriality derive from the category of allocation of property rights.
12. Two criteria were used to identify primary institutions in Parrat's (2012, p. 6) analysis: (1) states behave in accordance with a habit or (2) states argue against it.
13. Relating the concept of sovereignty to *right and authority*, historians, international lawyers and political theorists used it as "constitutional independence". This traditional approach deals with the *identity* of the actors who control the *decision-making mechanisms* of a state rather than its activities. Accordingly, sovereignty is considered a *qualification* for a state to be

eligible to take part in the international arena (Jackson 1999a, pp. 424–425; James 1999, p. 458). The traditionalist approach argues that the EU is still a union of sovereign states and there is no permanent or irreversible transfer of sovereignty among Member States. What they have done is a matter of choice. In this interpretation, sovereignty is a *legal status* rather than a resource to exchange (Jackson 1999b, pp. 450–453).

14. Relating the concept of sovereignty to *power and capability*, political economists and political sociologists use the term "autonomy". Dealing with the *activities* of a sovereign state rather than its identity, they consider sovereignty an *instrument* or *resource* to exchange rather than a status (Jackson 1999a, pp. 424–426). Therefore, in contrast to traditionalists' absolute character of sovereignty, which means that it either exists or does not exist (James 1999, p. 463), this approach argues that it is possible to retain some or all of sovereignty, as witnessed in the globalisation process. Accordingly, interpretation of the EU is not a unity of sovereign states, but a pooling of sovereignty (Jackson 1999a, p. 426).
15. He argued that whereas scholars in favour of continuity talk about the stable constitutive rules, those supporting change "talk about the development and change of substantial statehood, or development and change of sovereignty's regulative rules, or some mix of the two" (Sørensen 1999, pp. 596–597).
16. Sørensen argued that whereas the constitutive element which refers to "constitutional independence of states which has territory, people and government" (Sørensen 1999, p. 594) continues, the regulative element, which is indeed a framework of international law in the broadest sense (e.g. rules of non-intervention, recognition, reciprocity), changes. Furthermore, he mentioned "statehood" as the third element referring to the structure and content of both economy and polity and nationhood. Statehood together with regulative rules transforms in the perceptions of sovereignty.
17. Although this book relies extensively on Sørensen's understanding of sovereignty, it does not use the same concepts regarding the names of different sovereignty games. While Sørensen titled sovereignties as Westphalian, postcolonial and postmodern, this book uses the terms modern sovereignty, contemporary sovereignty and postmodern sovereignty. I am very grateful for discussions on biased definitions of sovereignty held in the seminar sessions at the University of Jyväskylä, Finland on 02.12.2010, and particularly to Tapani Turkka and Evgeny Roshchin for their recommendations.
18. Sørensen used the concept of postmodern sovereignty to refer to situations where states have intense co-operation and integration with each other (Sørensen 1999, p. 602). However, he included the EU and supranation-

ality in this type of sovereignty. Given that economy and polity are affected by international events as a result of globalisation without any necessity to transfer sovereignty to any organisation, the aims of this book require a distinction be made between the type of sovereignty in supranational cases (post-modern sovereignty) and the rest. Hence, three different terms for sovereignty are used in the book. The evolution of sovereignty is directly linked with the evolution of the concept of human rights in different periods such as the Enlightenment, post-Second World War, and post-Cold War (Klug 2001) (I am very grateful to Tapani Turkka for enlightening me on the evolution of the concept of sovereignty).

19. Within the framework of the Third Energy Package, when citizens have the right to choose their gas supplier companies, their influence on the decision-making processes of energy companies will increase. Similarly, actors will need to take into account external factors such as the structure of global energy markets, fluctuations in oil prices, liquefied natural gas (LNG) prices and developments in unconventional gas in their decisions and calculations.
20. One significant difference between this book and Sørensen's conceptualisation is the fact that whereas Sørensen considered the EU within the framework of postmodern sovereignty, this research argues that there are different sovereignty games inside the EU bearing in mind the principal of conferral. This principle is laid down in Article 5(2) of the Treaty of the European Union: "the Union shall act only within the limits of the competences conferred upon it ... Competences not conferred upon the Union in the Treaties remain with the Member States" (European Union 2012a, p. 18). As Kaczorowska (2011, p. 78) asserted, this principle provides a guarantee that the EU can only extend its competences if the Member States give consent.
21. "Ownership unbundling where all integrated energy companies sell off their gas and electricity networks. In this case, no supply or production company is allowed to hold a majority share or interfere in the work of a transmission system operator" (European Commission 2014).
22. Buzan (2004b, pp. 64–67) preferred to make a tripartite division of superpowers, great powers and regional powers, arguing that a simple polarity theory based on a differentiation between superpowers and regional great powers is not valid in the current global system. In this new classification, he made a distinction between system/global and regional levels where superpowers and great powers are considered within the former and regional powers the latter. Accordingly, superpowers and great powers have the ability to influence the global structure on which their securities also depend. On the other hand, regional powers play at the regional level whereas they are usually "takers" at the system level. The distinctive ele-

ment between a superpower and a great power in his classification rests on the size of expectations and realisation in terms of both capability and behaviour which are less demanding for a great power (Buzan 2004b, p. 69). In defining the systemic level of powers, whether it is a superpower or a great power, Buzan included Waltz's approach of *material capabilities* and Bull's approach of *self-declared status and acceptance of this status by others*. An important distinction between superpowers and great powers is the fact that the material capabilities of a superpower are observed in all sectors whereas expectations are more limited for a great power both in terms of material capabilities and behaviour. However, he did not consider capabilities, self-recognition and recognition by others as sufficient for defining either superpower or great power. Being active in securitisation and de-securitisation processes in almost all regions of the system is important for a superpower whereas it is not a required feature in all regions for a great power. Furthermore, superpowers also establish the universal values of the system (Buzan 2004b, p. 69). What counts as a difference between regional powers and great powers is not only the difference between regional and system levels but also the fact of how great powers "behave in a wider sense and that behaviour is treated by others" (Buzan 2004b, p. 67). Here, in addition to recognition by oneself and others, "observation of the practical mode of operation of states, particularly which actors are responded to by others on the basis of system level calculations" (Buzan and Waever 2003, p. 32) becomes significant. Therefore, *calculation* of a great power's behaviours at system level by others is the most distinctive element in Buzan's interpretation.

23. Balance of power is conceptualised in different ways by different theories. In neo-realism, for example, the structural anarchy in the states system prioritises survival and security which necessitates self-help. The need for self-help and competition between different units generates the concept of balance of power (Schroeder 1994, pp. 108–109). However, the concept is considered within the framework of co-operation rather than survival in Bull's understanding. According to him, balance of power can be realised in international society instead of international system since this primary institution needs shared beliefs and presence of common language (Little 2006, pp. 104–107).
24. Offering a broader conceptualisation, Buzan, Jones and Little argued that balance of power exists both in international system and international society. Whereas it refers to the same neo-realist conceptualisation in international system, it is interlinked with norms and rules in international society, and thus does not only mean balance of power (Rengger 2000, p. 53). Accordingly, Little (2006, pp. 100, 118–119) argued that there are two types of balance of power, one of which is "adversarial balance of power"

overlapping with the neo-realist conceptualisation of balance of power. The other type is "associative balance of power", which refers to co-operation within the balance of power. This type of balance of power is similar to Bull's contrived balance of power (Little 2006, p. 118) which refers to "one that owes its existence at least partly to the conscious policies of one or both sides" (Bull 2002, p. 100). It should also be underlined that co-operation in solidarist international societies invariably brings competition, as argued by Little (2006, p. 118).

25. If balance of power is realised by all partners, the concept refers to four different meanings: "1. An even distribution of power. 2. The principle that power ought to be evenly distributed. 3. The existing distribution of power. Hence, any possible distribution of power. 4. The principle of equal aggrandizement of the Great Powers at the expense of weak" (Wight 1966, p. 151).
26. If balance of power is realised by one particular power, the concept has four different meanings: "5. The principle that our side ought to have a margin of strength in order to avert the danger of power becoming unevenly distributed. 6. (When governed by the verb 'to hold') A special role in maintaining an even distribution of power. 7 ... A special advantage in the existing distribution of power. 8. Predominance" (Wight 1966, p. 151).
27. The concept refers to "[a]n inherent tendency of international politics to produce an even distribution of power" (Wight 1966, p. 151) when it is considered that the law distributes power evenly.
28. Regarding the concept of power, the research concurs with Bull's argument that there are different types of power which form many chessboards (Little 2006, pp. 101–102). Accordingly, Buzan's (2004b) criteria of material capabilities, self-declared status and acceptance of this by others, and calculation by others can be considered being a power in energy issues at systemic or regional level.
29. Contrary to the Commission, it is argued in an OECD paper that liberalisation may not automatically lead to diversification. Since the expectation is establishing a liquidity in the market with short term agreements, it is argued that these agreements will increase intermediary links with swaps and mini-swaps which will complicate contractual flows. There is even a risk of a decrease in diversification and an increase in regional dependencies if the cheapest gas is consumed in each location and if there is risk in transit routes or there are not sufficient wholesale suppliers (IEA 2000, pp. 52–54).
30. Inclusion of non-state actors is in line with the theoretical framework as it involves non-state actors (transnational domain). Accordingly, the argument that interplay between different integration domains (e.g. interstate and transnational) has an effect on the integration type in the interstate

domain (Buzan 2004a, pp. 231–233) necessitates taking into account Turkish non- state actors in addition to the State.

Bibliography

Aalto, P. (2009). European perspectives for managing dependence. In J. Perovic, R. Orttung, & A. Wenger (Eds.), *Russian energy power and foreign relations: Implications to conflict and cooperation* (pp. 157–180). London and New York: Routledge.

Aalto, P., & Korkmaz-Temel, D. (2012). Towards a European/Eurasian energy security society: From vulnerability and viability to sustainability. In P. Aalto, V. Harle, & S. Moisio (Eds.), *Towards the interdisciplinary study of global and regional policy problems* (pp. 79–104). Aldershot: Ashgate.

Akcollu, Y. (2006). Major challenges to the liberalization of the Turkish natural gas market. *Oxford Institute for Energy Studies, NG16*. Retrieved from https://www.oxfordenergy.org/wpcms/wp-content/uploads/2010/11/NG16-MajorChallengestotheLiberalizationoftheTurkishNaturalGasMarket-YesimAkcollu-2007.pdf.

Alasuutari, P. (1995). *Researching culture qualitative method and cultural studies*. London, Thousand Oaks, New Delhi: SAGE Publications.

Behrens, A. (2009). *Learning from the crisis: A market approach to securing European natural gas markets*. CEPS Policy Brief, 183. Retrieved from http://aei.pitt.edu/10768/1/1815.pdf.

Bellamy, A., & Mcdonald, M. (2004). Securing international society: Towards an English School discourse of security. *Australian Journal of Political Science, 39*(2), 307–330.

Belyi, A. (2003). New dimensions of energy security of the enlarging EU and their impact on relations with Russia. *European Integration, 25*(4), 351–369.

BP. (2018). *Statistical review of world energy*. Retrieved from https://www.bp.com/content/dam/bp/business-sites/en/global/corporate/pdfs/energy-economics/statistical-review/bp-stats-review-2018-full-report.pdf.

Bremmer, I. (2009). State capitalism comes of age. *Foreign Affairs, 88*(3), 40–55.

Bridgman, T., & Barry, D. (2002). Regulation is evil: An application of narrative policy analysis to regulatory debate in New Zealand. *Policy Sciences, 35*, 141–161.

Bull, H. (2002). *The anarchical society a study of world politics* (3rd ed.). New York: Palgrave.

Buzan, B. (2004a). *From international to world society*. Cambridge: Cambridge University Press.

Buzan, B. (2004b). *The United States and the great powers world politics in the twenty-first century*. Cambridge and Malden: Polity.

Buzan, B. (2005). International political economy and globalization. In A. J. Bellamy (Ed.), *International society and its critics* (pp. 115–133). New York: Oxford University Press.

Buzan, B., & Gonzalez-Pelaez, A. (Eds.). (2009). *International society and the Middle East: English School theory at the regional level.* Basingstoke: Palgrave Macmillan.

Buzan, B., & Waever, O. (2003). *Regions and powers: The structure of international security.* Cambridge: Cambridge University Press.

Buzan, B., Waever, O., & De Wilde, J. (1998). *Security: A new framework for analysis.* Boulder and London: Lynne Rienner Publishers.

Correlje, A., & Van Der Linde, C. (2006). Energy supply security and geopolitics: A European perspective. *Energy Policy, 34*, 532–543.

Czaputowicz, J. (2003). The English School of international relations and its approach to European integration. *Studies & Analyses, 2*(2), 3–55.

Diez, T., & Whitman, R. (2002). Analysing European integration: Reflecting on the English School—Scenarios for an encounter. *Journal of Common Market Studies, 40*(1), 43–67.

Diez, T., Manners, I., & Whitman, R. (2011). The changing nature of international institutions in Europe: The challenge of the European Union. *Journal of European Integration, 33*(2), 117–138.

Donnelly, J. (2006). *The constitutional structure of international societies.* Retrieved from http://mysite.du.edu/~jdonnell/papers.htm.

Enerji Piyasasi Duzenleme Kurumu. (2019). *Dogal Gaz Piyasasi 2018 Yili Sektor Raporu.*. Ankara.

Esterberg, K. (2002). *Qualitative methods in social research.* Boston: McGraw Hill.

Euractiv. (2009). *Liberalisation of the EU gas sector.* Retrieved from http://www.euractiv.com/energy/liberalisation-eu-gas-sector-linksdossier-188455.

Euractiv. (2010). *Nord Stream 'a waste of money' says Poland.* Retrieved from http://www.euractiv.com/energy/nord-stream-waste-money-poland/article-188727.

Euractiv. (2011). *Russia-EU energy politics.* Retrieved from http://www.euractiv.com/energy/russia-eu-energy-politics-analysis-508992.

European Commission. (2003). *Communication from the Commission to the European Parliament and the Council energy infrastructure and security of supply* (COM (2003) 743 final). Retrieved from http://ec.europa.eu/transparency/regdoc/rep/1/2003/EN/1-2003-743-EN-F1-1.Pdf.

European Commission. (2006). *Green paper—A European strategy for sustainable, competitive and secure energy* (COM (2006) 105 final) Retrieved from http://europa.eu/documents/comm/green_papers/pdf/com2006_105_en.pdf.

European Commission. (2007a). *Prospects for the internal gas and electricity market* (COM (2006) 841 final). Retrieved from http://www.europarl.europa.

eu/meetdocs/2004_2009/documents/com/com_com(2006)0841_/com_com(2006)0841_en.pdf.
European Commission. (2007b). *Energising Europe: A real market with security of supply* (MEMO/07/361). Retrieved from http://europa.eu/rapid/press-release_MEMO-07- 361_en.htm?locale=en.
European Commission. (2010a). *Commission staff working paper—Interpretative note on Directive 2009/72/EC concerning common rules for the internal market in electricity and Directive 2009/73/EC concerning common rules for the internal market in natural gas—The unbundling regime*. Retrieved from https://ec.europa.eu/energy/sites/ener/files/documents/2010_01_21_the_unbundling_regime.pdf.
European Commission. (2010b). *Energy infrastructure priorities for 2020 and beyond: A blueprint for an integrated European energy network* (COM (2010) 677 final). Retrieved from http://eur-lex.europa.eu/legal-content/EN/TXT/PDF/?uri=CELEX:52010DC0677&from=EN.
European Commission. (2010c). *Energy 2020: A strategy for competitive, sustainable and secure energy* (COM (2010) 639 final). Retrieved from http://eur-lex.europa.eu/LexUriServ/LexUriServ.do?uri=COM:2010:0639:FIN:En:PDF.
European Commission. (2011a). *Communication from the Commission to the European Parliament, the Council, the European Economic and Social Committee and the Committee of the Regions: Energy roadmap 2050* (COM (2011) 885/2). Retrieved from http://eur-lex.europa.eu/legal-content/EN/TXT/PDF/?uri=CELEX:52011DC0885&from=EN.
European Commission. (2011b). *Proposal for a decision of the European Parliament and of the Council setting up an information exchange mechanism with regard to intergovernmental agreements between Member States and third countries in the field of energy* (COM (2011)540 final). Retrieved from http://www.europarl.europa.eu/meetdocs/2009_2014/documents/com/com_com(2011)0540_/com_com(2011)0540_en.pdf.
European Commission. (2012). *Liberalisation*. Retrieved from http://ec.europa.eu/competition/liberalisation/overview_en.html.
European Commission. (2014). *Market legislation*. Retrieved from https://ec.europa.eu/energy/en/topics/markets-and-consumers/market-legislation.
European Commission. (2019). *The European citizen's initiative*. Retrieved from https://ec.europa.eu/citizens-initiative/public/competences/faq#q3.
European Council. (2007). *Brussels European Council 8/9 March 2007 Presidency Conclusions*. Retrieved from http://www.consilium.europa.eu/ueDocs/cms_Data/docs/pressData/en/ec/93135.pdf.
European Union. (2007). *An energy policy for Europe*. Retrieved from http://europa.eu/legislation_summaries/energy/european_energy_policy/l27067_en.htm.

European Union. (2011). *Security of supply of natural gas.* Retrieved from http://europa.eu/legislation_summaries/energy/external_dimension_enlargement/en0026_en.htm.

European Union. (2012a). Consolidated version of the treaty on European Union. *Official Journal of the European Union, C, 326*, 13–45.

European Union. (2012b). *Consolidated version of the treaty on the functioning of the European Union.* Retrieved from http://eur-lex.europa.eu/resource.html?uri=cellar:ccccda77-8ac2-4a25-8e66-a5827ecd3459.0010.02/DOC_1&format=PDF.

Fischer, F. (2003). *Reframing public policy discursive politics and deliberative practices.* Oxford, New York: Oxford University Press.

Gas Exporting Countries Forum. (n.d.). *Our objectives.* Retrieved from http://www.gecf.org/aboutus/gecf-objectives.

Gazprom. (2005). *Blue Stream project officially inaugurated.* Retrieved from http://www.gazprom.com/press/news/2005/november/article63323/.

Gilbert, N. (2008). *Researching social life* (3rd ed.). Los Angeles, London, New Delhi, Singapore: SAGE Publications.

Godzimirski, J. (2009). Energy security and the politics of identity. In G. Fermann (Ed.), *Political economy of energy in Europe: Forces of fragmentation and integration* (pp. 173–206). Berlin: Berliner Wissenschafts Verlag.

Holsti, K. J. (2004). *Taming the sovereigns: Institutional change in international politics.* New York: Cambridge University Press.

IEA. (2000). *Regulatory reform: European gas.* Paris: IEA. Retrieved from http://www.ipt.ntnu.no/~jsg/undervisning/naturgass/dokumenter/RegulatoryReformEuropeanGas2000.pdf.

IEA. (2018). *Key world energy statistics.* Paris: IEA.

IEA. (n.d.). *History.* Retrieved from http://www.iea.org/aboutus/history/.

Jackson, R. (1999a). Introduction: Sovereignty at the millennium. *Political Studies, XLVII*, 423–430.

Jackson, R. (1999b). Sovereignty in world politics: A glance at the conceptual and historical landscape. *Political Studies, XLVII*, 431–456.

James, A. (1999). The practice of sovereign statehood in contemporary international society. *Political Studies, XLVII*, 457–473.

Kaczorowska, A. (2011). *European Union law* (2nd ed.). New York and London: Routledge.

Klug, F. (2001). The Human Rights Act—A 'third way' or 'third wave' Bill of Rights. *European Human Rights Law Review, 4*, 361–372.

Kroes, N. (2006). *What's wrong with Europe's energy markets?* (Speech/06/137). Retrieved from http://europa.eu/rapid/press-release_SPEECH-06-137_en.htm.

Linklater, A., & Suganami, H. (2006). *The English School of international relations: A contemporary reassessment.* New York: Cambridge University Press.

Little, R. (2006). The balance of power and great power management. In R. Little & J. Williams (Eds.), *The anarchical society in a globalized world* (pp. 97–120). New York: Palgrave Macmillan.

Lowe, P. (2006). *The liberalisation of EU energy markets.* Retrieved from http://ec.europa.eu/competition/speeches/text/sp2006_017_en.pdf.

Makinda, S. (2005). Security in international society: A comment on Alex J. Bellamy and Matt McDonald. *Australian Journal of Political Science, 40*(2), 275–288.

Mayall, J. (2000). *World politics: Progress and its limits.* Cambridge: Polity.

Mcdonald, M. (2008). Constructivism. In P. Williams (Ed.), *Security studies: An introduction* (2nd ed., pp. 63–76). Abingdon, NY: Routledge.

Musacchio, A., & Lazzarini, S. (2014). *Reinventing state capitalism.* Cambridge: Harvard University Press.

Musacchio, A., Lazzarini, S., & Aguilera, R. V. (2015). New varieties of state capitalism? Strategic and governance implications. *The Academy of Management Perspectives, 29*(1), 115–131.

Natorski, M., & Surrallés, A. (2008). Securitizing moves to nowhere? The framing of the European Union's energy policy. *Journal of Contemporary European Research, 4*(2), 71–89.

Navari, C. (2013). *International organizations in the anarchical society: Interim report of an English School research project.* Retrieved from http://www.eisa-net.org/be-bruga/eisa/files/events/warsaw2013/navari_internationalorganisationintheanarchicalsociety.pdf.

O'Brien, R., & Williams, M. (2004). *Global political economy evolution and dynamics.* Hampshire and New York: Palgrave Macmillan.

Oatley, T. (2011). *International political economy.* New York: Routledge.

Oettinger, G. (2011). The necessity of ensuring the security of Europe's energy supply. *The European Files, 22*, 8.

OPEC. (2006). *Energy supply and demand security.* Retrieved from http://www.opec.org/opec_web/en/1097.htm.

OPEC. (2009). *OPEC Solemn declarations..* Retrieved from http://www.opec.org/opec_web/static_files_project/media/downloads/publications/Solemn_Declaration_I-III.pdf.

Parrat, C. F. (2012). *Understanding UN reform: Change in international society.* Retrieved from https://www.academia.edu/4557836/Understanding_UN_Reform_Change_in_International_Society.

Patterson, M., & Monroe, K. R. (1998). Narrative in political science. *Annual Review of Political Science, 1*, 315–331.

President of Russia. (2007). *Transcript of press conference with the Russian and foreign media..* Retrieved from http://archive.kremlin.ru/eng/text/speeches/2007/02/01/1309_type82915type82917_117600.shtml.

Rengger, N. J. (2000). *International relations, political theory and the problem of order*. London and New York: Routledge.

Roe, E. (1994). *Narrative policy analysis theory and practice*. Durham and London: Duke University Press.

Schmidt, V. A. (2002). *The futures of European capitalism*. New York: Oxford University Press.

Schouenborg, L. (2013). *The Scandinavian international society*. London: Routledge.

Schroeder, P. (1994). Historical reality vs. neo-realist theory. *International Security, 19*(1), 108–148.

Seyidoglu, H. (1992). *Ekonomik terimler ansiklopedik sozluk*. Ankara: Guzem Yayinlari.

Sørensen, G. (1999). Sovereignty: Change and continuity in a fundamental institution. *Political Studies, XLVII*, 590–604.

Soysal, C., Yucel, C. O., Koyuncu, T., & Tokgoz, E. (2012). *Dogalgaz sektor arastirmasi raporu*. Ankara: Rekabet Kurumu.

Stivachtis, Y. (2002). Understanding the European Union's enlargement: The international society approach of the English School. In H. Hensel (Ed.), *The United States of Europe* (pp. 55–77). Aldershot: Ashgate.

Strange, S. (2000). States, firms and diplomacy. In J. A. Frieden & D. Lake (Eds.), *International political economy perspectives on global power and wealth* (4th ed., pp. 60–67). London and New York: Routledge.

Talus, K. (2013). *EU energy law and policy: A critical account*. Oxford: Oxford University Press.

Tanap. (n.d.). *The project the world is talking about*. Retrieved from http://www.tanap.com/.

The Economist. (2012, January 24). *State capitalism—Debate*. Retrieved from http://www.lionelingram.com/561_Economist%20Debates_%20State%20capitalism_%20Statements.pdf.

Tradacete, A. (2000). *The role of EC competition policy in the liberalisation of EU energy markets*. Retrieved from http://ec.europa.eu/competition/speeches/text/sp2000_003_en.pdf.

Ungerer, H. (2007). *Competition policy and energy security—Some comments*. Retrieved from http://ec.europa.eu/competition/speeches/text/sp2007_09_en.pdf.

Watson, A. (1992). Diplomacy. In J. Baylis & N. J. Rengger (Eds.), *Dilemmas of world politics international issues in a changing world* (pp. 159–173). New York: Oxford University Press.

Westphal, K. (2006). Energy policy between multilateral governance and geopolitics: Whither Europe? *IPG, 4*, 44–62.

Wight, M. (1966). The balance of power. In H. Butterfield & M. Wight (Eds.), *Diplomatic investigations* (pp. 149–175). Cambridge and Massachusetts: Harvard University Press.

Yin, R. (2009). How to do better case studies (with illustrations from 20 exemplary case studies). In L. Bickman & D. J. Rog (Eds.), *The Sage handbook of applied social research methods* (pp. 254–282). Thousand Oaks: Sage Publications.

CHAPTER 3

European Energy Security and Turkey

In May 2010, Jerzy Buzek, President of the European Parliament, and Jacques Delors, former European Commission President, called for the creation of a European Energy Community (President of the European Parliament 2010). They argued that a common energy policy would overcome the current challenges in energy policy and create new opportunities just as the 1952 European Coal and Steel Community once replaced conflict with co-operation under similar circumstances. In February 2015, the European Commission (referred to as the Commission) announced the establishment of the Energy Union, which was expected to transform the energy system of the EU. While both documents referenced the EU's external energy relations, the latter emphasised the significance of ensuring a strategic energy partnership with Turkey (European Commission 2015b, pp. 2, 6).

This chapter[1] aims to explore the type of integration that the EU would like to establish with Turkey in the sphere of natural gas through a contextualisation of the theoretical framework of energy security society. By utilising primary institutions as analytical tools in our examination of EU narratives, this chapter aims to understand the cognitive map of the EU actors and in turn their main motivations in regard to their policies on Turkey in the sphere of natural gas. As mentioned in the methodological chapter, the analysis is based on policy papers and opinions written and produced by EU actors on Turkey's role in European energy security during the period between January 2001 and July 2019. Bearing in mind that

D. Korkmaz, *Turkey and the EU in an Energy Security Society*,
https://doi.org/10.1007/978-3-030-45774-7_3

the EU is not a homogeneous body, relevant EU actors in this research are considered to be the Commission, the European Council, the Parliament, the Council of the European Union and those Member States involved in the discussions in the Council of the European Union on Turkey and energy security. Therefore, this chapter analyses the narratives of each actor on Turkey's role in European energy security. The concept of energy security in EU narratives refers to competitive, secure and sustainable energy supplies.

Before delving into the narratives, the chapter begins by explaining the importance of natural gas for the EU and the role of Russia in the EU's efforts to secure its energy supply. The chapter then examines the EU's narratives on exporting liberal values and on the diversification of suppliers and the importance of Turkey within this context. From a theoretical standpoint, the market and the security of supply served as the foundational primary institutions in the EU narratives, while great power management functioned as a supportive primary institution. The chapter also explores the interrelationship between these primary institutions in order to illustrate the operation of the energy security society. The conclusion of the chapter discusses the type of integration that the EU desires to build with Turkey in the sphere of natural gas.

3.1 Significance of Natural Gas and the Role of Russia

Security of supply of constitutes one of the EU's major concerns due to the region's increasing external dependency. As of 2017, 74.3 per cent of natural gas was imported. Natural gas is a significant component of the EU's energy mix, accounting for 23.8 per cent of the gross inland consumption.[2] In the transformation sector, 21.1 per cent of electricity is generated from natural gas. The EU's declining indigenous production far from meets demand; while natural gas consumption[3] in 2017 was 442 bcm, production was only 114 bcm (European Commission 2019b, pp. 22, 76, 45, 90, 178). Furthermore, as shown in Fig. 3.1, production is expected to continue to decline, increasing external dependency. Although imports are expected to decline beginning in 2050, import dependency will continue owing to a parallel decrease in indigenous production (IEA 2018). While estimated shale gas resources, amounting to 89 tcm, have the potential to contribute to the EU's energy security, economic and technical difficulties make it difficult to determine the extent to

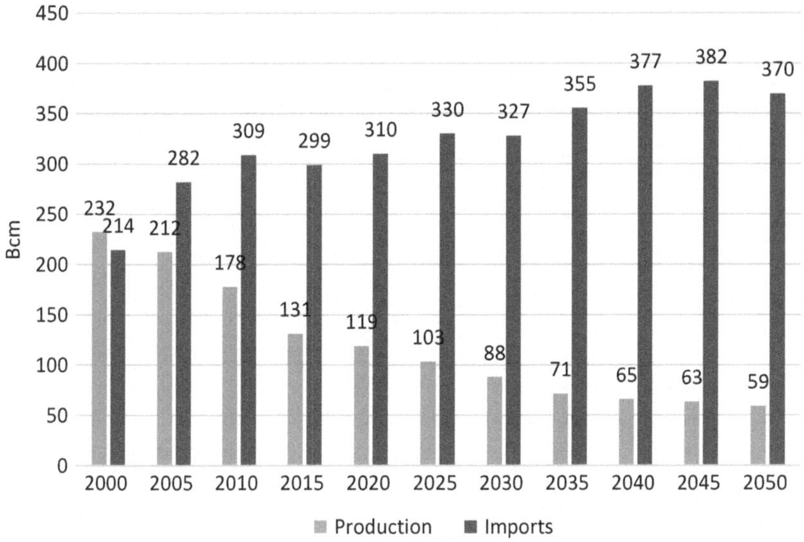

Fig. 3.1 EU production and import projections (Source: Data from European Commission, n. d.-c)

which the estimated resources can be recovered. Furthermore, environmental and regulatory concerns may prohibit the utilisation of shale gas resources as different Member States pursue diverging policies regarding shale gas. While Bulgaria and France have banned hydraulic fracturing, Poland has begun testing and explanatory drillings (European Commission n.d.-a). Additionally, natural gas is expected to replace oil and coal in the short and medium terms in the 2050 goal of reducing greenhouse gas emissions to 80–95 per cent below 1990 levels. For these reasons, the EU's strong dependency on external natural gas raises serious concerns about its secure supply.

The fact that the majority of imported gas comes from countries outside the European Economic Area is the real reason for the Commission's concern (European Commission 2014b, p. 61). Arguing that security of supply aims to reduce the risks related with dependency but does not necessarily create the absolute minimum level of risk, the Commission introduced the goal of "diversifying the various sources of supply (by product and by geographical region)" (European Commission 2000, p. 1) already in 2000. As illustrated in Fig. 3.2, 2017 saw an increase in the volume of

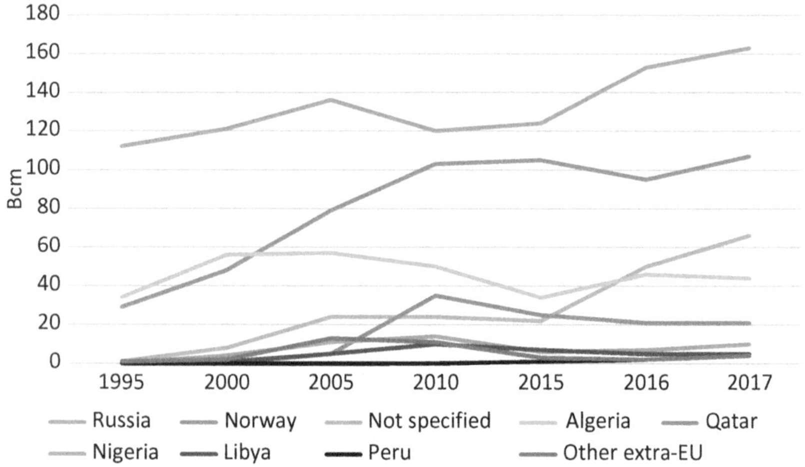

Fig. 3.2 Natural gas imports by country of origin (Source: Data from European Commission, 2018b, p. 65; 2019b, p. 69.)

imports from Russia. Although the Russian share in EU imports declined from 41 per cent in 2000 to 32 per cent in 2012 (European Commission 2014a, p. 26; 2000, p. 26), the share increased back to 38 per cent in 2017. Norway accounted for 25 per cent, Algeria 10, Qatar 5 and Nigeria 2 per cent in the same year (European Commission 2019b, p. 69). Russia accounted for 40.5 per cent of trade value in 2018 and 39.4 per cent in the first semester of 2019 (Eurostat 2019).

The dominance of Russian natural gas in northern, southern and central Europe increased concerns about dependency. The Commission's declaration that "… a number of Member States are highly or completely reliant on a single gas supplier" (European Commission 2007a, p. 10; 2008a, p. 9; 2010b, p. 7) was also highlighted by the Parliament: "…several Member States are highly dependent on a single supplier of natural gas…" (European Union 2010, p. 24). According to Eurostat data, Bulgaria, Czech Republic, Latvia, Estonia, Hungary, Austria, Romania, Slovenia, Slovakia and Finland imported more than 75 per cent of their natural gas imports from Russia and the share of Russian natural gas in Germany, Greece, Poland and Lithuania was more than 50 per cent in the first semester of 2019 (Eurostat 2019) (Table 3.1).

Russian gas flows through the following pipelines: Nord Stream 1 from Russia to Germany via the Baltic Sea; the Yamal pipeline via Belarus; the

Table 3.1 Share of Russia in national imports from outside the EU per member state (first semester 2019)

Share of Russia in national imports from outside the EU per member state (% of trade in value)	*Member states*
0–25	Belgium, Denmark, Ireland, Spain, Croatia, Cyprus, Luxembourg, Malta, Portugal, UK
25–50	Netherlands, Italy, France, Sweden
50–75	Germany, Greece, Lithuania, Poland
75–100	Bulgaria, Czech Republic, Latvia, Estonia, Hungary, Austria, Romania, Slovenia, Slovakia, Finland

Source: Eurostat (2019); © European Union, 1995–2019

Soyuz, Brotherhood and Trans Balkan pipelines via Ukraine; and TurkStream from Russia to Bulgaria via the Black Sea and Turkey. Although Russia aimed to halt gas flows via Ukraine at the end of 2019 and planned to transport Russian gas via Nord Stream 2 (a parallel pipeline to Nord Stream 1) and TurkStream, the Russian-Ukrainian transit deal of December 2019 envisages the continuation of Russian gas flows of a minimum of 65 bcm in 2020 and 40 bcm in 2021–2024 via Ukraine (Russia, Ukraine Reach Five Year 2019). While there is a delay in the Nord Stream 2 due to US sanctions against companies building the pipeline (So close 2020), Bulgaria began to receive Russian gas via TurkStream at the beginning of 2020 (Bulgaria starts 2020).

In addition to dependency, Russia's energy disputes with Ukraine, Belarus, Georgia, Azerbaijan and Moldova raised concerns about the EU's security of energy supply. After the gas disputes, which triggered declarations or reports from EU actors drawing attention to the need to diversify sources, routes and suppliers (European Council 2009, p. 10; 2008, p. 8; Council of the European Union 2009a; Eurlings 2006), the significance of diversification of suppliers became more visible. Javier Solana, then High Representative of the EU, described the effect of these disputes on the EU very clearly: "Energy security has shot to the top of the European and wider international agenda. It is easy to see why. … Russia's recent disputes with Ukraine, Georgia and Moldova over the terms of gas supplies have concentrated our minds" (Solana 2006). In order to prevent supply disruptions due to a lack of infrastructure or political or commercial problems, the Commission adopted measures such as the diversification of supplier countries and routes among others. Miguel Arias Cañete, the Commissioner for Climate Action and Energy, drew attention to the impact of energy disputes, saying that "after the gas crises of 2006 and 2009 that left many millions out in the cold, we said: 'Never again'" (European Commission 2016). Moreover, an increase in Russian gas prices to Ukraine of 80 per cent following the change in the Ukrainian government after Yanukovych's refusal of an Association Agreement with the EU, and the Russian annexation of Crimea (Burmistrova and Zinets 2014) further increased the EU's concerns and prompted the European Council to call for the Commission to prepare "a comprehensive plan for the reduction of EU energy dependence" (European Council 2014, p. 14).

Russian energy policies have also been considered by the EU as cause for concern. There is a strong connection between the Russian state and Gazprom, as exemplified by Prime Minister Medvedev, formerly Chairman of the Board of Gazprom. The Company holds a monopoly in exporting pipeline gas. The Commission clearly addressed the problem of the lack of liberal values in 2005: "it is essentially a seller's market; problems of non-liberalised supply market (e.g. Russia); we need to diversify our sources" (Council of the European Union 2005, p. 5). Russia's illiberal policies as a great power compelled the EU to adopt legislative measures. The third country clause, often called the Gazprom clause, of the Third Energy Package aims to prevent individuals or companies of third countries from gaining control over a transmission system unless permitted by an agreement between the EU and the third country.

Gazprom's illiberal policies resulted in a Commission investigation on the abuse of its dominant position in the Central and Eastern European gas markets. The suspected anti-competitive practices concerned the fact of whether Gazprom imposed unfair prices on its customers, made gas supplies conditional upon certain unrelated commitments, such as approval of Gazprom's control over a pipeline, and divided European markets by inhibiting the free flow of gas between Member States (European Commission 2015a; Euractiv 2012). Although the competition investigation against Gazprom was finalised without a fine, Gazprom agreed to reform its contracts by changing its pricing mechanism and removing contractual constraints (Chee and de Carbonnel 2018). Gazprom's strategy of controlling the downstream market must also be highlighted here. Gazprom has maintained extensive control over the gas network because of its shares in distribution and sales of gas in different countries (Bros

2014, pp. 11–12). Without mentioning the names Russia or Gazprom, the European Parliament (EP) referred to these cases as follows: "It cannot be excluded that sometimes the aim of the third country is to bind the Member States to assure the commercial contract or to secure a monopolistic position in energy supplies via particular infrastructure" (European Parliament 2011).

The EU's utilisation of regulatory tools towards Russia has initiated a discussion on whether the EU acts as a regulatory power or a market power (Andersen et al. 2017; Overland 2017). Regulatory power refers to the deployment of regulatory tools to correct or mitigate market failures and is thus not directed towards specific actors. In contrast, market power refers to the selective application of regulatory tools to gain broader economic and political goals. The Gazprom anti-trust case can be regarded within the scope of the EU's regulatory power owing to the requirement for all companies to obey EU rules and regulations (Goldthau and Sitter 2019, pp. 32–35). Similarly, the EU's antitrust case against Google, which ended with a fine of 495 million Euros, and decisions against major energy companies such as ENI, EDF and E.ON can be considered examples of regulatory power (Overland 2017, pp. 120–121). Likewise, the removal of destination clauses, which prevented the reselling of contracted gas to third parties, occurred in contracts with both Gazprom and other non-EU supplier companies such as Statoil (Andersen et al. 2017, p. 19).

However, Andersen et al. (2017, p. 20) cited examples such as the EU's different positions on the Russian-sponsored South Stream and the EU-sponsored Nabucco pipelines, financial support for the Nabucco project and the Gazprom clause as those reflecting the EU as a "liberal mercantilist". This term refers to cases in which the EU utilises regulatory tools to gain broader economic and political gains. Similarly, Goldthau and Sitter (2019) considered the Gazprom clause as an example of the EU acting as a "market power" owing to the fact that national transmission operators can reject certification of a non-EU energy company (such as Gazprom) by taking into account "security of supply risks". Furthermore, they offered the Commission's proposal to apply EU energy rules to offshore pipelines, the case of the South Stream in which the EU questioned the compliance of the pipeline with the EU *acquis communautaire* and the Commission's decision to apply third party access requirement to OPAL pipeline, which is an onshore extension of the Nord Stream 1 pipeline carrying Russian gas directly to Germany via Baltic Sea, as examples of EU market power. Although the Commission reversed its decision in 2016 and allowed Gazprom to book 80 or 100 per cent of capacity, the General Court ruled in September 2019 that the Commission's decision breached the principle of energy solidarity and thus Gazprom should be allowed to use only half of the capacity of the pipeline. The Court's decision is crucial, bearing in mind the possibility that it will be applied for prospective pipelines such as the EUGAL pipeline, which is planned to connect Nord Stream 2 to the Czech Republic, and the probable pipeline connecting TurkStream from the Turkey-Bulgaria border to the Balkan region (Assenova 2019). Taking into account the exemption from third party access for the TAP pipeline, which will transport Azeri gas from the Turkey-Greece border to Greece, Albania and Italy (Gotev 2015), the Court's decision provides an additional layer to the discussion of the extent to which the EU utilises regulatory tools for broader foreign policy goals and acts as a "market power". Last but not least, Goldthau and Sitter (2019, pp. 38–41) argued that energy sanctions against Iran and Russia, unsuccessful initiatives to establish the Caspian Development Corporation as "a European purchase vehicle for Caspian gas" (Andersen et al. 2017, p. 20) and "to pool EU consumer power for gas purchases from third countries" (Goldthau and Sitter 2019, p. 40) can be considered as attempts to transform the market power into a "hard economic power". This type of power refers to "direct use of economic power as a tool of foreign policy" (Goldthau and Sitter 2019, p. 39).

From a theoretical perspective, European dependency on Russian gas and the effect of Russian gas disputes and illiberal energy policies on Europe fulfil the criteria for Russia to be considered a great power in the EU's narratives. The Russian share among EU natural gas imports is high while gas disputes raise concerns on the EU's security of supply and Russian policies distort competition. Therefore, Russia is a part of the EU's calculations and influences the process of securitisation within the EU. The concerns related to Russia and the security of supply necessitate legislative measures, such as the third country clause, and efforts for further diversification of suppliers. This shows not only the functioning of great power management in the EU's narratives but also the interrelationship between great power management and security of supply as primary institutions.

3.2 Diversification of Suppliers: The Southern Corridor

Turkey's geographical location close to the world's proved gas reserves is significant for EU access to Middle Eastern and Caspian energy resources. So far, only Azeri gas, which amounted to 0.6 bcm in 2018, has been exported to Greece via Turkey. Therefore, as demonstrated in Fig. 3.3, Mediterranean, Middle Eastern and Caspian energy resources and increasing LNG supplies were deemed to be "emerging strategic suppliers" by the Commission, whereas Norway, Russia and Algeria were considered traditional strategic suppliers of natural gas. Accordingly, then Energy Commissioner Piebalgs argued that the proximity of the world's largest reserves in the Middle East and Caspian regions meant that "there is no reason holding back this development" (Piebalgs 2007a, p. 4).

As shown in Table 3.2, the Middle East has significant potential given the amount of known global natural gas reserves (38.4 per cent). However, while this share is greater than that of the CIS (31.9 per cent), Middle Eastern production is currently less (17.8 per cent) than total CIS

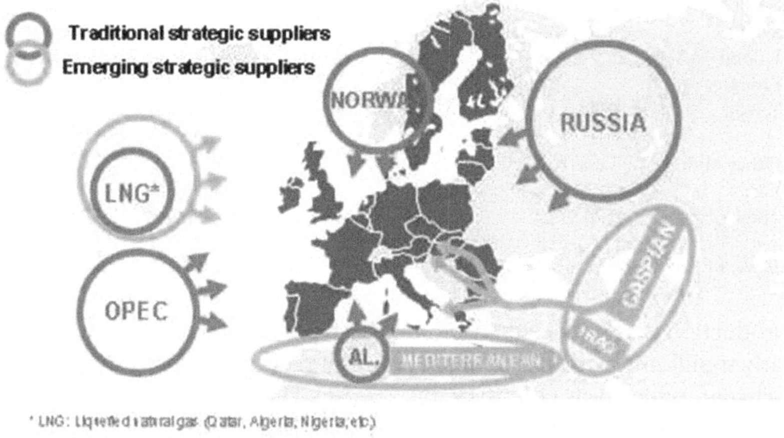

Fig. 3.3 The EU's traditional and emerging strategic suppliers. (Source: European Commission (2011a, p. 5); ©European Union, 1995–2019, http://eur-lex.europa.eu)

Table 3.2 Natural gas—proved reserves and production

	Proved reserves		*Production*		
	At the end of 2018 (trillion cubic metres)	*Share of total in 2018*	*2017 (billion cubic metres)*	*2018 (billion cubic metres)*	*Share of total in 2018*
Total CIS	62.8	31.9%	789.1	831.1	21.5%
Azerbaijan	2.1	1.1%	17.8	18.8	0.5%
Kazakhstan	1.0	0.5%	28.4	24.4	0.6%
Russian Federation	38.9	19.8%	635.6	669.5	17.3%
Turkmenistan	19.5	9.9%	58.7	61.5	1.6%
Uzbekistan	1.2	0.6%	53.4	56.6	1.5%
Other CIS	Less than 0.05	Less than 0.05%	0.3	0.3	Less than 0.05%
Total Middle East	75.5	38.4%	650.4	687.3	17.8%
Bahrain	0.2	0.1%	14.5	14.8	0.4%
Iran	31.9	16.2%	220.2	239.5	6.2%
Iraq	3.6	1.8%	10.1	13.0	0.3%
Israel	0.4	0.2%	n/a	n/a	n/a
Kuwait	1.7	0.9%	16.2	17.5	0.5%
Oman	0.7	0.3%	32.3	36.0	0.9%
Qatar	24.7	12.5%	172.4	175.5	4.5%
Saudi Arabia	5.9	3.0%	109.3	112.1	2.9%
Syria	0.3	0.1%	3.4	3.6	0.1%
United Arab Emirates	5.9	3.0%	62.0	64.7	1.7%
Yemen	0.3	0.1%	0.5	0.6	Less than 0.05%
Other Middle East	Less than 0.05	Less than 0.05%	9.5	9.5	0.3%
Total World	196.9	100%	3677.7	3867.9	100%

Source: BP Statistical Review of World Energy (2019, pp. 30, 32). Copyright © 1996–2020

production (21.5 per cent). Within this scope, Qatar and Iran are particularly significant, with shares of proved resources of 12.5 per cent and 16.2 per cent, respectively (BP 2019, pp. 30, 32). However, it is significant that the region does not contribute a major share of EU imports beyond the 5 per cent of LNG imports from Qatar in 2017 (European Commission 2019b, p. 69). This explains why Middle Eastern suppliers are considered within the context of "emerging strategic suppliers".

The EU does not import natural gas from Central Asian and Caspian countries. Although shares of proved gas reserves (12.1 per cent) and gas production (4.2 per cent) belonging to Azerbaijan, Kazakhstan, Turkmenistan and Uzbekistan (BP 2019, pp. 30, 32) are not high compared to Russia, they are crucial as alternative suppliers for consumers like the EU (Bilgin 2007, p. 6384). After their independence from the Soviet Union, the European Commission (1997, p. 6) highlighted the significance of these regions in terms of potential new suppliers. Thus, Turkey's geographical location and its significance for European energy security was already apparent in 2000: "A range of transport routes will also be necessary if the resources of the Caspian Sea Basin are to be fully exploited. Particular attention should therefore be paid to transit states such as Turkey, the CEEC countries, Ukraine, the Baltic States and the Caucasian countries" (European Commission 2000, p. 24).

EU concerns about Russia as a great power in the field of natural gas have accelerated efforts to diversify and reach the Middle Eastern and the Caspian resources. Within this context, different Energy Commissioners drew attention to Turkey's underutilised potential to transport natural gas in these regions. Piebalgs highlighted Turkey's geopolitical location and underlined the significance of resources in Turkey's east and south:

> From my perspective, being responsible for European energy security, the key questions facing the European Union and Turkey are in the East & South. Turkey is the link, the corridor, the bridge to those regions. To Turkey's East & South lies the greatest concentration of energy resources on the planet, far larger than those that lie in continental Europe. (Piebalgs 2007b, p. 3)

Similarly, Energy Commissioner Oettinger stated that "looking at the map, we can see that Turkey plays a significant role in energy security" (Turkey vital for energy 2012) and the Enlargement Commissioner Olli Rehn mentioned that "the EU has the market, Turkey has the geography" (Rehn 2009b, p. 2).

The Southern Corridor is the main geopolitical instrument in the EU's energy relations with Turkey. Considered a modern Silk Road and one of the projects of common interest, the Southern Corridor aims to link Caspian, Middle Eastern and Eastern Mediterranean natural gas resources with the EU (European Commission 2018a, p. 48; Council of the European Union 2009e, p. 3). It is expected that "the Southern Corridor would be-after the Northern Corridor from Norway, the Eastern corridor from Russia, the Mediterranean Corridor from Africa and besides LNG-the fourth big axis for diversification of gas supplies in Europe" (European Commission 2010b, p. 31). The Commission stated the goal for the development of the Southern Corridor as working together with gas suppliers and transit states to secure supplies and construct the necessary infrastructure:

> The operational objective for the development of the Southern Corridor strategy is that the Commission and Member States work with gas producing countries, as well as those countries which are key for transporting hydrocarbons to the EU, with the joint objective of rapidly securing firm commitments for the supply of gas and the construction of gas transportation infrastructures (pipelines, Liquefied/Compressed Natural Gas shipping) necessary at all stages of its development. (European Commission 2010b, p. 32)

The Southern Corridor consists of non-Russian gas transportation, connecting the Caspian and the Eastern Mediterranean basins with the EU, according to the Regulation numbered 2018/540 (European Commission 2018a). In the Caspian basin, the Southern Corridor includes the Trans-Caspian Gas Pipeline (from Turkmenistan to Azerbaijan), the South-Caucasus Pipeline Future Expansion (SCPFX) (from Azerbaijan to Georgia/Turkey border), TANAP[4] (from Georgia/Turkey border to Turkey/Greece border) and the Trans-Adriatic Pipeline[5] (TAP) (from Greece to Italy via Albania and the Adriatic Sea) (Fig. 3.4). In the Eastern

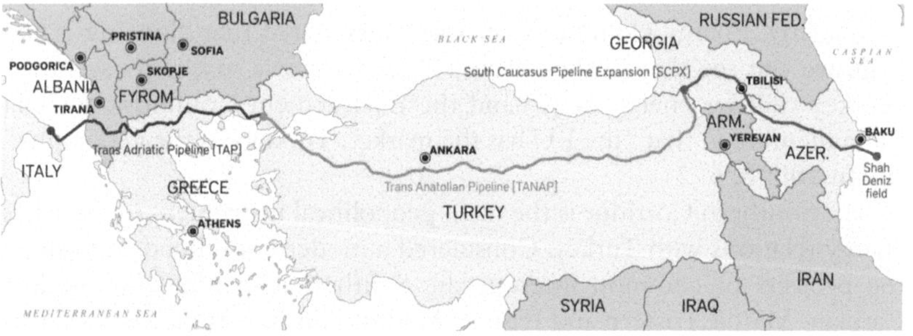

Fig. 3.4 The Southern Corridor. (Source: Petroleum Economist (2018). Reprinted with permission)

Mediterranean basin, the Corridor includes the EastMed Pipeline (from the Eastern Mediterranean gas reserves to Greece via Crete) and the Poseidon Pipeline (from Greece to Italy). Thus, the Corridor is not only limited to pipelines crossing through Turkey but also includes those bypassing the country. As of January 2020, construction was completed on the SCPFX and TANAP while construction of the TAP continues and the EastMed and Poseidon Pipelines are at the planning stage.

The European Commission (2010b, p. 32) designated Turkey as a "key transit state" in the Southern Corridor. The EU actors referred to Turkey's being a "transit" state rather than a "hub", which was preferred by Turkey with the exception of few occasions in the Commission papers (European Commission 2011c, p. 7; 2011f, p. 73). An interviewee representing the German government mentioned that the reference to Turkey as an energy hub in the 2016 EU-Turkey High Level Energy Dialogue was introduced by the Turkish side (Oner and Schröder 2017, pp. 187–194). Bearing in mind the gas reserves in North Africa and the Eastern Mediterranean, the EU sought to establish a Mediterranean gas hub to achieve diversification of suppliers and routes. Within this context, the Memorandum of Understanding with Egypt stipulated the development of an energy hub between 2018 and 2022 (Memorandum of Understanding n.d., p. 3). Furthermore, the establishment of a Balkan gas hub in Bulgaria was considered to be a project of common interest and received support from the European Commission, as underlined by the Commission Vice-President Šefčovič: "We want the Balkan gas hub to be efficient … to be the hub where the gas supplies are coming from different directions but the gas should be traded here, should be sold to the partner and shouldn't be just rushed through the territory to other countries" (Bulgaria launches gas hub 2018; European Commission 2017).

For the purposes of this chapter, it is significant to emphasise that the scope of the Southern Corridor has changed since its initiation, depending on the political and economic circumstances. Before TANAP, the Nabucco Pipeline planned to transport 30 bcm of natural gas from Middle Eastern and the Caspian energy resources to Austria via Turkey, Bulgaria, Romania and Hungary[6] (Fig. 3.5). The Southern Corridor also included the Interconnector Turkey-Greece-Italy[7] (ITGI) and the South-East Europe Pipeline[8] (SEEP). Furthermore, the European Commission (2010b, p. 32) discussed other transit routes through the Black Sea[9] and CNG/LNG options. In addition to the Caspian region, Iraqi sources were also considered as potential gas sources for transportation to Europe.

Fig. 3.5 Nabucco and the South Stream pipelines. (Source: Bailey (2009). @ Bailey/Wikimedia Commons/CC-BY-SA-3.0. The work of art can be freely copied, distributed and transmitted, always assuming that there is an attribution)

Ferrero-Waldner, the then Commissioner for External Relations and ENP, stated that "[t]he Mashreq countries, Turkey and Iraq are key energy partners for the EU, and it is important that we fully exploit the potential of our now well-established cooperation" (European Commission 2008b). Similarly, the Commission suggested in 2008 that the Arab Gas Pipeline[10] would open up "important possibilities as a new transport route for gas to the EU" (European Commission 2008b). Due to political problems, such as in the Arab gas pipeline project, and financial circumstances, often argued as one of the reasons for the failure of Nabucco project (Gloystein 2012), the pipelines under the umbrella of the Southern Corridor have changed. Furthermore, the Nabucco pipeline was considered in Azerbaijan to represent the interests of the consumer countries rather than Azerbaijan itself (Rzayeva 2012, p. 150; 2015, p. 191). As the country was willing to play a major role in energy projects and contribute to its economic growth, Azerbaijan believed that gaining direct access to European markets and having control of TANAP would serve better its national interests than selling its gas to a consortium. Although the names of pipelines have changed over time, any kind of delivery of Middle Eastern, Eastern Mediterranean and Caspian gas to Europe is significant for the EU as long as its supply remains competitive and secure.

Despite these criticisms on the potential of and the extent to which the Southern Corridor serves the interests of the EU (Siddi 2019; Pirani 2018), EU institutions provided continuing support for the Southern Corridor. On several occasions, the Council of the European Union (2018, 2011, pp. 6–7; 2009c, p. 3), the European Council (2009, p. 10) and the EP (European Parliament 2008; European Union 2010) backed the Corridor, underlining the significance of the diversification of energy suppliers and routes it would bring. Before arriving at the Advisory Council meeting in Baku, the Commission Vice-President Šefčovič highlighted the strategic importance of the Southern Corridor, particularly for South-East Europe and South Italy, which he called the "most vulnerable parts of Europe" (European Commission 2018c). In addition, the EP rejected by a large majority the proposal of the Green Group to oppose infrastructure projects based on fossil fuels, including the Southern Corridor (European Parliament backs 2018). While Šefčovič's position exemplified the concern about single source dependency, the Parliament's position confirmed the understanding that natural gas would serve the EU as a complementary source in transition towards renewables.

Although the EU Institutions referred to these pipelines or the LNG/CNG projects bypassing Russia for the purpose of achieving diversification of suppliers to be within the scope of the Southern Corridor, some Member States' preferences for Russian pipelines reflected the lack of a unilateral approach within the EU towards the Southern Corridor. This exemplifies one of the largest problems in establishing a unified external energy policy. Hungary signed an agreement with Gazprom to link the country with the TurkStream (Hungary joins 2017), which aims to supply 15.75 bcm/y Russian gas to Turkey and 15.75 bcm/y gas to Europe via Turkey (Fig. 3.6). Furthermore, both Greece and Bulgaria showed interest in the project following its announcement (Gotev 2017). TurkStream is in direct competition with the Southern Corridor, as both aim to supply the Southern and South Eastern European gas markets. A similar division with the EU occurred over the South Stream Pipeline, which was a Russian project to transport 63 bcm gas to Europe via Black Sea but was replaced by TurkStream owing to regulatory problems with the Commission (Fig. 3.5). At that time, the Italian and Slovenian delegations in the Council of the European Union (2010a, p. 3; 2010b, p. 3) showed their support in favour of the South Stream for the sake of the diversification of routes and several Member States signed intergovernmental agreements with Russia. On the other hand, the Commission insisted that the EU's

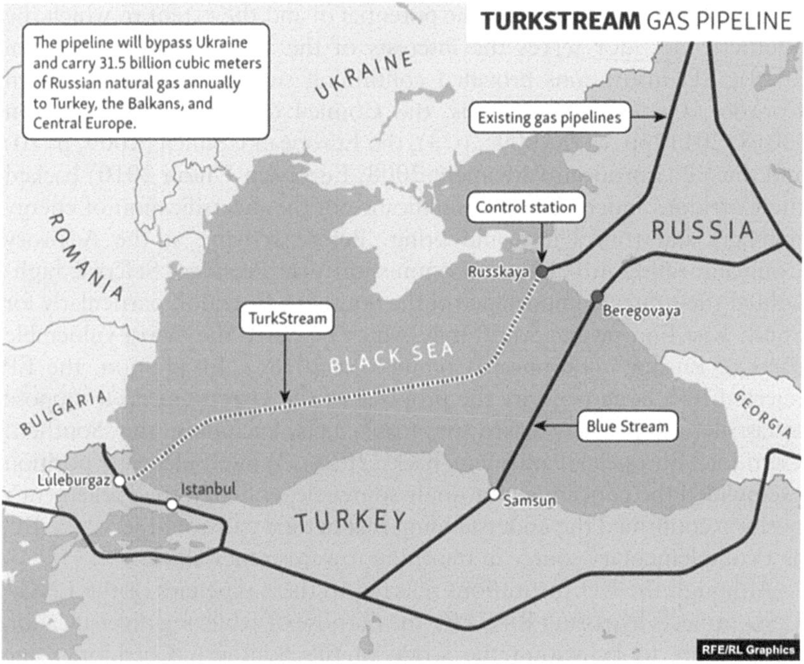

Fig. 3.6 TurkStream pipeline. (Source: Radio Free Europe/Radio Liberty (2020). Copyright © 2019. RFE/RL, Inc. Reprinted with the permission of Radio Free Europe/Radio Liberty)

dependency on Russian natural gas was the reason for the Southern Corridor. According to the Commission spokesperson, the "South Stream on the contrary has never been a European priority. Why? Because it diversifies routes but not supply as it is supposed to bring Russian gas to the EU" (Geropoulos 2012, May 11). Similarly, Solana characterised the problem and the solution very clearly in 2009: "We all know that excessive dependence on one source, one export route, or one company creates vulnerabilities. And vulnerabilities are a source for instability. This, then, is the main rationale for the Southern Corridor" (Council of the European Union 2009d). For the aims of this book, it is significant to underline that the contradictory attitudes of EU Member States' policies towards competing projects derive from their own national energy policies and relations with Russia and thus do not arise from opposition towards Turkey.

To achieve security of supply via diversification, many different elements must come together. Hesitation on the part of energy suppliers, political instability in regions, wars, terrorist attacks and adverse market and financial conditions might constitute obstacles for ensuring diversification of routes and suppliers. In the EU's case, the main obstacle to the Southern Corridor according to the European Commission was the difficulty in ensuring "that all elements of the corridor (gas resources, infrastructure for transport and underlying agreements) are available both at the right time and with significant scope" (European Commission 2010b, p. 32). These elements are directly related to political and economic conditions.

As previously mentioned, the Southern Corridor also includes Eastern Mediterranean gas. However, conflicts have arisen due to both the Cyprus conflict and disagreements on maritime jurisdiction zones in the region, which will be elaborated on in the next chapter. Here it is sufficient to mention that different EU actors have expressed their concerns on Turkey's exploration and drilling activities in the Eastern Mediterranean. Both the Commission[11] and the Council of the European Union[12] considered Turkey's activities to challenge the sovereign rights of Cyprus. The Council of General Affairs drew attention to the serious concerns and invited the Commission "to submit options for appropriate measures without delay" (Council of the European Union 2019a) in June 2019. Accordingly, the Council of the European Union decided in July 2019 to impose sanctions on Turkey in response to its drilling activities. The sanctions include the suspension of negotiations on the Comprehensive Air Transport Agreement and suspensions of meetings of the Association Council and EU Turkey High-Level Dialogues and the reduction of pre-accession assistance in 2020. The Council also invited the European Investment Bank to review its lending policy to Turkey (Council of the European Union 2019b). Turkey's position on the Eastern Mediterranean and the question of the extent to which the EU's sanctions have the potential to change Turkey's position will be analysed in the next chapter.

3.3 Extending Market Values

The EU's second goal in its relations with Turkey in the sphere of natural gas during the researched period was to extend its market values. Before delving into narratives, it is necessary to explain what is expected from a competitive market and why the EU wants to export its liberal values to neighbouring countries.

The main economic rationale behind the EU integration is to increase productivity, efficiency and innovation by benefitting from the principle of comparative advantage and economies of scale and by introducing competition to markets (El-Agraa 2007, p. 109). The strategy for economic prosperity is pursued not only at the internal but also the regional and global levels. At the regional level, the enlargement process and conditional market access to non-EU countries on its territory are tools to increase economic wealth. Therefore, liberal values are exported to neighbouring countries via various mechanisms such as the Euro-Mediterranean Programme. At the global level, the WTO trade regime is supported. However, the protection of some sectors, such as the agriculture, financial services and defence industries, are also pursued (Smith 2011, pp. 151–152).

In the field of energy, it is expected that competition in an integrated market will increase cross-border trade, productivity and efficiency and decrease costs. This is significant for the EU owing to the fact that energy prices can result in higher costs for households and industry, a crucial obstacle for European companies in terms of competitiveness. Furthermore, according to the liberal understanding, competition secures supplies by sending the right signals to investors, taking the necessary measures in the case of insecurity and promoting diversification. A well-interconnected network, which is necessary for an integrated market, contributes to the aim of securing supplies, which shows the interaction between the primary institutions of security of supply and the market from a theoretical perspective. Moreover, an integrated market is a large one, which attracts producers to the possibility of securing demand. The benefits for establishing an integrated market was articulated by the Commission: "a wider European internal market, properly implemented, will lead to increased competition and lower prices, will permit increased environmental protection over a wide area, and will enhance security of supply throughout Europe" (European Commission 2003, p. 5).

Similar to the export of the EU's liberal grand strategy to non-EU countries at the regional level via different tools (Smith 2011), the EU aims to export its rules and principles in the field of energy. This is one of the policy tools the Commission uses to secure investments in external production (upstream) and transit of gas and oil supplies (midstream), ensure competition via external supplies and contribute to the operation of the single market. In addition to extending the market values to non-EU countries, the Commission uses its regulatory tools in the form of giving exemptions from the third-party access requirement and its financing mechanisms to be influential in the decision-making process of external pipelines and investments. Furthermore, with the help of the competition policy, the Commission executes its power in downstream markets by applying the same rules to all EU and non-EU energy companies operating in the single market (Andersen et al. 2016, pp. 57–60). The discussion on the extent to which the EU acts only as a regulatory power or a market power/hard economic power, which was briefly articulated in the previous sub-section, relies on the EU's utilisation of these tools.

Why does the EU want to export its liberal values to neighbouring countries, including Turkey? First of all, interdependence among energy producers, consumers and transit states inevitably necessitates some form of co-operation. The type of co-operation depends on whether or not the state concerned pursues a market approach (Padgett 2011, p. 1071). As an energy dependent consumer, the EU pursues the market approach, which is based on the idea that "markets are the best way of ensuring safe and affordable energy supplies" (European Commission n.d.-d, p. 3). While adopting a liberalisation policy inside its own territories, the EU considers the exportation of this policy as important for its relationships with producer and transit countries in order to speak in the same language and secure supplies. Difficulties in cooperation may occur if "the market" drives the EU's motives for co-operation but "state capitalism" drives those of the producer or transit state. This was also highlighted in some of the narratives given by EU actors. For example, the European Economic and Social Committee argued that "the increasing concentration of dependence on suppliers which do not play by the same rules as Europe, as well as still increasing demand of gas, increases risk of problems in supply" (European Union 2009, p. 85). Within this scope, the EU's energy relations with its neighbours were deemed "fundamental to European security and stability" (European Commission 2007a, p. 19) and "cooperation with the energy suppliers and transit countries based on reciprocity, clear rules and market economy" (Council of the European Union 2009b, p. 6) was considered a priority for energy security in the Lithuanian contribution to the Second Strategic Energy Review.

The second reason for the EU's desire for a wide energy market around Europe is related to the economic assumption that an internal market is easier to achieve when regional energy markets are established. Accordingly, there are currently three regional gas markets within the EU as an interim step in establishing an internal energy market. The Energy Community, which is an international organisation bringing the EU together with the Balkan countries, Georgia, Moldova and Ukraine, is the fourth region with which the EU aims to build this kind of integration by extending its rules to non-EU countries (Hunt and Karova 2010, p. 52). The Commission formulated this as follows: "The Energy Community has three levels of ambition: national, regional and pan European" (European Commission 2011d, p. 2). Here, the pan-European level refers to the wider European market and its possible integration with the EU's internal energy market. It is significant to highlight the fact that non-EU members of the Energy Community do not have the opportunity to influence the European *acquis communautaire* according to their preferences. Therefore, members not in the EU must "accept the relevant EU rules, including the cost of adaptation, without having a 'voice' in future rule-setting or even the perspective of EU membership" (Prange-Gstöhl 2009, p. 5299).

EU actors underlined the significance of creating a wider market and extending market values to third countries in their narratives. According to the Commission "The EU should aim to build up a wide network of countries around the EU, acting on the basis of shared rules or principles derived from the EU energy policy" (European Commission 2007a, p. 19). Similarly, the EP called on the Commission in 2010 "to step up, through trade agreements, the process of *adopting EU-compatible safety and energy-efficiency rules* for the generation, transmission, transit, storage and processing/refining of energy imports and exports" (European Parliament 2010a) (author's emphases). Likewise, the Council of the European Union (2011, p. 7) considered enhancing energy security through promoting forms of cooperation with North African, Middle Eastern, Caspian, Eastern Mediterranean and Black Sea countries. Accordingly, the Council argued that regulatory co-operation and convergence with neighbours had "a key role to play in order to build a wide energy market while ensuring a level playing field" (Council of the European Union 2011, p. 3). As Table 3.3 shows, the EU refers to its neighbours as market integration partners in the EU's set of co-operation formats with third parties. All issues covered in the EU's energy policy are mentioned when speaking of relations with market integration partners.

There is an interrelationship between the two goals of the diversification of suppliers/routes to secure supplies and the exportation of liberal values, which also shows the linkage between the primary institutions of

Table 3.3 The scope and instruments for co-operation with other actors

	With neighbours/ market integration partners	*With key energy suppliers and transit countries*	*With key energy players worldwide*	*With developing countries*
Scope	All issues covered by the EU energy policy	Priority to: Security of supply/demand, investment promotion, stability and security, trade and investments cooperation, promotion of sustainable development policies and common energy standards	Priority to: Security of global energy supply chain, common actions towards enhancing investment promotion, stability and security, promotion of sustainable development policies and common energy standards, R&D cooperation	Priority to: energy market reforms, promotion of sustainable development policies and common energy standards
Instruments	Energy Community Treaty	Strategic energy dialogues	Strategic energy dialogues	Ad hoc energy cooperation
	Instruments under the ENP; crisis response and prevention mechanisms		Instruments under EU development policy, where appropriate crisis and response instruments	
	Partnership and cooperation agreements covering inter alia energy, Energy Charter Treaty, Trade Agreements, Union for the Mediterranean			

Source: Council of the European Union (2011, p. 13); ©European Union, 1995–2019

security of supply and the market. Diversification of suppliers and routes paves the way for establishing partnerships, which makes it possible to implement similar rules and principles: "While pursuing diversification of import sources and routes, reinforced energy partnerships will be established by the EU with key suppliers and transit countries" (European Commission 2010a, p. 19). Moreover, creating energy partnerships with third parties contribute to the goal of diversification, as similar rules would enable competitive gas resources to come to Europe and necessitate the construction of new pipelines. Accordingly, the Council of the European Union underlined the necessity for a single mechanism, in line with the EU competition rules, to facilitate diversification and provide access to new energy resources in the Caspian region (Council of the European Union 2009c, p. 3).

As illustrated in Table 3.4, the EU's tools to export liberal values to Turkey included the Baku Initiative, the Union for the Mediterranean, the accession process, the Energy Community, the Energy Charter and the WTO. However, this chapter focuses only on the Energy Community and the accession process, as both anticipate deeper integration than do the others. Together these were seen as means to achieve the goal of creating "a wide network of countries around the EU, acting on the basis of shared rules or principles derived from the internal market" (European Commission 2006, p. 5). Among these shared rules and principles, competition is key as seen in the provisions for third party access and unbundling. The Energy Charter and the WTO framework include less integration than the EU legislation. While the Charter foresees the facilitation of energy transit as means to promote the freedom of transit, the Treaty does "not oblige any Contracting Party to introduce mandatory third party access" (Energy Charter Secretariat 2015, p. 37). Although WTO rules are applied to trade in energy goods and services, these rules do not provide a proper regime for trade in energy. The specific characteristics of energy, which have an impact on storage, transportation and distribution, the existence of natural monopolies and state-owned companies, dual energy prices and export restrictions make it difficult to apply the WTO rules properly in the sector (Cottier et al. n.d.). Last but not least, while the Baku Initiative and the Union for the Mediterranean aim for the harmonisation of legislation, the Energy Community endeavours to create a regional energy market to be incorporated into the EU's single energy market, thus obliging its members to adopt the EU legislation. The accession process aims at full membership of the EU, which also makes the adoption of the EU *acquis communautaire* obligatory.

The Energy Community aims to establish an integrated energy market in the participating countries which would attract investment, improve the security of supply and sustainability and increase competition by exploiting economies of scale (The Energy Community 2010). The contracting parties of the Energy Community are Albania, Bosnia and Herzegovina, North Macedonia, Moldova, Montenegro, Serbia, Ukraine, Kosovo and

Table 3.4 The EU's existing instruments relevant to the energy sector

	Political instruments				*Bilateral legal instruments*				*Multilateral legal instruments*				
Country	*Energy dialogue*	*MoU*	*ENP Action Plan / Roadmap /Association Agenda*	*Other*	*PCA/ Association Agreement /SAA/ Framework Agreement*	*FTA / Non-preferential Agreements / TA/EEA*	*Euratom agreements*	*Science and technology Cooperation agreement*	*Energy Community*	*Energy Charter Treaty*	*WTO*	*Non-proliferation treaty*	*ITER agreement*
Turkey				Baku Initiative, the Union for the Mediterranean	x	x		Associated to Framework Programme 7	Observer	x	x	x	

Source: European Commission (2011a, pp. 13, 26); ©European Union, 1995–2019

Georgia. Armenia, Norway and Turkey are observers. The EU, represented by the Commission, is a party to the Treaty. The geopolitical scope of the Energy Community is worth a mention as the contracting parties include candidate countries, potential candidate countries or transit states around the EU. There is an interconnection between the economic and geopolitical goals of the Energy Community, which shows itself with the necessity of creating an integrated energy market in the wider Europe and that of building a strategic energy infrastructure connecting the energy-rich regions with the EU. Within this scope, the extension of the Energy Community would provide access to new energy resources. The linkage with geopolitics becomes evident in the quotation from Ferrero-Waldner, then Commissioner:

> We should strongly support and facilitate the creation of such a Community [Energy Community] by strengthening physical infrastructure such as pipelines and electricity cables. *Strategic energy infrastructure linking the Mediterranean Sea, African Sub-Sahara, the Caspian Basin, Central Asia and the Middle East should be the cement of our common energy security* (emphases in original). (Ferrero-Waldner 2006)

To achieve the goal of establishing an integrated market in Southeast Europe, the Energy Community Treaty sets three targets. First, the EU aims to extend the *acquis* on electricity, gas, environment, competition and renewables to the participating countries. Extending liberal values is expected to ensure the competitiveness, sustainability and security of supply. Adoption of the EU's *acquis* reassures investors and furthers common rules in the event of the disruption of energy supplies. Moreover, harmonisation with the EU legislation prevents third parties such as Gazprom from extending its operations in European markets (Tekin and Williams 2009, p. 2) and leads to third-party access to infrastructure.

Second, the Treaty aims to establish a regulatory framework for the efficient implementation of rules in participating countries and to create a single mechanism for the cross-border transmission and/or transportation of energy. It is expected that this mechanism would allow closer integration in local energy markets and develop strategic routes from new suppliers, such as the Southern Corridor and Southern Mediterranean. Within this context, the Commission specified that "[s]upply issues, including network development and possibly grouped supply arrangements as well as regulatory aspects, notably concerning the freedom of transit and investment security, would be covered" (European Commission 2010a, p. 22).

Last but not least, the Treaty aims to create an internal energy market with no frontiers and to enhance mutual co-operation in the event of problems in supply or infrastructure (The Energy Community 2010; European Commission 2005). Accordingly, to the European Economic and Social Committee, the goal of the Energy Community is "to progressively create a European electricity and gas market, including potentially more than 35 countries and a population over 600 million" (European Union 2004, p. 17). Therefore, the Commission deemed the Treaty to be a "reference point for the majority of the EU's neighbours willing to be a part of the European energy system" (European Commission 2011c, p. 6). Within the context of internal market, the Treaty refers to an external energy trade policy and Article 43 foresees that the Energy Community "may take measures necessary for the regulations of imports and exports of Network Energy [gas] to and from third countries..." (The Energy Community 2010, p. 22).

EU narrators emphasised the impact of the Energy Community on secure supplies and integrated competitive markets, which again displays the interrelationship between the primary institutions of the market and security of supply. Exporting liberal values to the region is expected to "assist in assuring both the European Union's security of supply and that of the region" (European Commission 2005). The European Council also stated the aim of securing energy supplies through extending liberal values: "The Union will work to ensure long-term security of energy supply through. ... the extension of its internal energy market principles to neighbouring countries, in particular on the basis of the Energy Community Treaty and the European Neighbourhood Policy" (European Council 2006, p. 15). Similarly, the Italian position given below clearly summarises the rationale behind multilateral institutions such as the Energy Community, and the linkage between diversification, security of supply and the establishment of an integrated market. It was argued that the need for co-operation on energy issues was best ensured through mutual interdependence. Diversification of energy suppliers and routes, access for European companies to producers and transit country markets, promotion of innovation and sustainability and secure energy supplies are best achieved via integration of energy markets:

> Cooperation in the energy sector is multifaceted, a feature which should be used to engage with producer countries in a framework of mutual interdependence; we should capitalise on cooperation to diversify energy sources and transport routes in a concerted manner, to promote technological innovation and new energy sustainability platforms, to increase security of supply, and to open up access to the producer and transit countries' markets for European companies on conditions of reciprocity. To achieve this, the European Union should maximise the role played by existing multilateral fora, such as the Southeast Europe Energy Community and the Energy Charter Treaty, in facilitating the process of integrating energy markets. (Council of the European Union 2008, p. 5)

Likewise, France declared its full support for the Commission's proposal to extend the Energy Community and considered the Community and the Energy Charter to be the main tools for "the progressive establishment of a harmonized legal area around the EU" (Council of the European Union 2010c, p. 12). Furthermore, when fully implemented, the Commission expected the Energy Community to serve as "an appropriate framework to boost business and favour sustainable growth. ... to ensure that citizens and companies benefit from fair competition on energy markets" (European Commission 2011b, p. 1).

Regarding Turkey, all EU narrators agreed that more intense co-operation would benefit both parties (Tekin and Williams 2009, p. 12) and placed a clear emphasis on interdependency and mutual benefits (Piebalgs 2007b; European Commission 2007c). According to EU actors, more intense co-operation begins with the liberalisation of energy markets, which would help Turkey to secure supply, have an energy market and develop its role in international politics. Piebalgs clearly summarised the connection between security and the market: "Turkey can help the EU secure its energy supply, while integration into the EU's internal market will enable Turkey to build the domestic energy market and infrastructure needed for its rapid economic growth" (European Commission 2007c). Similarly, then Commissioner Rehn underlined the economic benefits of liberalisation for Turkey and argued that liberalisation of the Turkish energy market would "create a transparent, open and competitive domestic energy market for the benefit of the Turkish consumer" (Rehn 2009b). He also highlighted the role of liberalisation from the point of view of both security of supply and Turkey's position in international politics and stated that the intense co-operation between the two parties could "help

Turkey develop its role as energy crossroads and address concerns about its security of supply" (Rehn 2009a).

From the EU's point of view, the Energy Community provided a rationale for this type of intense co-operation and integration, which necessitated the harmonisation of the EU's internal market legislation. Then Energy Commissioner Piebalgs portrayed Turkey's accession to the Energy Community Treaty as the best tool to strengthen co-operation and facilitate integration. However, he also emphasised that there was no direct connection between energy policy and the accession process:

> Currently observer, Turkey has a standing invitation to join the European Energy Community. ... this is a process that of course has nothing to do with the EU accession—the one does not prejudge the other or vice versa ... these two processes have a common ground in the fact that they both stem from the understanding that further cooperation is needed between EU and Turkey in a number of fields. ... I invite my Turkish colleagues to reflect on the possibilities for strengthening of our energy co-operation. This could cover the following elements. ... A broad-based agreement to exchange best practice in energy market reform and regulation, as well as a commitment to implement an internal market in network energy sources, inspired by EU internal market principles, within Turkey. The best means for this in my view would be Turkey's accession to the Energy Community Treaty as an equal partner with full rights and influence on our common external energy policy. (Piebalgs 2007b)

Considering Turkey an essential strategic partner, the European Commission (2006, p. 16; 2007a, p. 24; 2007b, p. 5; 2010a, p. 18) urged expanding the Energy Community to transit countries, including Turkey. The Commission highlighted the economic benefits and argued that Turkey's possible accession to the Energy Community would facilitate "energy sector reforms and result in a mutually beneficial enlarged energy market based on common rules" (European Commission 2008a, p. 7). Similar references came from other EU narrators, including the Council of the European Union. The Council underlined the importance of "continuing cooperation with Turkey, aiming at integration of the country into the Energy Community" (Council of the European Union 2011, p. 5) and the European Parliament deemed Turkey's accession to the Energy Community crucial (European Parliament 2012). Furthermore, the Commission's public consultation dated 2011 showed support for the Energy Community's extension to Turkey. According to the stakeholders,[13] Turkey's "effective integration into the Energy Community was necessary" (European Commission 2011e, pp. 3, 5) and was considered a short-term priority.

Turkey's membership in the Energy Community is crucial for the EU to be able to gain access to Caspian and Middle Eastern energy resources. In the EU's efforts to access new suppliers, transit states play a significant role:

> The EU seeks to ensure safe, transparent, reliable and secure transit systems for energy, from whatever direction. We also believe that transit countries themselves stand to benefit from such transit conditions and we work to further develop our co-operation with the EU's transit countries to this effect. (Piebalgs 2007c, p. 6)

In its relations with transit countries, the EU aims to secure the transportation of energy supplies. Within this scope, it is expected that adoption of liberal values by these countries, harmonisation of legislation with the EU's *acquis communautaire* on energy and competition and participation in the single mechanism for cross-border transmission and transportation of energy would contribute to competitive and secure supplies. The European Parliament stated very clearly the necessity for all-energy network leading to the EU to be governed by internal market rules:

> ...all external pipelines and other energy networks entering the territory of the European Union should be governed by transparent intergovernmental agreements and subject to internal market rules, including rules on third party access, destination clauses, supervision of allocation and bottleneck management, the duration of the contracts and take or pay clauses. (European Parliament 2010a)

Adoption of the EU *acquis* would allow third-party access to Turkey's transit network as the EU legislation foresees the elimination of borders and treats transit as transmission (see Chap. 5) (Yafimava 2011, p. 117). This entails the risk of abolishing the exclusive right of the Turkish government to decide on the transit of natural gas passing from the country's territories (see Chaps. 4 and 5). When the pipeline crossing from Turkey is not regulated by the EU's internal market rules such as third-party access, security of supply would be at risk from the EU's point of view. The inclusion of liberal values in its transit agreements is significant for the

EU's securing of supply. The European Commission stated that normal transit flow, even in the periods of political tension, should be guaranteed through "innovative approaches such as joint management and even ownership of pipelines by companies of supplier, transit and consumer countries" (European Commission 2008a, p. 8).

While the EU narrators fully support Turkey's membership in the Energy Community, there was no consensus on the status of Turkey's accession to the EU, which is the second tool for extending the EU's liberal rules. There are 35 chapters with which Turkey must harmonise its legislation, including one on energy, for accession to the EU. Energy is one of the chapters that Cyprus blocks unilaterally. The EU actors' positions on opening the energy chapter for negotiations were divided. The Commission, some Member States such as the UK and some parties in the EP favoured opening the chapter while Cyprus and some other parties were against it. As an example of the narrative in favour of opening the energy chapter, the European Commission underlined the significance of the accession process in extending the EU's rules and principles: "...the enlargement process can play important role in developing the wide application of the community *acquis* in the energy sector, thus following the EU's energy security objectives and contributing to the security of enlargement countries" (European Commission 2008a, p. 8). After opening negotiations in 2005, the then Enlargement Commissioner Rehn mentioned energy strategy "as an area where both the EU and Turkey can gain from deeper cooperation" (European Commission 2007c, June 1). According to the Commission, the "progress towards the opening of the energy chapter in the accession negotiations would help deepen cooperation and establish a solid framework for gas transport through Turkey" (European Commission 2011c, p. 7). The Commission's support in favour of opening the energy chapter was best explained in the words of Stefan Fule, then Commissioner for Enlargement and European Neighbourhood Policy: "The Commission thinks that Turkey is ready to negotiate the energy chapter" (EU Commission calls 2013).

The narrative in favour of opening the energy chapter could also be found among some Members of the European Parliament (MEPs), some of whom brought the issue to Parliament and questioned why the energy chapter was blocked given the significance of Turkey for European energy security. For example, the Socialist Group in the Parliament declared that it was in favour of opening the energy chapter, which was deemed a possible step for "more intensive energy dialogue" (European Parliament

2009a) between the EU and Turkey by the European People's Party (EPP). Traian Ungureanu, an MEP from the EPP, welcomed "the call made by the rapporteur to harmonise energy policies between Turkey and the EU, in particular, by opening the accession negotiations on the energy chapter and by including Turkey in the European Energy Community" (European Parliament 2010b). Likewise, Geoffrey Van Orden from the European Conservatives and Reformists (ECR) party showed his support for opening the energy chapter in negotiations and questioned why it had not yet been opened considering the problem of energy security in the EU and Turkey's significant geographical location:

> At a time when, in all our countries, we have serious concerns about energy security, and Turkey is in such a key geographical position in providing the routes for pipelines from the Caspian, why is the energy chapter not open? (European Parliament 2010b)

A similar question came from Libor Rouček from the Party of European Socialists (PSE): "I cannot understand why it is not possible to negotiate with Turkey over the 'Energy' chapter, for example, which is vitally important, both for the EU and Turkey" (European Parliament 2009a).

As for the Member States' positions, the Commissioner Fule stated very clearly that "not every member of the EU approved of the opening of the energy chapter" (EU Commission calls for opening 2013). However, some Member States, such as the United Kingdom, were in favour of opening the energy chapter in the accession process. For example, David Lidington, the EU Minister of the UK, said that "all blocks on chapters should be lifted in the shortest time possible and the path for Turkey's EU membership should be smoothed" (EU urged to open energy chapter 2014). He showed the British support by adding that "positive steps in UK-Turkey energy co-operation can help Turkey open the energy chapter and reach the EU membership goal" (EU urged to open energy chapter 2014).

On the other hand, opening negotiations on the energy chapter was a controversial issue among Member States and MEPs in the European Parliament. Some MEPs argued for the continuance of Cyprus' blocking of negotiations. Kyriakos Mavronikolas from the Progressive Alliance of Socialists and Democrats (S&D) openly stated that "the Republic of Cyprus, as a small state, needs to look after its interests and to request sanctions against Turkey, one of which is, of course, to prevent chapters from being opened" (European Parliament 2009b). Similarly, Adamou and Hatzigeorgiou, MEPs from the European United Left-Nordic Green Left (EUL-NGL), argued that the energy chapter "cannot be opened unless Turkey stops preventing the Republic of Cyprus from exercising its sovereign rights in its exclusive economic zone" (European Parliament 2009a, 2009b).

It was often argued by some of the MEPs that the EU did not need Turkey as a full member to benefit from the country's potential contributions. They mentioned that a form of closer co-operation rather than the accession process could also provide the necessary framework. Accordingly, Andreas Molzer, MEP from Non-Inscrits (NI), argued that "the positive aspects, such as an improvement in energy security, can also be achieved by means of a privileged partnership. It is high time that we began speaking honestly and clearly" (European Parliament 2009b). More precisely, Molzer argued that energy pipelines could cross Turkey even though it is not a member of the EU:

> Important though considerations of the security of the European Union's energy supply might be, energy policy cannot be a reason for promoting, on a massive scale, the accession of Turkey to the EU. I do not believe that any country outside Europe should be allowed to become an EU Member State if the only reason for it being allowed in is the desire to extend the EU to the boundaries of the energy-rich regions in the Middle East and around the Caspian Sea. Even if Turkey does not become a member, the mooted oil pipelines will still be able to run through it and it will still be possible to realise the gas infrastructure projects. I believe that these things will be possible even if Turkey becomes no more than a privileged partner of the European Union rather than a fully-fledged Member State. (European Parliament 2006)

Similarly, Bastiaan Belder, MEP from the Europe of Freedom and Democracy (EFD), stated that negotiations with Turkey on energy should "be kept strictly separate from the country's accession negotiations. It should not be the case that Turkey receives an entry ticket for the Union in exchange for being cooperative" (European Parliament 2009c).

In summary, in its goal to extend market values to Turkey, the EU used two main tools, the Energy Community and the accession process, specifically the energy chapter. While all EU actors underlined the significance of Turkey's membership in the Energy Community, Turkey's preference to remain an observer, which will be examined in the fifth chapter, was the main obstacle for this tool to be effective. The different positions of the EU actors on opening negotiations of the energy chapter were the main obstacle preventing the EU from achieving progress on the accession process. Having identified that the market and security of supply functioned in the EU narratives and elaborated on the differences among the narratives, the conclusion of this chapter determines the type of integration the EU actors want to build with Turkey in the sphere of natural gas.

3.4 Conclusion

In its aim to answer the question of "what type of integration does the EU want to achieve with Turkey in the sphere of natural gas", this chapter analysed different EU actors' narratives on Turkey's role in European energy security, based on the data for the research period of January 2001 to July 2019. Analysing the primary institutions in the EU narratives and determining the type of integration the EU desires to build with Turkey provide a background against which to discuss the Turkish narratives and understand the extent to which the narratives of the Turkish actors coincide with those of the EU. Furthermore, from a theoretical perspective, the chapter examined the functioning of the primary institutions of security of supply, great power management and the market, and the interaction amongst them.

As summarised in Table 3.5, EU actors articulated three narratives on Turkey's role in the European energy security over the reviewed period, although references to Turkey decreased in the later years. From a geopolitical perspective, the first narrative's goal was ensuring the secure supply of natural gas and the diversification of suppliers. Security of supply functioned as the foundational primary institution and great power management operated as a supportive one. While the EU's high degree of external dependency in natural gas increased concerns about its secure supply, the EU's dependency on Russia, Russian energy disputes and energy policies affected the Russian influence in the EU's securitisation. Within this context, all EU narrators agreed on Turkey's significance in the EU's ability to access new suppliers, owing to its geographic location next to untapped energy resources. The support of EU actors for competing energy projects arose from their national energy policies and relations with Russia, rather than any opposition to Turkey.

The second and third narratives, in which the market institution functions, had the goal of exporting liberal values to third countries. Extending

Table 3.5 Summary of the analysis in the chapter

EU narratives	*Narrators*	*Primary institutions*	*Goals*	*Means*
Narrative on diversification	All EU narrators	Security of supply (foundational) Great power management (supportive)	Maintaining security of supply, diversification	The Southern Corridor
Narrative on extending market values	All EU narrators	The market (foundational)	Extending market values	Energy Community
Narrative on extending market values	Directorate-General for Neighbourhood and Enlargement Negotiations of the European Commission, some Member States (for. Example, the UK), some parties in the Parliament	The market (foundational)	Extending market values	Accession process

liberal values to third parties was expected to contribute to the operation of a competitive market and security of supplies, and to facilitate the establishment of an internal market via regional market initiatives. This also illustrated the interaction between the primary institutions of the market and security of supply, as examined in the theoretical framework. There was a strong emphasis on close co-operation with mutual benefits in the EU's narrative on Turkey. However, narrators differed on the ways to achieve such close co-operation. While all EU narrators agreed on the necessity of extending the Energy Community to Turkey, there was not a consensus on the use of the accession process as a means to do so and on opening the energy chapter for negotiations within this context. While some narrators blocked the opening of the energy chapter, others questioned why the harmonisation of legislation was not achieved via opening the energy chapter for negotiations when the concept of energy security was gaining increasing significance.

Turkey's geopolitical location next to energy-rich regions makes the country strategically significant for the EU in its efforts to diversify energy suppliers. Because of this, it is necessary for the EU to develop common rules for the operation of pipelines and energy markets. It is expected that competitive energy markets in the wider Europe would better secure energy supply and contribute to the effective operation of the European energy markets. As converging energy security societies are based on shared values, harmonisation of energy legislation with the EU energy *acquis* via negotiations within the accession process or the Energy Community allows a converging energy security society to be realised. Therefore, the role of market institution in the EU narratives and the consensus among the EU actors on Turkey' inclusion in the Energy Community show that the EU wanted to have at least a converging energy security society with Turkey.

The likelihood of a confederative energy security society between Turkey and the EU in the sphere of natural gas should be investigated. As elaborated in the theoretical framework, a confederative energy security society requires the transfer of competence in both internal and external affairs. In the Energy Community, non-EU members are not involved in the EU legislative process and a majority of votes is needed for the extension of the *acquis* in the Energy Community. Therefore, the obligation for the contracting parties to adopt the EU energy *acquis* in the Energy Community introduces a transfer of competence in internal affairs. Regarding the transfer of competence in external affairs, the Article in the Energy Community Treaty in favour of an "external energy trade policy" allows us to consider the possibility of the Energy Community's role in foreign energy relations of the contracting parties. This Article necessitates the consideration of a converging energy security society close to the confederative one. However, according to the Energy Community Treaty, decisions on external energy trade requires unanimity. Thus, there is not a direct transfer of competence in external issues and this type of integration cannot be labelled as a confederative energy security society.

For the aims of this book, it is important to remember that the EU and its Member States have shared competences on energy issues, as elaborated on in the theoretical chapter. The Member States' references to sovereignty show their reluctance to establish a supranational body in energy affairs and to conduct their energy policies with third parties. In external affairs, some co-operation may take place, as long as it does not harm Member States` national policies (Aalto and Korkmaz-Temel 2014, pp. 765–771), as demonstrated by the Commission's mandate to negotiate a legally binding treaty with Azerbaijan and Turkmenistan to construct a trans-Caspian pipeline (European Commission n.d.-b). However, this kind of co-operation does not lead to the transfer of competence in external energy affairs, which allows us to consider the EU to be a converging energy security society. This shows us that the type of integration the EU prefers to have with Turkey is the same regardless of Turkey's EU membership status.

Notes

1. I'd like to thank an anonymous reviewer for his/her comments on the earlier version of this chapter.
2. Gross inland consumption refers to the "total energy demand of a country or region. ... Gross inland energy consumption covers: consumption by the energy sector itself; distribution and transformation losses; final energy consumption by end users; statistical differences. ... Gross inland consumption does not include energy (fuel oil) provided to international maritime bunkers" (Eurostat 2013).
3. The conversion rate is: 1mtoe = 1.11 bcm (European Commission 2008a, p. 4).
4. In June 2018, TANAP began delivering Azeri gas from the Shah Deniz II field to Turkey. The aim is to reach the plateau level of 6 bcm supplies to Turkey in 2021 and transport 10 bcm to Europe by 2021–2022. An increase in capacity through the contribution of other fields in the Caspian Sea is foreseen. The shareholders are SOCAR (58 per cent), BOTAS (30 per cent) and BP (12 per cent).
5. TAP's shareholders are as follows: BP (20 per cent), SOCAR (20 per cent), Snam (20 per cent), Fluxys (19 per cent), Enagas (16 per cent) and Axpo (5 per cent) (TAP'S shareholders n.d.). Transport of 10 bcm of Azeri gas from the Turkish Greek border to Southern Italy is planned, while the capacity may be expanded to 20 bcm.
6. The Nabucco Company consisted of Bulgargas, Transgas, OMV, MOL, RWE and BOTAS, with a share of 16.67 per cent each. The parties signed an intergovernmental agreement in July 2009 and project support agreements in June 2011. However, when Turkey and Azerbaijan signed an intergovernmental agreement in October 2011 to transport Azeri natural gas from the Shah Deniz II field to Turkey via TANAP, the idea of transporting Azeri gas (which would come to the western border of Turkey) from Bulgaria to Austria, named the Nabucco West pipeline, was developed to replace original Nabucco. The Shah Deniz Consortium decided in June 2013 to supply 10 bcm of Azeri gas to the Trans Adriatic Pipeline instead of Nabucco West.

7. An intergovernmental agreement for the Turkey-Greece-Italy pipeline project, which aimed to transport 11.6 bcm of Caspian natural gas to Greece (3.6 bcm) and Italy (8 bcm) via Turkey, was signed in 2007. The Turkey-Greece Interconnector has been in operation since.
8. BP proposed to transport the Azeri gas, which would be supplied via TANAP to the western border of Turkey and on to Europe in 2011. This plan was in competition with Nabucco West, ITGI and TAP to transport the Shah Deniz II gas. BP had a share of 25.5 per cent in the Shah Deniz consortium (Blair 2011).
9. For example, the Azerbaijan-Georgia-Romania Interconnector aims to carry Azeri gas to Europe via pipelines from Azerbaijan to Georgia and in LNG form from the Georgian coasts to Romania. SOCAR, the Georgian Oil and Gas Corporation, MVM (Hungary) and Romgaz (Romania) are shareholders of the project (Romania reveals possible financing 2018).
10. The Pipeline aims to bring 10 bcm/y Egyptian gas to Turkey via Syria. However, the war in Syria and decline in relations between Syria and Turkey prevented the finalisation of the Arab gas pipeline, the final stage of which was expected to be built between Homs (Syria) and Kilis (Turkey).
11. The Commission highlighted that "Turkey's actions and statements continued to challenge the rights of the Republic of Cyprus to exploit hydrocarbon resources in the Cyprus Exclusive Economic Zone (European Commission 2019a, p. 7).
12. "The Council calls on Turkey to show restraint, respect the sovereign rights of Cyprus and refrain from any such action" (Council of the European Union 2019a).
13. Over 90 contributions from seven Member States, four regulators' associations, two Transmission System Operators, industry players, associations, non-governmental organisations, think-tanks, individual citizens, academia and consumers' associations in the EU Member States.

Bibliography

Aalto, P., & Korkmaz-Temel, D. (2014). European energy security: Natural gas and the integration process. *Journal of Common Market Studies, 52*(4), 758–774.

Andersen, S., Goldthau, A., & Sitter, N. (2016). The EU regulatory state, commission leadership and external energy governance. In J. Godzirmirski (Ed.), *EU leadership in energy and environmental governance* (pp. 51–68). Basingstoke: Palgrave.

Andersen, S., Goldthau, A., & Sitter, N. (2017). From low to high politics? The EU's regulatory and economic power. In S. Andersen, A. Goldthau, & N. Sitter (Eds.), *Energy Union Europe's new liberal mercantilism?* (pp. 13–26). London: Palgrave.

Assenova, M. (2019). Since EU Court ruling, Moscow in a weaker position in gas transit talks with Kyiv. *Eurasia Daily Monitor, 16*(133) Retrieved from https://jamestown.org/program/since-eu-court-ruling-moscow-in-a-weaker-position-in-gas-transit-talks-with-kyiv/.

Bailey, S. (2009). *File: Nabuccostream.png*.. Retrieved from https://commons.wikimedia.org/wiki/File:Nabuccostream.png.

Bilgin, M. (2007). New prospects in the political economy of inner-Caspian hydrocarbons and western energy corridor through Turkey. *Energy Policy, 35*, 6383–6394.

Blair, D. (2011). *BP plans gas pipeline to Europe from Azerbaijan*. Retrieved from http://www.ft.com/intl/cms/s/0/ed9151b8-e84c-11e0-ab03-00144feab49a.html#axzz1pm09chpg.

BP. (2019). *Statistical review of world energy*. Retrieved from https://www.bp.com/content/dam/bp/business-sites/en/global/corporate/pdfs/energy-economics/statistical-review/bp-stats-review-2019-full-report.pdf.

Bros, A. (2014). Gazprom in Europe: A business doomed to fail? *IFRI Russie. Nei. Reports*, No. 18. Retrieved from https://www.ifri.org/sites/default/files/atoms/files/ifri_rnr_18_gazprom_aurelie_bros_july2014.pdf.

Bulgaria launches gas hub feasibility study. (2018, March 15). *Reuters*. Retrieved from https://www.reuters.com/article/bulgaria-gas-hub/bulgaria-launches-gas-hub-feasibility-study-idUSL8N1QW5VE.

Bulgaria starts receiving Russian gas via TurkStream pipeline. (2020, January 1). *TASS*. Retrieved from https://tass.com/economy/1105309.

Burmistrova, S., & Zinets, N. (2014). UPDATE 3-Russia raises gas prices for Ukraine by 80 percent. *Reuters*. Retrieved from http://www.reuters.com/article/2014/04/03/ukraine-crisis-gas-idUSL5N0MV2WL20140403.

Chee, Y. F., & de Carbonnel, A. (2018, May 24). EU ends antitrust case against Gazprom without fines. *Reuters*. Retrieved from https://uk.reuters.com/article/uk-eu-gazprom-antitrust/eu-ends-antitrust-case-against-gazprom-without-fines-idUKKCN1IP1K4.

Cottier, T., Malumfashi, G., Matteotti-Berkutova, S., Nartova, O., De Sépibus, J. and Bigdel, Z.S. (n.d.). *Energy in WTO law and policy*. Retrieved from http://www.wto.org/english/res_e/publications_e/wtr10_forum_e/wtr10_7may10_e.pdf.

Council of the European Union. (2005). *High level energy event 3–4 November 2005* (14777/05). London.

Council of the European Union. (2008). *Second strategic energy review—An EU energy security and solidarity action plan—Contribution from the Italian delegation* (16345/08 ADD 4). Brussels.

Council of the European Union. (2009a). *Second strategic energy review—An EU energy security and solidarity action plan—Contribution form the Polish delegation* (16345/08, ADD 7). Brussels.

Council of the European Union. (2009b). *Second strategic energy review—An EU energy security and solidarity action plan—Contribution form the Lithuanian delegation* (16345/08, ADD 9). Brussels.

Council of the European Union. (2009c). *Council conclusions on the commission communication 'Second strategic energy review—An EU energy security and solidarity action plan'* (6692/09). Brussels.

Council of the European Union. (2009d). *Remarks by Javier Solana at the 'Southern Corridor—New silk road' Summit* (S120/09). Brussels.

Council of the European Union. (2009e). *International relations in the field of energy* (9852/09). Brussels.

Council of the European Union. (2010a). *Towards a new energy strategy for Europe 2011–2020—Contribution from the Slovenian delegation* (16303/10 ADD 5). Brussels.

Council of the European Union. (2010b). *Towards a new energy strategy for Europe 2011–2020—Contribution from the Italian delegation* (16303/10 ADD 12). Brussels.

Council of the European Union. (2010c). *Towards a new energy strategy for Europe 2011–2010—Contribution from the French delegation* (16303/10 ADD 20). Brussels.

Council of the European Union. (2011). *Council conclusions on communication on security of energy supply and international cooperation—'The EU energy policy: Engaging with partners beyond our borders'* (17615/11). Brussels.

Council of the European Union. (2018). *The fourth ministerial meeting of the Southern Gas Corridor Advisory Council—Joint Declaration.* ENER 29, COEST 18. Brussels.

Council of the European Union. (2019a, June 18). *Council conclusions on enlargement and stabilisation and accession process.* Retrieved from https://www.consilium.europa.eu/en/press/press-releases/2019/06/18/council-conclusions-on-enlargement-and-stabilisation-and-association-process/.

Council of the European Union. (2019b, July 15). *Turkish drilling activities in the Mediterranean: Council adopts conclusions.* Retrieved from https://www.consilium.europa.eu/en/press/press-releases/2019/07/15/turkish-drilling-activities-in-the-eastern-mediterranean-council-adopts-conclusions/.

El-Agraa, A. (2007). The theory of economic integration. In A. El-Agraa (Ed.), *The European Union economics and policies* (pp. 109–129). New York: Cambridge University Press.

Energy Charter Secretariat. (2015). *The International Energy Charter Consolidated Energy Charter Treaty with related documents.* Retrieved from http://www.energycharter.org/fileadmin/DocumentsMedia/Legal/ECTC-en.pdf.

EU Commission Calls for Opening of Energy Chapter in Turkish Accession Process. (2013, April 16). *Hurriyet Daily News*. Retrieved from http://www.hurriyetdailynews.com/eu-commission-calls-for-opening-of-energy-chapter-in-turkish-accession-process-45042.

EU Urged to Open Energy Chapter. (2014, February 27). *Hurriyet Daily News*. Retrieved from http://www.hurriyetdailynews.com/eu-urged-to-open-energy-chapter-62981.

Euractiv. (2012). *Commission opens antitrust case against Gazprom*. Retrieved from http://www.euractiv.com/energy/commission-opens-antitrust-case-news-514613.

Eurlings, C. (2006). *Report on Turkey's progress towards accession* (2006/2118(INI)) FINAL A6–0269/2006. Retrieved from http://www.europarl.europa.eu/sides/getDoc.do?pubRef=-//EP//TEXT+REPORT+A6-2006-0269+0+DOC+XML+V0//EN&language=ga.

European Commission. (1997). *The external dimension of trans-European energy networks* (COM (97) 125 final). Retrieved from http://aei.pitt.edu/4732/1/4732.pdf.

European Commission. (2000). *Green paper on the security of energy supply* (COM/2000/0769 final). Retrieved from http://eur-lex.europa.eu/legal-content/EN/TXT/?uri=CELEX%3A52000DC0769.

European Commission. (2003). *Communication from the Commission to the Council and the European Parliament on the development of energy policy for the enlarged European Union, its neighbours and partner countries* (COM (2003) 262 final/2). Retrieved from http://ec.europa.eu/dgs/energy_transport/international/doc/2003_communication_en.pdf.

European Commission. (2005). *An integrated market for electricity and gas across 34 European countries* (MEMO/05/397). Retrieved from http://europa.eu/rapid/pressReleasesAction.do?reference=MEMO/05/397&language=en.

European Commission. (2006). *Green paper—A European strategy for sustainable, competitive and secure energy* (COM (2006) 105 final). Retrieved from http://europa.eu/documents/comm/green_papers/pdf/com2006_105_en.pdf.

European Commission. (2007a). *Communication from the Commission to the European Council and the European Parliament an energy policy for Europe* (COM (2007) 1 final). Retrieved from http://www.europarl.europa.eu/meetdocs/2004_2009/documents/com/com_com(2007)0001_/com_com(2007)0001_en.pdf.

European Commission. (2007b). *Black Sea synergy—A new regional cooperation initiative* (COM (2007) 160 final). Retrieved from http://eeas.europa.eu/enp/pdf/pdf/com07_160_en.pdf.

European Commission. (2007c). *Turkey and the EU: Together for a European energy policy* (IP/07/748). Retrieved from https://europa.eu/rapid/press-release_IP-07-748_en.htm?locale=en.

European Commission. (2008a). *Second strategic energy review: An EU energy security and solidarity action plan* (COM (2008) 781 final). Retrieved from http://eur-lex.europa.eu/LexUriServ/LexUriServ.do?uri=COM:2008:0781:FIN:EN:PDF.

European Commission. (2008b). *Commissioners host meeting to boost energy co-operation with Mashreq countries, Iraq and Turkey*. Retrieved from http://europa.eu/rapid/press- release_IP-08-677_en.htm?locale=en.

European Commission. (2010a). *Energy 2020: A strategy for competitive, sustainable and secure energy* (COM (2010) 639 final). Retrieved from http://eur-lex.europa.eu/LexUriServ/LexUriServ.do?uri=COM:2010:0639:FIN:En:PDF.

European Commission. (2010b). *Energy infrastructure priorities for 2020 and beyond: A blueprint for an integrated European energy network* (COM (2010) 677 final). Retrieved from http://eur-lex.europa.eu/legal-content/EN/TXT/PDF/?uri=CELEX:52010DC0677&from=EN.

European Commission. (2011a). *Commission staff working paper key facts and figures on the external dimension of the EU energy policy* (SEC (2011) 1022 final). Retrieved from http://eur-lex.europa.eu/LexUriServ/LexUriServ.do?uri=SEC:2011:1022:FIN:EN:PDF.

European Commission. (2011b). *Energy community: Five years of regional cooperation* (IP/11/1223). Retrieved from http://europa.eu/rapid/press-release_IP-11- 1223_en.htm.

European Commission. (2011c). *On security of energy supply and international cooperation—'The EU energy policy: Engaging with partners beyond our borders'* (COM (2011) 539 final). Retrieved from http://eur-lex.europa.eu/legal-content/EN/TXT/PDF/?uri=CELEX:52011DC0539&from=EN.

European Commission. (2011d). *Report from the Commission to the European Parliament and the Council under Article 7 of Decision 2006/500/EC (Energy Community Treaty)* (COM (2011) 105 final). Retrieved from http://eur-lex.europa.eu/legal-content/EN/TXT/PDF/?uri=CELEX:52011DC0105&from=EN.

European Commission. (2011e). *Commission staff working paper results of the public consultation on the external dimension of the EU energy policy* (SEC (2011) 1023 final). Retrieved from http://eur-lex.europa.eu/legal-content/EN/TXT/PDF/?uri=CELEX:52011SC1023&from=EN.

European Commission. (2011f). *Commission staff working paper Turkey 2011 Progress Report* (SEC (2011) 1201 final). Retrieved from http://ec.europa.eu/enlargement/pdf/key_documents/2011/package/tr_rapport_2011_en.pdf.

European Commission. (2014a). *EU energy in figures: Statistical pocketbook 2014*. Luxembourg: Publications Office of the European Union.

European Commission. (2014b). *Commission staff working document in depth study of European energy security* (SWD (2014) 330 final/3). Retrieved from

http://ec.europa.eu/energy/sites/ener/files/documents/20140528_energy_security_study.pdf.
European Commission. (2015a). *Antitrust: Commission sends statement of objections to Gazprom for alleged abuse of dominance on Central and Eastern European gas supply markets.* Retrieved from http://europa.eu/rapid/press-release_IP-15-4828_en.htm.
European Commission. (2015b). *Energy Union package—A Framework Strategy for a Resilient Energy Union with a Forward-looking Climate Change Policy* (COM(2015) 80 final). Retrieved from https://eur-lex.europa.eu/resource.html?uri=cellar:1bd46c90-bdd4-11e4-bbe1-01aa75ed71a1.0001.03/DOC_1&format=PDF.
European Commission. (2016, February 16). *Towards Energy Union: The Commission presents sustainable energy security package.* Retrieved from https://europa.eu/rapid/press-release_IP-16-307_en.htm.
European Commission. (2017). *Feasibility study on the Balkan gas hub.* Retrieved from https://ec.europa.eu/inea/sites/inea/files/6.25.4-0015-bg-s-m-16_action_fiche_gas.pdf.
European Commission. (2018a). Commission Delegated Regulation (EU) 2018/540 of 23 November 2017 amending Regulation (EU) No 347/2013 of the European Parliament and of the Council as regards the Union list of projects of common interest. *Official Journal of the European Union, L 90/38.* Retrieved from https://eur-lex.europa.eu/legal-content/EN/TXT/PDF/?uri=CELEX:32018R0540&from=EN.
European Commission. (2018b). *EU Energy in figures.* Luxembourg: Publications Office of the European Union.
European Commission. (2018c, February 15). *Vice-President Šefčovič in Azerbaijan to attend the Southern Gas Corridor Advisory Council.* Retrieved from https://ec.europa.eu/info/news/vice-president-sefcovic-azerbaijan-attend-southern-gas-corridor-advisory-council-2018-feb-15_en.
European Commission. (2019a). *Commission staff working document—Turkey 2019 report* (SWD(2019) 220 final). Retrieved from https://ec.europa.eu/neighbourhood-enlargement/sites/near/files/20190529-turkey-report.pdf.
European Commission. (2019b). *EU energy in figures.* Retrieved from https://op.europa.eu/en/publication-detail/-/publication/e0544b72-db53-11e9-9c4e-01aa75ed71a1/language-en.
European Commission. (n.d.-a). *Shale gas and other unconventional hydrocarbons.* Retrieved from https://ec.europa.eu/energy/en/topics/oil-gas-and-coal/shale-gas.
European Commission. (n.d.-b). EU starts negotiations on Caspian pipeline to bring gas to Europe. Retrieved from http://europa.eu/rapid/press-release_IP-11-1023_en.htm.

European Commission. (n.d.-c). *Excel sheets with EU and EU country results*. Retrieved from https://ec.europa.eu/energy/en/data-analysis/energy-modelling/eu-reference-scenario-2016.

European Commission. (n.d.-d). *An external policy to serve Europe's energy interests* (S160/06). Retrieved from http://ec.europa.eu/dgs/energy_transport/international/doc/paper_solana_sg_energy_en.pdf.

European Council. (2006). *Brussels European Council 14–15 December 2006 Presidency Conclusions*. Retrieved from https://www.ab.gov.tr/files/ardb/evt/1_avrupa_birligi/1_4_zirveler_1985_sonrasi/2006_12_bruksel_zirvesi_baskanlik_sonuc_bildirgesi_en.pdf.

European Council. (2008). *Brussels European Council 15–16 October 2008 presidency conclusions.*. Retrieved from http://www.consilium.europa.eu/uedocs/cms_data/docs/pressdata/en/ec/103441.pdf.

European Council. (2009). *Brussels European Council 19/20 March 2009 presidency conclusions*. Retrieved from http://www.consilium.europa.eu/uedocs/cms_data/docs/pressdata/en/ec/106809.pdf.

European Council. (2014). *European Council 20–21 March 2014 presidency conclusions*. Retrieved from http://www.consilium.europa.eu/uedocs/cms_data/docs/pressdata/en/ec/141749.pdf.

European Parliament. (2006). *Guidelines for trans-European energy networks (debate)*. Retrieved from http://www.europarl.europa.eu/sides/getDoc.do?type=CRE&reference=20060403&secondRef=ITEM-010&language=EN&ring=A6-2006-0071.

European Parliament. (2008). *European Parliament resolution of 17 January 2008 on a Black Sea regional policy approach* (2007/2101 (INI)). Retrieved from http://www.europarl.europa.eu/sides/getDoc.do?type=TA&reference=P6-TA-2008-0017&language=EN.

European Parliament. (2009a). *Croatia: Progress report 2008—Turkey: Progress report 2008—Former Yugoslav Republic of Macedonia: Progress report 2008 (debate)*. Retrieved from http://www.europarl.europa.eu/sides/getDoc.do?pubRef=-//EP//TEXT+CRE+20090311+ITEM-012+DOC+XML+V0//EN&language=EN.

European Parliament. (2009b). *Enlargement strategy 2009 concerning the countries of the Western Balkans, Iceland and Turkey (debate)*. Retrieved from http://www.europarl.europa.eu/sides/getDoc.do?pubRef=-//EP//TEXT+CRE+20091125+ITEM-012+DOC+XML+V0//EN&language=EN.

European Parliament. (2009c). *Energy security (Nabucco and Desertec) (debate)*. Retrieved from http://www.europarl.europa.eu/sides/getDoc.do?pubRef=-//EP//TEXT+CRE+20090917+ITEM-003+DOC+XML+V0//EN&language=EN.

European Parliament. (2010a). *European Parliament resolution of 25 November 2010 on towards a new energy strategy for Europe 2011–2020* (2010/2108

(INI)). Retrieved from http://www.europarl.europa.eu/sides/getDoc.do?type=TA&reference=P7-TA-2010-0441&language=GA.

European Parliament. (2010b). *2009 progress report on Croatia—2009 progress report on the Former Yugoslav Republic of Macedonia—2009 progress report on Turkey (debate)*. Retrieved from http://www.europarl.europa.eu/sides/getDoc.do?pubRef=-//EP//TEXT+CRE+20100210+ITEM-008+DOC+XML+V0//EN&language=EN.

European Parliament. (2011). *European Parliament resolution of 5 July 2011 on energy infrastructure priorities for 2020 and beyond* (2011/20134(INI)). Retrieved from http://www.europarl.europa.eu/sides/getDoc.do?pubRef=-//EP//TEXT+TA+P7-TA-2011-0318+0+DOC+XML+V0//EN.

European Parliament. (2012). *Resolution of 12 June 2012 on engaging in energy policy cooperation with partners beyond our borders: A strategic approach to secure, sustainable and competitive energy supply* (2012/2029(INI)). Retrieved from http://www.europarl.europa.eu/sides/getDoc.do?pubRef=-//EP//TEXT+TA+P7-TA-2012-0238+0+DOC+XML+V0//EN&language=EN.

European Parliament backs Southern Gas Corridor. (2018, March 24). *Azernews*. Retrieved from https://www.azernews.az/oil_and_gas/129148.html.

European Union. (2004). Opinion of the European Economic and Social Committee on a 'proposal for a decision of the European Parliament and of the Council laying down guidelines for trans-European energy networks and repealing Decisions No 96/391/EC and No 1229/2003/EC' (COM(2003) 742 final). *Official Journal of the European Union, C, 241*, 17–18.

European Union. (2009). Opinion of the European Economic and Social Committee on the Communication from the Commission on the second strategic energy review—An EU energy security and solidarity action plan (COM (2008) 781 final). *Official Journal of the European Union, C, 228*, 84–89.

European Union. (2010). European Parliament resolution of 17 September 2009 on external aspects of energy security (2010/C 224 E/06). *Official Journal of the European Union, C, 224*(E), 23–27.

Eurostat. (2013). *Glossary: Gross inland energy consumption*. Retrieved from http://ec.europa.eu/eurostat/statistics-explained/index.php/Glossary:Gross_inland_energy_consumption.

Eurostat. (2019). *EU imports of energy products-recent developments*. Retrieved from https://ec.europa.eu/eurostat/statistics-explained/index.php/EU_imports_of_energy_products_-_recent_developments#Overview.

Ferrero-Waldner, B. (2006). *Opening address of the conference: Towards an EU external energy policy to assure a high level of supply security* (SPEECH/06/710). Retrieved from http://europa.eu/rapid/pressReleasesAction.do?reference=SPEECH/06/710&format=HTML&aged=0&l anguage=EN.

Geropoulos, K. (2012). *EU calls for 'non-Russian sources' of gas*. Retrieved from http://www.neurope.eu/article/eu-calls-non-russian-sources-gas.

Gloystein, H. (2012). Snap analysis: Nabucco gas pipeline must shrink or die. In *Reuters*. Retrieved from https://uk.reuters.com/article/uk-energy-europe-gas-nabucco/snap-analysis-nabucco-gas-pipeline-must-shrink-or-die-idUKBRE83P10K20120426.

Goldthau, A., & Sitter, N. (2019). Regulatory or market power Europe? EU leadership models for international energy governance. In J. Godzimirski (Ed.), *New political economy of energy in Europe* (pp. 27–48). Cham: Palgrave.

Gotev, G. (2015). TAP pipeline secures exemption from Third Energy Package. In *Euractiv*. Retrieved from https://www.euractiv.com/section/energy/news/tap-pipeline-secures-exemption-from-third-energy-package/.

Gotev, G. (2017). Russian PM: Turkish Stream will enter EU via Bulgaria or Greece. In *Euractiv*. Retrieved from https://www.euractiv.com/section/global-europe/news/russian-pm-turkish-stream-can-enter-eu-via-bulgaria-or-greece/.

Hungary joins Gazprom pipeline, as Trump touts US LNG. (2017, July 6). *Euractiv*. Retrieved from https://www.euractiv.com/section/energy/news/hungary-joins-gazprom-pipeline-as-trump-touts-us-lng.

Hunt, M., & Karova, R. (2010). The energy acquis under the Energy Community Treaty and the integration of south east European electricity markets: An uneasy relationship? In B. Delvaux, M. Hunt, & K. Talus (Eds.), *EU energy law and policy issues* (2nd ed., pp. 51–86). Rixensart: Euroconfidentiel.

IEA. (2018). *Outlook for natural gas*. Retrieved from https://www.iea.org/publications/freepublications/publication/WEO2017Excerpt_Outlook_for_Natural_Gas.pdf.

Memorandum of Understanding on a Strategic Partnership on Energy Between the European Union and the Arab Republic of Egypt 2018–2022. (n.d.). *European Commission*. Retrieved from https://ec.europa.eu/energy/sites/ener/files/documents/eu-egypt_mou.pdf.

Oner, N., & Schröder, M. (2017). 'Turkey as a future energy hub'—A comparative analysis of the hub narratives in Turkey and in the EU. In M. Schroder, M. O. Bettzuge, & W. Wessels (Eds.), *Turkey as an energy Hub? Contributions on Turkey's role in EU energy supply* (pp. 185–202). Baden-Baden: Nomos Verlagsgesellschaft.

Overland, I. (2017). The hunter becomes the hunted: Gazprom encounters EU regulation. In S. Andersen, A. Goldthau, & N. Sitter (Eds.), *Energy Union Europe's new liberal mercantilism?* (pp. 115–130). London: Palgrave.

Padgett, S. (2011). Energy co-operation in the wider Europe: Institutionalizing interdependence. *Journal of Common Market Studies, 49*(5), 1065–1087.

Petroleum Economist. (2018, April 16). *Southern Gas Corridor Project defies sceptics*. Retrieved from https://www.petroleum-economist.com/articles/midstream-downstream/pipelines/2018/southern-gas-corridor-project-defies-sceptics.

Piebalgs, A. (2007a). *Nabucco pipeline and security of supply* (SPEECH/07/531). Retrieved from http://europa.eu/rapid/press-release_SPEECH-07- 531_en.htm?locale=en.

Piebalgs, A. (2007b). *EU and Turkey: Together for a European energy policy* (SPEECH/07/368). Retrieved from http://europa.eu/rapid/press-release_SPEECH-07-368_en.htm.

Piebalgs, A. (2007c). *Key note speech at the conference: 'East meets west: New frontiers of energy security'* (SPEECH/07/437). Retrieved from http://europa.eu/rapid/press- release_SPEECH-07-437_en.htm.

Pirani, S. (2018). *Let's not exaggerate: Southern Gas Corridor prospects to 2030.* OIES Paper, NG 135.

Prange-Gstöhl, H. (2009). Enlarging the EU's internal energy market: Why would third countries accept EU rule export? *Energy Policy, 37*, 5296–5303.

President of the European Parliament. (2010). *Buzek and Delors declaration on the creation of a European Energy Community.* Retrieved from http://www.europarl.europa.eu/former_ep_presidents/president-buzek/en/press/press_release/2010/2010-May/press_release-2010-May-3.html.

Radio Free Europe/Radio Liberty. (2020). TurkStream gas pipeline map. Retrieved from https://www.rferl.org/a/russia-launches-itself-into-new-export-territory-with-turkstream-natural-gas-pipeline/30364755.html.

Rehn, O. (2009a). *EU and Turkey-tackling economic downturn through partnership* (SPEECH/09/148). Retrieved from http://europa.eu/rapid/press-release_SPEECH-09-148_en.htm.

Rehn, O. (2009b). *Turkey as an energy hub for Europe: Prospects and challenges* (SPEECH/09/89).Retrievedfromhttp://europa.eu/rapid/press-release_SPEECH-09-89_en.htm.

Romania Reveals Possible Financing Sources for AGRI project. (2018, August 13). *Azernews.* Retrieved from https://www.azernews.az/oil_and_gas/136127.html.

Russia, Ukraine Reach Five-Year-Gas Transit Deal. (2019, December 31). *Radio Free Europe/ Radio Liberty.* Retrieved from https://www.rferl.org/a/long-russia-ukraine-reach-five-year-gas-transit-deal/30353000.html.

Rzayeva, G. (2012). A complicated corridor: Gas to Europe—It's not just economics. *Caucasus International, 2*(2), 141–159.

Rzayeva, G. (2015). Azerbaijan-Turkey relations and Baku's energy strategy for Southeastern Europe. In M. Assenova & Z. Shiriyev (Eds.), *Azerbaijan and the new energy geopolitics of Southeastern Europe* (pp. 179–202). Washington, DC: Jamestown Foundation.

Siddi, M. (2019). The EU's botched geopolitical approach to external energy policy: The case of the Southern Gas Corridor. *Geopolitics, 24*(1), 124–144.

Smith, M. (2011). A liberal grand strategy in a realist world? Power, purpose and the EU's changing global role. *Journal of European Public Policy, 18*(2), 144–163.

So close: Nord Stream 2 gas link completion trips at last hurdle. (2020, January 7). *S&P Global Platts.*. Retrieved from https://blogs.platts.com/2020/01/07/nord-stream-2-gas-pipeline-trips-at-last-hurdle/.

Solana, J. (2006). Why Europe must act collectively on energy. *Financial Times.* Retrieved from http://www.ft.com/intl/cms/s/0/76e72606-aed1-11da-b04a-0000779e2340.html#axzz3wHPcMGrb.

TAP's shareholders. (n.d.). *Trans Adriatic pipeline.* Retrieved from https://www.tap-ag.com/about-us/our-shareholders.

Tekin, A., & Williams, A. (2009). *Europe's external energy policy and Turkey's accession process.* Center for European Studies, Working Paper Series #170. Retrieved from http://aei.pitt.edu/11786/1/CES_170.pdf.

The Energy Community. (2010). *Legal framework.* Retrieved from http://www.energy-community.org/pls/portal/docs/808177.PDF.

Turkey vital for energy, EU Commissioner says. (2012, February 10). *Hurriyet Daily News.* Retrieved from http://www.hurriyetdailynews.com/turkey-vital-for-energy-eu-commissioner-says.aspx?pageID=238&nid=13451.

Yafimava, K. (2011). *The transit dimension of EU energy security.* Oxford and New York: Oxford University Press.

CHAPTER 4

Turkey's Energy Security and Pipelines

This chapter aims to determine how the Turkish actors perceive the EU's narratives on diversification, which can best be achieved by analysing Turkish narratives on the Southern Corridor. Turkish actors in the field of energy consist of state and non-state actors. The book considers the views of the AKP, which has been in power since 2002, the opposition parties, public authorities concerned with energy matters such as the Ministry of Foreign Affairs, the Ministry of Energy and Natural Resources (hereinafter Ministry of Energy), the Energy Market Regulatory Authority (EMRA), the state owned Petroleum Pipeline Company (BOTAS) and the Turkish Competition Authority as state actors. Furthermore, the book considers representatives of the private sector[1] such as the Turkish Industry and Business Association (TUSIAD) and the Petroleum Platform Association (PETFORM), the union Petrol-Is, think-tanks and non-governmental organisations such as the Union of Chambers of Turkish Engineers and Architects (TMMOB) and the World Energy Council Turkish National Committee as non-state actors in the energy field. Since the scope of the chapter is delimited to the Turkish actors' positions on pipelines, it does not focus on all Turkish non-state actors interested in energy issues.

Like the previous chapter, this chapter uses primary institutions as analytical tools to examine Turkish narratives on pipelines. An examination of primary institutions in the Turkish narratives make it possible to comprehend the domestic discussions in Turkey on pipelines, the cognitive maps

D. Korkmaz, *Turkey and the EU in an Energy Security Society*,
https://doi.org/10.1007/978-3-030-45774-7_4

of the Turkish actors and their main motivations in their policy with the EU in the sphere of natural gas. This allows for the understanding of the extent to which the Turkish narratives on pipelines coincide with those of the EU on diversification and the position in which Turkish actors aim to reside in the energy security society.

Commonalities in different actors' narratives provide a useful starting point. The emphasis on "national interest" was one of the significant common points underlined by different Turkish actors. For example, the AKP mentioned protecting the national interest in its Manifesto on energy policy (AK Parti n.d.-a) while the Republican People's Party (CHP), the main opposition party, promised "an understanding prioritising ***national interest*** in international relations" to be pursued within the scope of energy politics (Cumhuriyet Halk Partisi n.d., p. 242) (emphases in original). In addition to the country's interest, the Chamber of Mechanical Engineers underlined the significance of "society's interest" (Turkyilmaz and Aytac 2018, p. 589) and argued that "energy planning should aim to protect the national and public interest" (Makina Muhendisleri Odasi 2012a, p. 207). However, commonalities also involved differences within themselves. Accordingly, as this chapter aims to demonstrate, the context of "national interest" differed in each narrative.

The chapter begins with an analysis of different actors' definitions of the concept of energy security. This provides an understanding of what Turkish actors refer to when dealing with energy security and serves as a comparison with the definitions described by the EU actors. This section is significant as a starting point in showing how actors' understanding of energy security is reflected in their narratives on pipelines and the market, which will be examined in the next chapter. After an examination of the concept of energy security and examination of each component of the concept with reference to different narrators, the chapter continues by analysing the AKP's story on pipelines, constituted by the balance of power. The chapter then scrutinises the functioning of security of supply in the Turkish narratives and analyses the functioning of modern sovereignty. Within this context, domestic discussions on the extent to which the natural gas pipelines crossing Turkey contribute to Turkey's security of supply and the Turkish position on the Eastern Mediterranean are scrutinised.

4.1 The Concept of Energy Security for Turkish Actors

The AKP referred to maintaining secure and continuous energy supplies, establishing a competitive energy market and protecting the environment and human health in its Manifesto (AK Parti n.d.-a). The Presidency also included the goal of achieving a competitive energy sector, which would strengthen Turkey's strategic position in international energy trade and reduces energy intensity (Cumhurbaskanligi 2018, p. 235). The Ministry of Energy referred to sustainability as a framework that considers environmental, economic and social aspects (Enerji ve Tabii Kaynaklar Bakanligi 2017a, pp. 19–21). However, the Party prioritised security of supply over sustainability in its energy policy. The significance of security of supply was highlighted in the Party's Election Program in which energy was considered a "strategic sector" (AK Parti 2018, p. 218). The prioritisation of security of supply became visible in the "National Energy and Mining Policy", declared in 2017. It consists of three pillars: security of supply, foreseeable energy markets and indigenisation, which refers to the development of domestic energy technology. Within the scope of the National Energy and Mining Policy, the AKP pursued the "more indigenous, more renewables" policy (Enerji ve Tabii Kaynaklar Bakanligi 2017a, p. 5), which included domestic coal in addition to wind, solar, geothermal and hydro power. Targets included increasing the indigenous energy production and the share of renewables in electricity generation and developing local technology in energy and mining sectors, including clean coal technology. Accordingly, Berat Albayrak, then Minister of Energy, stated that strategies within the scope of security of supply included increasing the share of coal and renewables in the energy mix, investing in infrastructure, increasing the supply capacity, being active in exploration and diversifying suppliers and routes (Enerji ve Tabii Kaynaklar Bakanligi 2017b). Highlighting the significance of indigenous coal in electricity generation and comparing with other countries, Albayrak confirmed that Turkey will continue to use domestic coal despite criticisms:

> As stakeholders, we are aware of the significance of coal. There are anti-coal people. They are not very significant ... The USA has been consuming [coal] ... the UK has been consuming. ... for electricity production. Sorry about that, we will be using [consuming] our source. (Kilavuzoglu 2016b)

The AKP's energy policy aimed to ensure security of supply by establishing a competitive energy market. Bearing in mind the interaction between the primary institutions of security of supply and the market, the Party's position was that a competitive energy market reduces the risks for security of supply and creates efficiency in generating and consuming energy. To overcome the increase in energy demand, an annual 4.2 per cent on average during 2003 to 2016 (Enerji ve Tabii Kaynaklar Bakanligi 2017b, pp. 1–2), the AKP considered developing an investor-friendly environment based on competition as strategy. The Party deemed the private sector to be the main actor for energy investments to meet the rise in energy demand (Enerji ve Tabii Kaynaklar Bakanligi 2017b, p. 9). Not surprisingly, the private sector, as highlighted by a TUSIAD representative, also included "securing supply-liberalisation and climate-energy integration" (Altan 2010, p. 62) within the scope of the three pillars on which the Turkish energy policy should be based. The private sector's narrative shows an interaction between security of supply and the market as primary institutions, as they believed that security of supply is achieved in a competitive energy market.

The union Petrol-Is also prioritised security of supply although it did not consider competitiveness to be a tool. Petrol-Is rejected the interaction between the primary institutions of security of supply and the market and stated that the "strategic importance of natural gas for countries highlights the security of supply to become more prominent than price" (Petrol-Is 2007, p. 65). According to the union, private firms might prefer to opt out when new or additional gas is received with higher prices (Petrol-Is 2007, p. 65) due to concerns about demand. This could create a risk to security of supply, which should be prioritised. Petrol-Is' narrative underlined that liberalisation did not guarantee security of supply or lower price and that it was difficult to find a price equilibrium in a free market due to the weak natural gas demand elasticity. Arguing that the private sector prioritises profit over public benefit, the union stated that liberalisation would pave the way for higher prices (Petrol-Is 2008, p. 2) and prepare the grounds for the privatisation of BOTAS (Petrol-Is 2009). A similar narrative came from the People's Democratic Party (HDP), which stated in its Manifesto that the Party was against "energy policies and projects based on the market … privatisation of public goods and commercialisation and marketisation of public services" (Halkların Demokratik Partisi n.d.).

The two other actors that indicated the significance of the public benefit were the Union of Chambers of Turkish Engineers and Architects (TMMOB) and the CHP. The TMMOB referred to security of supply, sustainability and low-cost energy in their definition of energy security: "supplying energy to all consumers in an adequate, high quality, continuous, low-cost and sustainable way should be the main energy policy" (Turkyilmaz and Aytac 2018, p. 587). Although the TMMOB agreed that the public and private sectors should co-exist (interview 2018) and referred to the rights of the private sector to import gas, they envisaged a strong vertically integrated state company. This company would not only be a monopoly in transmission but also powerful in imports and storage and would be re-structured based on a new understanding of "public ownership and governance" (Turkyilmaz and Aytac 2018, pp. 590–594).

The CHP's energy policy was based on high quality, sufficient, affordable and continuous energy supplies. The Party emphasised prioritising human-centred and sustainable energy production by indigenous sources (Cumhuriyet Halk Partisi 2016, p. 5) and underlined in its Manifesto the significance of an understanding based on public benefit and economic and technological efficiency in regulating the energy market. It considered establishing a competitive market to encourage investors while it placed an emphasis on the involvement of the state by highlighting that public ownership would "not be an alternative to the market mechanism but a complementary part of it" (Cumhuriyet Halk Partisi n.d., p. 146).

Among the other opposition parties, the Good Party (IP) prioritised the ensuring of security of supply and reducing external dependency while domestic and renewable energy sources would be prioritised to achieve this goal. The Party welcomed domestic coal as long as technological solutions were sought for electricity generation. In general, they set their main goal for energy policy as the high quality, on time, sufficient, cheap and continuous supply of energy. Although the Party did not elaborate on the methods with which to achieve a cheap energy supply, it can be assumed that they favoured the establishment of a competitive market as the IP's Manifesto called for a free market (Iyi Parti, pp. 46, 61, 62). Similarly, the Nationalist Movement Party (MHP), aligned with the AKP, included a call for secure, continuous, sufficient, environmentally friendly and low-cost supplies in their 2011 Manifesto which included a reference to establishing a competitive energy market and encouraging domestic and foreign investments (Milliyetci Hareket Partisi 2011, pp. 97–98).

Security of supply can be considered the most significant element in energy policy in countries such as Turkey that are experiencing rising energy demands. Turkey's energy demand has increased due to its growing population and economy. The average annual growth in GDP for the years 2002 to 2017 was 5.8 per cent (Why Invest n.d.), which caused an annual growth average of 5.5 per cent for electricity consumption (Enerji ve Tabii Kaynaklar Bakanligi 2017b, p. 18). Security of supply in natural gas is crucial for Turkey due to the significance of natural gas in the primary energy demand and electricity generation. In 2018, the share of natural gas in the primary energy demand was 29 per cent (Enerji Isleri Genel Mudurlugu n.d.). Natural gas is a significant component of electricity production, amounting to a share of 37 per cent in 2017 and 30.8 in 2018 (Enerji Piyasasi Duzenleme Kurumu 2019b, p. iii). If Turkey were able to utilise indigenous natural gas for its electricity production, such a high share would be significantly less of a problem. However, Turkey produced only 0.428 bcm of natural gas in 2018, meeting just 0.86 per cent of natural gas consumption. Imports covered 99.16 per cent of natural gas[2] demand (Enerji Piyasasi Duzenleme Kurumu 2019a, p. 19) in the same year. This high import dependency has a negative impact on the current account deficit (Fig. 4.1). If we exclude energy imports from the current account deficit, it decreases in significant amounts and even

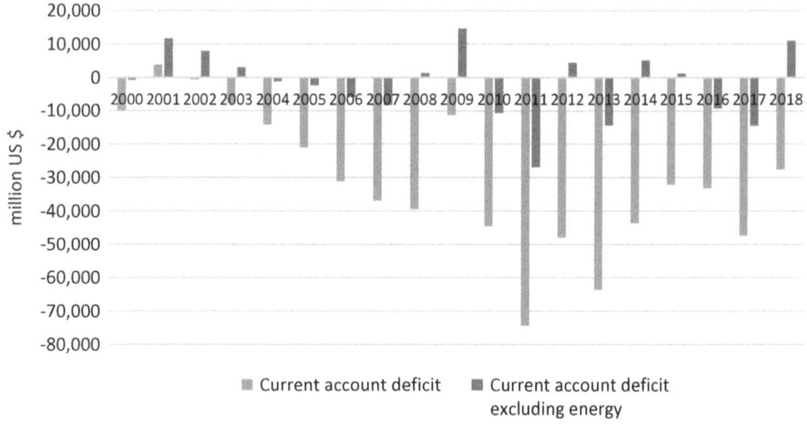

Fig. 4.1 Comparison of current account deficit and current account deficit excluding energy. (Source: Data from Central Bank of the Republic of Turkey n.d.)

reaches positive values in some years, including 2018. While the total current account deficit between 2010 and 2018 was $414.50 billion net energy[3] was $360.73 billion. A comparison for the shorter period is even more striking. The total current account deficit during the period between 2013 and 2018 was $247.51 billion and net energy was $226.71 billion (Central Bank of the Republic of Turkey n.d.).

The AKP aimed to reduce the current account deficit by increasing diversification in energy sources, investing in exploration in the Black Sea and the Mediterranean and increasing energy efficiency and domestic energy production. At the same time, the CHP drew attention to Turkey's growing energy dependency from 67 per cent in 2000 to 75 per cent in 2015, the increase in imported coal under the AKP governance and the high import dependency on Russian natural gas (Cumhuriyet Halk Partisi 2016, pp. 13–14). Likewise, the Union of Turkish Bar Associations stated that import dependency was an inevitable consequence of profit-oriented policies and poor policy and resource choices rather than the consideration of national and public interests (Basa and Pamir 2014, p. 20). The AKP's narrative on increasing energy demand was also questioned. Cetin Kocak (2018), a member of the Energy Working Group of the TMMOB, highlighted the differences between the projections and the real-time primary energy and electricity demand. While this difference in primary energy demand was 65 per cent in 2010 and 24 per cent in 2015, the deviation for electricity production was 37 per cent in 2010 and 23 per cent in 2015. He argued that such gaps might be the result of unrealised expectations for high economic growth (Makina Muhendisleri Odasi 2018, pp. 11–12). Similarly, the TMMOB drew attention to the fact that Turkey has historically faced a serious economic crisis every 7 to 8 years and that electricity demand changes according to the country's economic circumstances (Makina Muhendisleri Odasi, Enerji Calisma Grubu 2018, p. 56). Accordingly, the TMMOB proposed structural economic change from energy intensive sectors such as cement, ceramic and iron-steel towards industries with high added value such as electronics, nanotechnology and software. Recommendations in favour of energy efficiency within the scope of demand management, increased efficiency in facilities, decreased share of electricity loss in the network and the shift to less energy intensive industries were presented as remedies to ensure secure supplies (Turkyilmaz and Aytac 2018, p. 587). Similarly, Mustafa Sonmez (2018, p. 46), the Adviser of the Chamber of Mechanical Engineers, claimed that increasing oil and natural gas prices and loss of value in the Turkish Lira revealed the necessity of shifts in energy policies based on imports. Briefly, while all actors underlined the significance of security of supply, their strategies differed and ranged from investing in domestic coal to adopting structural changes in the economy to decrease energy demand.

All narrators included sustainable energy in their definitions of energy security. Although this book excludes domestic discussions on sustainability, a separate topic in Turkey-EU energy relations, it is necessary to describe the consumption of renewable energy in electricity production, which could serve as an alternative to natural gas in Turkey. Renewable-based installed capacity and electricity production increased by approximately 211 per cent and 152 per cent in 2017, respectively, compared to 2002 (TEIAS n.d.). The share of renewable energy in electricity production in 2018 was 32.5 per cent while the target for 2023, the 100th anniversary of the foundation of the Republic of Turkey, was set at 38.8 per cent (Cumhurbaskanligi Strateji ve Butce baskanligi 2019, p. 121). Bearing in mind estimations of an approximate annual increase of 5 per cent in the electricity demand until 2023 and continuing support for investing in renewables, the estimation of a slight decrease in the share of renewables shows that the expected increase will come from fossil fuels. Given the target of increasing the coal-fired installed capacity to 30 GW in 2023 (Why invest n.d.) and decreasing the share of natural gas in electricity production from 29.85 per cent in 2018 to 20.7 per cent in 2023, it is expected that coal will be primary fossil fuel source.

Arguing that the AKP's increase in the share of renewables far underperformed Turkey's potential, the CHP suggested the establishment of energy co-operations run by municipalities to generate electricity from renewables and supply secure and cheap energy without seeking profit (Cumhuriyet Halk Partisi 2016, pp. 5, 10, 14, 15). Necdet Pamir (2016b, p. 472), the Chairman of the Energy Commission of the CHP, argued that Turkey's lack of sufficient energy resources and utilisation of its renewable potential was a political argument. TMMOB also highlighted Turkey's potential for renewables, which amounted to approximately 614 billion Kwh (Makina Muhendisleri Odasi Enerji Calisma Grubu 2018, p. 129), bearing in mind the 2016 electricity consumption of approximately 280 billion Kwh (Enerji ve Tabii Kaynaklar Bakanligi 2017b, p. 23). In addition, it was argued that measures for energy efficiency could cause an increase in electricity supply equal to 25 per cent of total energy consumption while 100–150 billion Kwh could be added with the rehabilitation of current power plants (Makina Muhendisleri Odasi, Enerji

Calisma Grubu 2018, p. 129). According to the Union of Chambers, Turkey's main energy goal should be the increasing the share of hydropower to 20 to 25 per cent, other renewables to 20 to 25 per cent and decreasing the share of natural gas to 20 to 25 per cent of electricity consumption in the medium term and generating electricity mainly from renewables in the long term (Makina Muhendisleri Odasi, Enerji Calisma Grubu 2017, p. 158).

The last component of energy security is "competitive/affordable/cheap/low-cost" energy. As highlighted above, Turkish actors did not reach a consensus on the extent to which a competitive market results in low prices. Natural gas prices for industries and households are relatively cheaper in Turkey than most countries (Fig. 4.2). However, this is not due to cheap import prices. On the contrary, Turkey pays relatively high prices for Russian gas and thus price discounts have dominated the negotiations so far. Turkey has long-term oil indexed import contracts with not only Russia but also other suppliers. While the share of long-term contracts was 89.79 per cent of total imports in 2018, the remaining 10.21 per cent were in LNG imported from spot markets (Enerji Piyasasi Duzenleme Kurumu 2019a, p. 14). Relatively cheaper prices are due to pricing policy

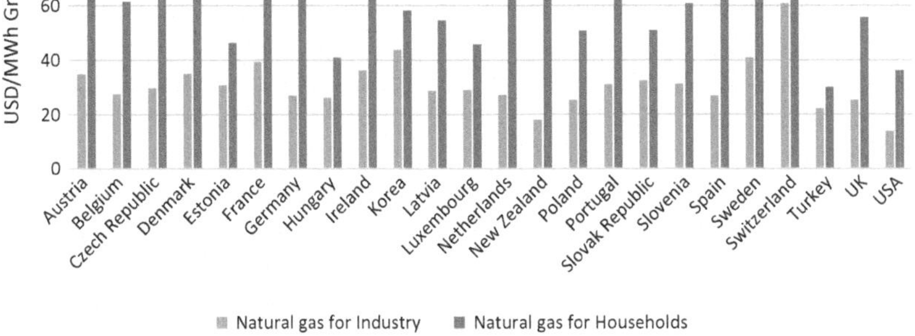

Fig. 4.2 Natural gas prices for industries and households in OECD countries (USD/Unit) (2017). (Source: Data from IEA 2018, p. 25)

based on subsidisation. Since the pricing mechanism will be examined in the next chapter, it is sufficient here to state that different actors criticise this pricing policy for different reasons.

In sum, although all actors included secure and sustainable energy in their definitions of energy security, the means by which to achieve competitive or low-cost energy varied in different narratives. The differences regarding competitive or low-cost energy in the actors' narratives were related to how to structure the market. This will be analysed in the next chapter. The next sections examine the Turkish narratives on natural gas pipelines, which are tools to secure supplies, and on the Turkish position in the Eastern Mediterranean.

4.2 Balance of Power: The AKP's Narrative

The AKP pursues a foreign policy of which energy forms a significant part. Due to the interlinkage between Turkey's foreign and energy policies, the main motivations behind Ankara's foreign policy must first be examined to understand how Turkey situates itself in the energy game. The AKP's foreign policy can be examined in two time periods: the Davutoglu period, in which Ahmet Davutoglu acted as the foreign policy adviser of Prime Ministers Abdullah Gul and Recep Tayyip Erdogan between 2002 and 2009, the Minister of Foreign Affairs between 2009 and 2014 and the Prime Minister between 2014 and 2016; and the post-Davutoglu period, which has continued since 2016. As the research data ended in July 2019, the post-Davutoglu period in the book refers to the period between 2016 and July 2019. Although Turkish foreign policy in the post-Davutoglu period shows a rupture rather than a continuity with the Davutoglu period, continuity in energy policy on natural gas pipelines, conceptualised with Turkey being a transit state[4] and an energy hub, continued (Devlet Planlama Teskilati 2006, p. 125; Kalkınma Bakanligi 2013, p. 119; Keyman 2017, pp. 56, 65).[5]

In both the Davutoglu and post-Davutoglu periods, Turkey's foreign policy was based on the assumption of a change in the order of the world, which accelerated even more after the 2008 financial crisis, in the post-Cold War period. According to this understanding, rising new powers, such as China, and an increasing multi-polarity constituted the character of the new international system, which lacks defined principles among state actors. There was a belief that Turkey should actively take part in influencing the process of building a new world order. The architecture of this thinking was Ahmet Davutoglu. Being critical of the narrow spatial and geographic perception prevalent in Turkey throughout the Cold War, Davutoglu claimed that Turkey should be an order-building actor in this period, instead of serving merely as a bridge between the East and West and adapting itself to the order. He proposed a multidimensional foreign policy based on the hypothesis that Turkey's geopolitical, geo-cultural and geo-economic location can influence the transformation of the international system and world politics (Yesiltas and Balci 2011, pp. 12–18). This new perspective foresaw the redesigning of relations with the great powers and the establishment of a hinterland in which cultural, economic and political links are consolidated with Turkey as the central country. The concept of a central country refers to Turkey as an order-building country influencing the transformation of the international system. Therefore, taking part in the existing distribution of power was part of Turkey's new perspective on foreign policy. The merits of this new perspective remain highly controversial.[6]

Drawing from Davutoglu's conceptualisation, Ali Aslan from the SETA think-tank, which has direct links with the AKP, framed the AKP's foreign policy as Turkey's struggles to move from a negative to a positive autonomy, and from a determined state to a determining one. According to Aslan, Turkey used to be a determined state before the AKP with a negative autonomy and did not have an establishing role in the international system but retained a limited autonomy. Under AKP governance he argued, Turkey aimed for a positive autonomy in which the state has the power to shape international structure and establish a kind of power over others. Becoming a determining state which would strive for stability and peace in its region and a significant actor in the global balance of power was also part of the party's 2023 vision (AK Parti n.d.-b). To be a determining state, the AKP pursued policies to develop both its ideational[7] and material capacities. Energy falls into the category of material capabilities, which include not only economic growth and investments in military technology but also energy pipelines and technology (Aslan 2018, pp. 31–39). Furthermore, prospective explorations in the Eastern Mediterranean and investments on nuclear energy and renewables were deemed as steps for Turkey to become an active energy actor (Ertem 2017; Aslan 2018), decrease its energy dependency and ensure its security of supply. Last but not least, bearing in mind the goal to transform Istanbul into a finance centre, Turkey aims to establish "an energy center having power for price formation. … in the Black Sea and the Mediterranean in which Ceyhan and Aliaga products are processed" (Ministry of Energy n.d., p. 78). Briefly, Turkey's goals in its energy policy are expected to contribute to Turkey's role in the existing distribution of power, which shows the functioning of the balance of power as a primary institution.

Regarding energy, Davutoglu drew attention to the necessity for Turkey to make long-term strategic plans for the transportation of energy sources. This was deemed important not only for active diplomacy on energy sources but also adaptation to regional geopolitics (Davutoglu 2001, pp. 118, 139). This emphasis on being a central country rather than a bridge was voiced by AKP MP: "...Turkey [is to be considered] not only as a transit state, due to its location between energy consuming countries and energy producing countries, but also as a terminal which would make trade..." (Turkiye secime giderken 2007, p. 44). However, as will be elaborated on later in this chapter, while the government welcomed energy pipelines crossing Turkey, they considered them to be contributing to the country's power and ability to transform itself into a central country instead of simply serving as a bridge. Accordingly, the AKP narrative also referenced being a secure and stable transit country and energy hub (Disisleri Bakanligi 2011, p. 1).

The narrative on Turkey becoming a central country and an active energy actor was so strong in AKP circles that Turkey's domestic and economic problems were portrayed as challenges by "others", who were not pleased with Turkey's rising power and attempts to change the energy game in the region. Accordingly, the events of "Gezi Park" and "17–25 December", coup attempt in July 2016 and loss of value in the Turkish Lira were considered to be attacks of these actors (Altun 2016; Kilavuzoglu 2016a; Tatliyer and Ozkir 2018). According to the narrators, this linkage confirmed the need to become even more powerful, which was best exemplified in the words of Erdogan:

> If we are not powerful, they will not give us the opportunity to have a drink of water, get a bite, the possibility to have a breath. When we show a little weakness or act in a way perceived in this way, you will also see how they descend upon us like vultures, hooded crows. Some unwary people among us think that the issue is on Tayyip Erdogan. They think that the issue is on AKP. No, the issue is on Turkey. The issue is on the Islam, which they personalised on our nation. (Duran 2018)

In both periods, the AKP clearly referred to Turkey's increasing role in the balance of power and effective utilisation of Turkey's geopolitical location within this context. Emphasis was placed on the significance of Turkey's geopolitical location connecting the East and the West, and the North and the South, which increases Turkey's significance (Karagol 2016a). This understanding was articulated clearly in the MUSIAD journal by journalist Abdullhamit Bilici: "Turkey's geopolitical location provided an opportunity for Turkey to have a say in the great game [on energy]" as it had happened in the years of Cold War" (Bilici 2008, p. 31). Similarly, several references to the significance of Turkey's geopolitical location close to rich energy reserves and Europe as a consumption centre were made in many public documents and declarations (BOTAS n.d., pp. 38–39, 47; Yildiz 2010a, p. 7; Enerji ve Tabii Kaynaklar Bakanligi 2017a, pp. 40, 42; Kalkinma Bakanligi 2013, p. 119; Devlet Planlama Teskilati Mustesarligi 2006, p. 69), as openly articulated by Albayrak: "… although Turkey does not have much oil and gas resources of its own, we are in the middle of the reserves and the market" (Ovunc 2016). Turkey's energy diplomacy was described by the Energy Ministry as being conducted with an understanding of its status as "a rising power and a key state" between suppliers and consumers (Enerji ve Tabii Kaynaklar Bakanligi 2017b, p. 67). This narrative was symbolised with the motto "TurKEY for Energy".

The AKP governments openly stated that Turkey, as a neighbour of energy producers and consumers, pursued a co-operative approach in its relations with producers, consumers and transit states. In this approach, pipeline projects and market integration became instruments for achieving co-operation and energy security (Yildiz 2010b, 2011, p. 8). This liberal narrative should be deemed as a toolkit to strengthen Turkey in the existing distribution of power. Thus, one should not underestimate that the AKP considered being an active key energy actor, with transit pipelines and energy hub, in co-operative energy diplomacy as a part of its strategy to increase Turkey's regional and global power. This co-operative approach based on a pragmatic understanding and cost-benefit analysis (Bacik 2006, pp. 298–305) was named by Davutoglu (2008, p. 92) as "rational calculation". This was considered a requirement for a "multidimensional foreign policy", which advocated the development of relationships with different actors at the same time, arguing that such relationships are complementary and increase interdependencies rather than strategic alternatives (Yesiltas and Balci 2011, p. 16). Davutoglu underlined the necessity of making rational calculations when referring to Turkey's continuing gas imports from Iran, despite sanctions, and Turkey's position towards Russia in the Georgia-Russia war of 2008:

> Here all our allies should take into consideration Turkey's unique position. As a growing economy and surrounded by energy resources, Turkey needs Iranian energy as a natural extension of its national interests. Therefore, Turkey's energy agreements with Iran cannot be dependent upon its relationships with other countries. ... Turkey shares common interests with Russia, Iran, and the United States for the successful operation of natural gas and oil pipelines that run in various directions through the Turkish territory. Hence, Turkish analysts try to combine all these interests in one single picture. This is a rational calculation, not an ideological account. Turkey's relations with Iran will continue, and efforts will be made to preserve its understanding with Russia, based on mutual interest. (Davutoglu 2008, pp. 91, 92), (original language)

Reflecting Turkey's geopolitical location and co-operative approach, AKP and pro-AKP narratives specifically emphasised on Turkey being involved in both the East-West pipelines, supported by the US and the EU to bypass Russia, and in the North-South energy projects, initiated by Russia (Karagol 2016a, 2017; Ertem 2016; Guler 2008; Yildiz 2010a).

The first opportunity in which the AKP attempted to pursue its energy policy in the sphere of natural gas pipelines was the Nabucco Pipeline, which planned to transport 31 bcm natural gas from Middle Eastern and the Caspian energy resources to Austria via Turkey, Bulgaria, Romania and Hungary (Fig. 3.6). The Intergovernmental Agreement (IGA) foresaw the allocation of 2.5 bcm/y for each shareholder and a maximum of 15 bcm/y in case of a lack of demand, without any re-export rights and with tariffs decided by the Nabucco Company. Although the provisions far from met Turkey's demands to secure its supply and contribute to its goal of becoming an energy hub, the pipeline was still presented as a "success story" (Ozalp 2009) in AKP circles. This argument was based on the viewpoint that energy pipelines were tools to strengthen Turkey's material capacities, and thus its power in the region. Accordingly, the Prime Ministry referred to the link between European security of supply and the contribution of transit pipelines to Turkey's power in the Preamble of the Draft Law on Nabucco as follows: "efforts of the European Union for developing its security of supply by diversifying sources and routes create an opportunity for Turkey to increase its effectiveness in the international arena in the field of energy" (Turkiye Buyuk Millet Meclisi 2009, p. 1). The references to Turkey's being a significant partner in the EU's energy policy (Ozalp 2009) should be read within this context.

A similar understanding prevailed on the TANAP, referred to as the Silk Road of Energy and introduced as "the project by which Turkey becomes more powerful" (TANAP n.d.). The AKP considered energy projects opportunities for Turkey to increase its role in the existing distribution of power in this new game. Yildiz's reference to pipelines crossing Turkey as tools to increase Turkey's strategic significance in the Grand National Assembly should be considered within this context: "we know that the more [pipelines] cross [Turkey], the more Turkey's strategic significance increase, this is, no doubt, a significant fact" (Turkiye Buyuk Millet Meclisi Disisleri Komisyonu 2012, p. 11). Similarly, Cemil Ertem, adviser to President Erdogan, argued that energy pipelines such as TANAP represent a new strategy for countries like Turkey, who have begun to control regional energy sources via new pipelines. Ertem remarked that this strategy has helped these countries to retain their sovereignty and considered it one of the indicators of the new energy game, which referred to the decline of not only the petro-dollar system but also the dominance of western multinational companies. According to Ertem, "even this explains why stable democracies in the region, such as Turkey, is not wanted and Erdogan is being targeted" (Ertem 2017). Similarly, Minister of Treasury and Finance Albayrak underlined the importance of TANAP as a critical point of a significant chain connecting the East with the West in a new economic order in which the East has been gaining power (Bakan Albayrak 2017). Therefore, according to this narrative, TANAP is a tool to remake Turkey into a strategic route, as it used to be in the historical Silk Road, and to turn it into a centre of energy networks (Karagol 2016b, 2016c; Karagol and Kaya 2014, p. 36; Kavaz 2018).

According to the AKP narrators, TANAP was considered to be strategic owing to its potential contribution to not only increasing Turkey's power in the new energy game but also developing participating countries` economic and political independence and solving regional conflicts. Indeed, Turkish foreign policy since the end of the Cold War has been based on the idea that cooperation in the field of energy would enable integration of the Southern Caucasian countries into the world economy through Turkey, increase Turkey's power in the region vis-à-vis Russia and Iran and contribute to Turkey's economic growth (Alpour 2015, p. 207; Aras and Akpinar 2011, p. 54). The Ministry of Foreign Affairs referred to the

South Caucasus as a “bridge” connecting Turkey with Central Asia and thus Turkey’s influence in the region would also help it strengthen its position in Central Asia. Trilateral dialogues at the presidency level between Turkey-Azerbaijan-Georgia and Turkey-Azerbaijan-Turkmenistan aimed to increase economic and political cooperation (Disisleri Bakanligi n.d.). Within this context, Erdogan referred to energy projects in the region such as the Baku-Tbilisi-Ceyhan oil pipeline, the Baku-Tbilisi-Erzurum gas pipeline and TANAP as well as to the Baku-Tbilisi-Kars railway project, a segment of the railway from China to London, as the new Silk Road (Presidency of the Republic of Turkey 2017). A typical narrative regarded Turkey’s position in the Caucasus as a “buffer country” in the Cold War, a “model country” in the post-Cold War (which went unfulfilled) and a “central country” in the AKP era (Abakan 2018; Aras and Akpinar 2011, p. 64).

Along with TANAP, nuclear power plants and investments on renewable energy, the TurkStream was also considered to be one of Turkey’s energy mega-projects (Furuncu 2018a). The significance of the first line, which will transport Russian gas via the Black Sea to Turkey, was mentioned within the context of security of supply (Berat Albayraktan 2016). The second line, which will transport Russian gas to Europe via Turkey, and its contribution to increasing interdependence between Russia and Turkey was emphasised (Enerjide Turkiye 2015; Furuncu 2018b; Turkiye Buyuk Millet Meclisi Disisleri Komisyonu 2016b, p. 16). Energy Minister Yildiz addressed the significance of increasing interdependeny with Russia as follows: “One of our main targets with Russian Federation is, to speak frankly, to form mutual interdependencies, not one-sided” (Turkiye Buyuk Millet Meclisi Disisleri Komisyonu 2012, pp. 2, 8). Although the extent of the interdependency was controversial (see Chap. 5), TurkStream was expected to result in increasing mutual interdependency, as highlighted by AKP MP Talip Kucukcan: “Russia has been becoming dependent on us” (Turkiye Buyuk Millet Meclisi Disisleri Komisyonu 2016b, p. 16). It was argued that with the second line Turkey became a necessary actor for Russia at a period of emerging natural gas suppliers, including the USA, and developing energy technologies, such as fracturing (Gur 2017; Atesoglu Guney 2018, pp. 45–52; Kilavuzoglu 2016b). Furthermore, the AKP narrative deemed TurkStream to be not only an energy project but also a tool that, together with TANAP, would increase Turkey’s political power and autonomy in global politics.

In sum, the new global system characterised by the rise of non-Western powers, increasing multi-polarity and pragmatic and output-focused coalitions provided opportunities for the AKP to pursue its ambitious foreign policy. Within this context, the AKP took advantage of an increasing multi-polarity in global politics by seeking autonomy in its relations with other actors, including Russia and Iran, and pursued a foreign policy to increase its economic relations with other countries (Ozel 2019, pp. 9, 14; Oguzlu 2018; Keyman 2017; Kirisci and Toygur 2019, p. 7; Unay 2016). Turkey's chairmanship of the Energy Club of the Shanghai Cooperation Organisation (SCO) and President Erdogan's assertion that the SCO serve as Turkey's alternative to the EU (Turkey to Chair 2016) should be considered within this context. Examination of the linkage between the AKP's foreign and energy policies and narratives on pipelines crossing Turkey show that balance of power functioned strongly in the narratives as a primary institution. The AKP narratives strongly emphasised increasing Turkey's power in the new energy game with the help of transit pipelines and establishing an energy hub. This geopolitical narrative on the energy hub overshadowed the significance of establishing a competitive market to become an energy hub when there was lack of progress in the liberalisation of the market. Criticism of the AKP narrative was driven by concerns about security of supply, which is examined in the next section.

4.3 Security of Supply: Other Actors' Narratives

Security of supply constituted the Turkish narratives on pipelines in two ways. First, all Turkish narrators considered pipelines and other transportation facilities (such as LNG) to be means to achieve the goal of security of supply. This goal was crucial for Turkey, as mentioned in the previous section, since the country is heavily dependent on imports. Turkey's high external dependency necessitated diversification not only of resources but also suppliers. Turkey imported 46.95 per cent of its natural gas from Russia, 15.61 per cent from Iran, 14.95 from Azerbaijan, 8.98 per cent from Algeria, 3.31 per cent from Nigeria and 10.71 per cent from spot markets in 2018 (Enerji Piyasasi Duzenleme Kurumu 2019a, p. 9). Turkey's geographic proximity to energy rich countries was regarded as a big opportunity for Turkey to reduce its market dependency. Countries close to Turkey possess 70.3 per cent of proved reserves and 39.3 per cent of total production in the world (Table 3.2) (BP 2019, pp. 30, 32).

Bearing in mind its significant external dependency, all Turkish narrators underlined the importance of security of supply and diversification of suppliers. According to Emre Engur, the then Head of Strategy Development and International Projects Department of BOTAS, "Our priority has always been ensuring the supply security of Turkey first" (Engur 2010, p. 5). The CHP also drew attention to the significance of decreasing external dependency on Russia and placed the diversification of suppliers as a target (Cumhuriyet Halk Partisi 2017, p. 25). The Chamber of Mechanical Engineers considered the high external dependency to be harmful not only for economy but also in terms of national security. Within this context, decreasing dependency on Russia and Iran and ensuring diversification of supplies from new and secure sources were recommended (Turkyilmaz and Aytac 2018, p. 594).

For the aims of this book, it is significant to mention that all Turkish narrators supported the idea of contributing to the EU's energy security while still prioritising Turkey's security of supply. Albayrak, the then Minister of Energy, stated that Turkey would continue to be a significant partner to Europe in ensuring security of supply and diversification (Bakan Albayrak 2017). This position was revealed in the preambles of the laws on pipelines to cross Turkey. For example, the Preamble of the Nabucco Agreement included language that the pipeline would show Turkey's trustworthiness (Turkiye Buyuk Millet Meclisi 2009, p. 2) while the Preamble of TANAP ensured both Turkey's and the EU's security of supply (Turkiye Buyuk Millet Meclisi 2012, p. 5). Contributing to Europe's security of supply by acting as a bridge between energy rich countries and Europe and establishing an energy trade centre in this unique position were also mentioned in the narratives of the private sector (Enerji Ticaret Dernegi ve Petform n.d.), the CHP (Cumhuriyet Halk Partisi 2017, p. 23), Good Party (Iyi Parti n.d., p. 62) and the Chamber of Mechanical Engineers (Turkyilmaz and Aytac 2018, p. 593).

The second way in which security of supply constituted Turkish narratives of non-AKP narrators was related to its criticisms of AKP policies. Indeed, Turkey's international gas projects were usually discussed domestically in terms of security of supply. Other actors questioned the extent to which each natural gas pipeline contributed to Turkey's own security of supply. Although all Turkish narrators supported Turkey's contribution to the EU's security of supply, the critical question, as stated openly by one of the interviewees, was whether or not the transit pipelines merely "meet the needs of consumers in the countries the gas arrives at" (interview,

December 2011). According to this narrative the pipelines do not address Turkey's security of supply as, "none of them is for solving Turkey's energy problem" (interview, December 2011). Similarly, Mehmet Ogutcu, a representative from the private sector, argued that the security of demand of Russia and the Caspian and Middle Eastern countries and the EU's security of supply are not "more important than our [Turkey's] obligation to supply continuous, low cost, clean and secure energy to our consumers and to industry" (Ogutcu 2011, p. 28). Ogutcu considered Turkey's security of supply as paramount and criticised the pipelines based on the understanding that Turkey would be supplying gas it needed to Europe via transit pipelines "in return for a small transit fee and [a] 'well done'" (Ogutcu 2009, p. 29). Arguing that transit projects would not contribute to achieving the goal of the establishment of a competitive market, the Turkish Competition Authority stated that the "pipeline projects mentioned within the context of the fourth corridor and crossing Turkey matter in terms of EU's policies for the security of supply" (Soysal et al. 2012, pp. 62–63). Therefore, to establish a competitive market and guarantee gas-to-gas competition, the entry and exit of gas and the re-export of gas,[8] which would increase the amount of imports and diversification of suppliers, had to be ensured (Soysal et al. 2012, pp. 63–64). Erdinc Ozen, a consultant and a former senior expert at BOTAS, also mentioned the significance of Turkey's security of supply and advised "a more proactive manner than usual on taking necessary steps for facilitating natural gas trade between Turkey's east and west via pipelines for both its own supply security and the realisation of the vision of becoming an energy terminal" (Ozen 2012, p. 76). Therefore, then Foreign Minister Davutoglu received harsh criticism over his aims of "facilitating the transit of energy across its territory, which is central to an East-West energy corridor" (Davutoglu 2008, p. 91), and being a "bridge" or "corridor" between energy producers and consumers.

The Union of Chambers of Turkish Architects and Engineers and the related Chambers within the Union raised similar concerns over the security of supply when it comes to Turkey's transit status. Accordingly, the Chamber of Mechanical Engineers advised "being an 'energy terminal' rather than an 'energy corridor'" (Makina Muhendisleri Odasi 2012b, p. 41). The Chamber complained that "no more developments than Turkey's being a transit route have been achieved in transporting oil, natural gas and electricity to international markets" (Makina Muhendisleri Odasi 2012b, p. 23). Within this context, it was proposed that projects which envisage transportation of Middle Eastern and the Caspian energy to energy consumers should be reorganised so that these projects contribute to Turkey's security of supply. For example, the National Committee argued that pipeline projects transporting Caspian and Middle Eastern natural gas to Europe via Turkey "should be regulated in a way that envisages Turkey as a transportation and trade centre, excluding the idea that Turkey is a simple transit state" (Dunya Enerji Konseyi Turk Milli Komitesi 2012, p. 95). Referring to Turkey's geopolitical position for supplying gas to Europe and other consumers, the Chamber of Mechanical Engineers (Makina Muhendisleri Odasi 2012a, p. 218) advocated that Turkey should become a centre for the transportation of natural gas resources located in its northern, eastern and southern close/far neighbours to Turkish and European markets. Accordingly, they suggested that Turkey should take steps in order to ensure the security of supply, price stability and competition in supply sources.

Although the Republican People's Party highlighted the necessity for investments to facilitate Turkey becoming a critical energy transit and terminal country (Cumhuriyet Halk Partisi 2011a, p. 45), it prioritised securing Turkey's own energy needs while contracting gas and oil pipelines crossing Turkey. Furthermore, it was highlighted that geopolitical and economic interests would be pursued (Cumhuriyet Halk Partisi 2011b, p. 244). Therefore, while the Party used the terminology of "transit" and "bridge", it also emphasised the need for actions that "added value to Turkey" (Turkiye secime giderken 2007, p. 33). Moreover, the Party opposed Turkey being restricted to a role as a transit country through the development of its transit role in pipeline agreements during the discussions on the Nabucco Pipeline in the Grand National Assembly. Criticising Turkey's transit role, Taciser Seyhan, an MP at that time, argued that Turkey needed to play a leading role in gas contracts due to its geopolitical location. He added that Turkey would lose if it were to consider itself as a transit country, as advocated by Europe, and argued that pipeline projects should be considered "to be trade agreements, instead of transit agreements, providing strategic priorities" (Turkiye Buyuk Millet Meclisi 2010, p. 28). Although there was a consensus among narrators from the opposition on Turkey becoming energy corridor or a transit state, the discourse on the "establishment of an energy hub" differed in terms of their views on the establishment of a competitive energy market. Whereas the government's narrative emphasised Turkey's increasing significance and role in the current distribution of power as a goal, showing the balance of power institution, the Chamber of Mechanical Engineers referred to the establishment of an energy terminal as a goal. However, their definition of energy terminal did not include a liberal market. In contrast to both the government's story and the Chamber's narrative, the Competition Authority and representatives of the private sector considered the establishment of an energy hub to be a consequence of successful liberalisation policies, showing the market institution to be functioning (see Chap. 5).

The difference between these narratives arises from the government's emphasis on balance of power. Although all narratives included the linkage between the establishment of an energy terminal, no matter its definition or scope, and security of supply, their narratives differed in the way in which they perceived primary institutions other than security of supply. The Specialisation Commission, which was composed of different stakeholders in the energy field, acknowledged the linkage between an energy terminal and security of supply as follows: "Our country's becoming an energy corridor and terminal is one of the biggest projects related also to security of supply" (Devlet Planlama Teskilati 2006, pp. 125). However, when referring to the energy hub/energy terminal, the government narrative placed balance of power as a primary institution and connected the establishment of an energy hub/energy terminal to Turkey's significance in the region. This shows the linkage between Turkey's energy policy and foreign policy, which aims for Turkey to serve as the central country.

While the Chamber of Mechanical Engineers also considered an energy terminal to serve the goal of securing supplies, balance of power or the market institutions were not apparent in its narrative. The Chamber of Mechanical Engineer's narrative was based on the idea that such an energy terminal would secure supply. The Chamber referred to the need to ensure the security of supply of Turkey and other consumers, including Europe, within the context of the energy terminal. They advised Turkey to become "a centre for natural gas sources in Turkey's close/far neighbours in its north, east and south. … realise security of supply, price stability and competition of supply sources for achieving this goal" (Makina Muhendisleri Odasi 2012a, p. 218; 2014, p. 211). Thus, while the Chamber considered the establishment of an energy trade centre in Turkey as a goal, it discussed in reference to concerns of security of supply.

Although other narrators in the private sector and the Competition Authority used the term "energy hub" in addition to "trade centre" and "energy terminal" in their narratives, they considered the establishment of an energy hub/trade centre/energy terminal to be a consequence of successful liberalisation policies. Therefore, instead of balance of power, their narrative centred the market institution. Stating that a hub affords both opportunities and threats to security of supply and price levels, the Competition Authority highlighted that the "establishment of a trade centre in Turkey is a consequence of success in creating a competitive natural gas market together with only developments in international natural gas markets, rather than a policy goal" (Soysal et al., p. 63). Similarly, mentioning the lack of co-ordination in strategic plans and the different approaches of different government institutions, private sector narrator Arif Akturk argued that Turkey vacillated between the targets of being a transit and a terminal while it did not establish the legal ground for the latter (Akturk 2010, pp. 5–6). Questioning the extent to which transit pipelines could contribute to Turkey's security of supply, he advised policymakers to adopt the "discourse of a trade centre. … instead of transit of gas" (Aydilek 2008). This would make Turkey "a big market in which price dynamics of natural gas in the Mediterranean basin is determined, and also a centre of attention for gas sources within the neighbourhood" (Akturk 2010). Likewise, Rıdvan Ucar, Chairman of the Gas Group of PETFORM, drew attention to the significance of establishing a liberal market rather than considering establishing an energy hub a goal, arguing that it was possible to create the circumstances to entice trade. He asserted that a transit pipeline contributed to the development of the target market rather than the transit state and that transit was not a necessity in an energy hub as the trading takes place in the hub (Ucar 2017, pp. 12–24). Therefore, in their narratives the market rather than balance of power functioned as a primary institution.

In addition to security of supply, domestic discussions on pipelines revolved around the issue of pricing and the extent to which pipelines contributed to the goal of establishing an energy hub. This most likely resulted from the fact that security of supply, cheaper gas and establishing an energy hub in addition to transit fees were mentioned as goals of Turkey in international gas projects in BOTAS presentations in 2009 and 2010 (Pamir 2016b, p. 358). Accordingly, the Nabucco, TANAP and TurkStream pipelines were also discussed within these three dimensions.

4.3.1 Nabucco Pipeline

The Nabucco Pipeline, intended as a transit pipeline connecting Caspian and the Middle Eastern energy sources with the EU, drew considerable criticism about its impact on security of supply. Article 3 of the IGA stipulated the allocation of 50 per cent of the 31 bcm/y volume of natural gas to the shareholders (Bulgargas, Transgas, OMV, MOL, RWE and BOTAS) and the rest to third parties (Ministry of Foreign Affairs 2009). If all shareholders were willing to buy gas, then their shares would be 2.5 bcm/y each, lower than Turkey's imports of 39 bcm in 2009 (Enerji Piyasasi Duzenleme Kurumu 2010, p. 24), the year in which the IGA was signed. The deal was heavily criticised by some on the grounds that the agreement did not meet Turkey's needs and made Turkey a transit state. For example, an MP from the MHP asked how much the Nabucco Pipeline would contribute to Turkey's security of supply during Parliamentary discussions: "Is there anything related to Turkey's security of supply? No. Is there anything related to natural gas supply? No ... Let's solve Turkey's energy problem first" (Turkiye Buyuk Millet Meclisi 2010, p. 33). Similarly, provisions on exit points envisaging only one point of exit in Turkey for 2–3 bcm, two exits in Romania and one exit each in Bulgaria, Hungary and Austria (Akturk 2009a) were also criticised as contrary to Turkey's security of supply. As one of the interviewees clearly explained, "the biggest part of the pipeline crosses Turkey but there is only one point of exit in Karacabey for Turkey. This does not meet Turkey's own requirements" (interview, December 2011). These criticisms contrasted with the AKP's argument that the pipeline would contribute to solving Turkey's problem of security of supply (Turkiye Buyuk Millet Meclisi 2010, p. 77).

In addition to criticisms of the AKP's pipeline politics in terms of security of supply, narrators also argued that pipeline politics was successful neither in ensuring cheaper gas nor establishing an energy hub. The metaphor of Turkey becoming a 'traffic police in the highway' was usually used to draw attention to a "transit" status in opposing narratives (Pamir 2007, p. 20). Furthermore, there was a disagreement with the AKP's understanding that all pipelines crossing Turkey served as strategic tools to increase Turkey's significance. Nabucco was criticised heavily within this context as the IGA stipulated the construction of a new pipeline from the eastern borders of Turkey to Austria without any re-export rights and at real prices. While the AKP considered Nabucco to be an integral part of increasing Turkey's "effectiveness in the international arena in the field of energy" (Turkiye Buyuk Millet Meclisi 2010, p. 1), other narrators disagreed. According to Mehmet Gunal, then Member of the Parliament from the MHP, "Turkey should not be an energy corridor, an energy bridge. Turkey should be a centre of the energy market. ... We are in a position of being a 'transit state' only" (Turkiye Buyuk Millet Meclisi 2010, pp. 34–35). Arif Akturk, a private sector representative, argued that the report by the Co-ordinator of the Pipeline Van Aartsen was "significant proof of Turkey being considered just a transit state" (Akturk 2009b) due to the proposal of a joint Azeri—Georgia—Turkey—EC Gas Corridor Transmission Agreement based on free transit and four price points, excluding Turkey, in Azerbaijan, Romania, Greece and Austria. While Turkey's demands to secure 15 per cent of the gas at discounted prices were not met, the preamble of the intergovernmental agreement noted Turkey's request for natural gas at competitive prices (Turkiye Buyuk Millet Meclisi 2009, p. 7). This was heavily criticised by Pamir (2016b, p. 685). Similarly, one of the interviewees questioned why BOTAS participated in the project rather than investing in its own infrastructure:

> BOTAS, why do you create a rival to yourself? Why do you become a shareholder for 16.6 per cent in Nabucco? ... instead of paying ... to a project which needs investment for 7.9 billion, it is better to reconstruct your pipelines, build 2 compressors, ... so that you can reach a transportation capacity for 25 bcm. (interview, December 2011)

Narrators criticised the Nabucco Agreement, which was presented by AKP sympathisers as "the agreement of the century" (Turkiye Buyuk Millet Meclisi 2010, p. 84), on the grounds that the Agreement did not prioritise Turkey although more than 2000 km of the pipeline was to cross the country. One of the interviewees expressed this frustration openly:

> The longer the pipeline the greater the obligation, therefore, it is argued that it was not fair in Nabucco to have the same rights as Germany or Romania which has 200 km. This was unfair to Turkey. ... Turkey had the idea, so it was the originator of the Project, two thirds of the pipeline cross Turkey's territory, which increases the risk and obligations. (interview, January 2012)

Therefore, the criticism by the opponents of the Nabucco Pipeline was based on lack of prioritisation of Turkey's own interests and security of supply.

4.3.2 TANAP

Security of supply also functioned as a primary institution in the narratives on TANAP. The fact that TANAP supplies 6 bcm/y of Azeri gas for Turkey's own needs was perceived positively, as Pamir stated: "This difference [6 bcm/y in TANAP and 2.5 bcm/y in Nabucco] should be considered a significant advantage in terms of decreasing our dependence on Russia" (Girgic 2012). He also underlined the fact that TANAP would reduce Turkey's import dependency on Russia by bringing more Azeri gas (Pamir 2016b, p. 358).

Although narrators acknowledged TANAP's contribution to Turkey's security of supply and to reducing dependency on Russia, the AKP was criticised on the grounds that the pipeline did not contribute to the goals of establishing an energy hub and obtaining cheaper energy prices. TANAP is a pipeline connecting the Turkey-Georgia border to the Turkey-Greece border, which was already connected via BOTAS' own network. Therefore, construction of a separate pipeline in which BOTAS has a share of 30 per cent rather than transporting Azeri gas via BOTAS` own transmission system in essence means entering into competition with itself (Ozdemir et al. 2015, p. 102). Furthermore, according to the Host Government Agreement, the TANAP Project Company will not pay any transit fees, is exempted from taxes such as value added and withholding tax, but is subject to corporation tax (Kilinckiran 2015, p. 12; Turkiye Cumhuriyeti Hukumeti 2012, pp. 26–28). Therefore, noting that transit states transport imported gas via its own network while such a pre-requisite is not required for energy corridors, Volkan Ozdemir (2017, pp. 186–191), an expert from the think-tank EPPEN, argued that TANAP made Turkey into an energy corridor and not a transit state, let alone an energy hub.

Some controversy existed over the extent to which Turkey has the right to re-export Shah Deniz II gas (Rzayeva 2018, p. 13; Ozdemir 2015). The confidentiality of gas sales and purchase contracts between SOCAR and BOTAS prevent us from exploring the details here. However, the main criticisms facing TANAP centred around the pricing issue of the Shah Deniz II gas transported via the project. According to the Agreement, Turkey will pay \$79/'000 m^3 and \$103/'000 m^3 in Eskisehir and Thrace, where it will receive natural gas for its domestic consumption. While the price of the Azeri gas is 12 per cent less than Russian gas, the high transportation costs increase the total price. Therefore, other narrators questioned how oil indexed Azeri gas could be competitive considering its expensive transportation fees (Karbuz 2018a; Simsek 2018). Ozdemir (2017, pp. 189–190) argued that, with the $3 billion to be invested in TANAP, BOTAS would have instead been able to renovate its infrastructure and transport 16 bcm/y additional gas by investing in its own network. In that case, transportation costs would lower to $30/'000 m^3 according to an interviewee (interview, October 2018). Therefore, according to critical narrators, investing in the company's own transmission system would have better served Turkey's interests despite the fact that BOTAS would earn back some of the transportation cost as a shareholder (Ozdemir 2015).

4.3.3 TurkStream Pipeline

The AKP highlighted the significance of the first line of TurkStream for eliminating transit risks for Turkey's security of supply and argued that the pipeline would not increase external dependency as it replaces the Western Line. In contrast, the CHP lodged a statement of opposition stating that the TurkStream consolidated Turkey's dependency on Russia (Turkiye Buyuk Millet Meclisi Disisleri Komisyonu 2016a, pp. 7–8). Accordingly, stating that Turkey would import 1.75 bcm more gas via TurkStream, Pamir (2016a) argued that Turkey's goal should be to decrease dependency on Russia. He argued that its high external dependency on Russia makes Turkey insecure, bearing in mind that the "Turkish economy will experience serious problems if Russia wants to punish Turkey by cutting the gas, due to "technical" or any other reason" (Yivciger 2017). Within this context, Seyit Ali Dastan recalled reductions in the Russian gas flows via the Western Line and normalisation of flows after Putin's announcement of the TurkStream project on December 1, 2014 (Dastan 2018, pp. 756–758; Umbach 2017). To sum up, from a theoretical point of view, the opponents' narrative described a negative relationship between great power management and security of supply, while the AKP narrative constructed a positive relationship between the primary institutions of balance of power, great power management and security of supply.

Karbuz considered the AKP's emphasis on the significance of TurkStream's second line to be an overestimation, bearing in mind the fact that the transportation of Russian gas to Europe via Ukraine did not make the country an energy hub (Turk Akim 2018). While Putin's first declaration on TurkStream in December 2014 referenced the establishment of a natural gas hub "on Turkish territory near the border with

Greece" (News conference 2014), the idea of creating natural gas hub was replaced by that of transporting Russian gas via the second line of TurkStream to Bulgaria (Gotev 2019). According to Ozdemir et al. (2015), it would have been more rational if Turkey had taken advantage of the souring relations between the EU and Russia and suggested the establishment of a virtual hub in the country with Gazprom and other suppliers (Gazprom Export n.d.).

Rather than joining the AKP in considering TurkStream as a tool to increase Turkey's role in the current balance of power, CHP MP Ekmeleddin Ihsanoglu argued that "Russia has been gaining a very significant strategic leverage against Ukraine, against NATO, against the West" (Turkiye Buyuk Millet Meclisi Disisleri Komisyonu 2016b, p. 15). Thus, the MPs from the CHP questioned why Turkey had not re-negotiated the gas price in return for ensuring the secure transportation of Russia gas to European markets and giving Russia the strategic and political advantage of bypassing Ukraine (Turkiye Buyuk Millet Meclisi Disisleri Komisyonu 2016b, pp. 11, 15). Similarly, Dastan underlined Turkey's strong negotiating power and referred to the transit fees of $1.5 billion/y Russia would be paying to Ukraine and the Russian sunk cost of $4.7 billion in the Black Sea it had already invested for the South Stream. Furthermore, Russia aimed to secure its supplies by circumventing Ukraine and continuing to provide 31 bcm/y gas, which amounts to $10 billion/year and accounts for approximately 15 per cent of Russian gas income. He argued that Turkey could have negotiated the establishment of a virtual hub in Turkey (Dastan 2018, pp. 756–758). Likewise, the Chamber of Mechanical Engineers opined that constructing a parallel offshore pipeline to the Blue Stream in the Black Sea and transporting Russian gas via BOTAS' own network would better serve Turkey' interests (Makina Muhendisleri Odasi 2019, p. 16).

Indeed, the talks on TurkStream were suspended in September due to a disagreement on price discounts. Sefa Sadık Aytekin, then Deputy Undersecretary of the Ministry of Energy, explained the disagreement rising from Russian's offer of a 10.25 per cent discount for the project and Turkey's position that this discount was merely a starting point in negotiations:

> Russia offered a gas discount of around 10.25, but we did not accept this, as we saw this as a beginning price to start negotiations. This was not a prerequisite to start talks over a gas pipeline project for us. ... if Russia had made a

> further gas discount without naming it as a perquisite [prerequisite] for the project we could have been in a better position. (Moscow and Ankara 2015; Erdil 2015)

However, the IGA on TurkStream was signed in October 2016 without any publicised Russian concessions. Accordingly, opponents' narratives criticised the high prices Turkey pays for Russian gas compared to European customers and the continuation of oil indexed take or pay gas contracts at a time of a global shift to contracts indexed to spot markets (Pamir 2016a; Ozdemir 2017, p. 193). Russia and Turkey agreed on a retrospective price discount of 10.25 per cent in May 2018 (Albayrak 2018). The timing for the IGA is significant bearing in mind the deterioration in relations between Russia and Turkey with the crisis in November 2015 following the Turkish downing of a Russian jet and the beginning of the rapprochement in June 2016 and intensifying relations after the coup attempt in Turkey in July 2016. Russian sanctions after the jet crisis may have forced Turkey to abandon its policy to consider a 10.25 per cent discount as a starting point. These sanctions had a significant impact on the Turkish economy, which also shows Turkey's sensitivity to Russian policy changes and the asymmetry of the relationship, as Turkey's exports fell from $5.9 billion in 2015 to $1.7 billion in 2016 and the number of Russian tourists fell from 4 million in 2014 to seven hundred thousand in 2016 (Kostem 2018, p. 13). Therefore, considering the TurkStream to be a "concession" of the AKP, Ahmet Akin, an MP from the CHP, queried whether the pipeline agreement was made to return to normalise relations with Russia (Turkiye Buyuk Millet Meclisi Disisleri Komisyonu 2016b, p. 11).

Briefly, security of supply functioned as a primary institution in all narratives due to Turkey's high dependency on external sources. Furthermore, it was one of the main concerns of the actors criticising the AKP's narrative on the Nabucco pipeline owing to the fact that the amount of gas Turkey would get was minimal compared to its own consumption. Turkey's continuing dependency on Russia with the TurkStream pipeline was also criticised on the grounds that such a high level of dependency would risk maintaining security of supply. Moreover, TANAP's high transportation costs and the lack of success in negotiating flexibility in gas contracts which are oil indexed with take or pay conditions and destination clauses (with the exception of Shah Deniz I gas for the latter) formed the basis of criticisms of other actors since gas-to-gas competition was not possible within these circumstances.

4.4 Modern Sovereignty: The Eastern Mediterranean and Control of the Transit Pipelines

Modern sovereignty prevailed in the Turkish actors` narratives on two issues: Eastern Mediterranean hydrocarbon resources and the extent to which Turkey have control of the natural gas pipelines crossing Turkey.

Narratives about the Eastern Mediterranean focused on the two main problems of the maritime jurisdiction zones and the hydrocarbon resources around Cyprus. While the Cyprus conflict has continued since the 1960s, the disagreement on exclusive economic zone began in the 2000s when the Greek Cypriots signed exclusive economic zone delimitation agreements with Egypt, Israel and Lebanon, established offshore license areas and opened them for international tender. Turkey's offshore drilling operations began in May 2019 in its continental shelf, which Cyprus also claims, and have raised concerns in the EU (European Union External Action Service 2019).

The disagreement on the exclusive economic zones arises from contrasting views on the role of islands in determining maritime jurisdiction areas. The main disagreement centres around the extent to which the Greek islands in the Eastern Mediterranean, including the tiny 12 km^2 island of Castellorizo (Meis island), which is 2 km away from the Turkish mainland, have maritime jurisdiction areas. Greece argues that the "islands, regardless of their size, have full entitlement to maritime zones (continental shelf/exclusive economic zone), as other land territory" (United Nations 2019a) and the delimitation of exclusive economic zone should take place based on the principle of equidistance/median line.[9] The immediate consequence is a reduction in Turkey's maritime jurisdiction zone in the Eastern Mediterranean in this interpretation (Fig. 4.3) compared to that of Turkey's interpretation (Fig. 4.4, red areas).

The Turkish position on the Eastern Mediterranean, which is a state policy supported by other actors, relied on the fact that the semi-enclosed character of the Eastern Mediterranean Sea necessitated the conclusion of bilateral agreements for maritime delimitation without violating third party rights. Turkey argued that the "entitlement of islands to continental shelves and exclusive economic zones, and their effect to maritime boundary delimitation are two different issues" (Erciyes 2019, p. 7). This meant that islands may have full effect, reduced effect or no effect on delimitation depending on the main principle of the international law principle of "equity". An equitable solution could be achieved via either bilateral/

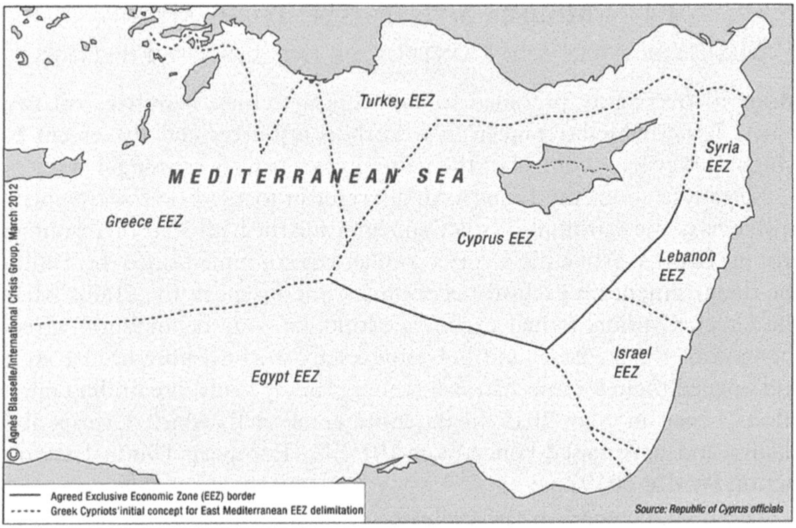

Fig. 4.3 Exclusive economic zones according to Greece. (Source: International Crisis Group 2013. Reprinted with permission.)

multilateral agreements among coastal states or international jurisprudence. The special circumstances of each island should be agreed upon by paying attention to its geographical (for ex. configuration of the coasts, size and position of islands and rocks) and non-geographical circumstances (for ex. historical rights, environment), and other factors (for ex. proximity and proportionality). Otherwise, islands may distort the principle of equity, especially in semi-enclosed seas such as the Eastern Mediterranean, on which Turkey's coastline is the longest (Baseren 2013, p. 259; Erciyes 2012, 2019, p. 8).

The Turkish interpretation of its own maritime jurisdiction zone (Fig. 4.4, red area) is based on the argument that "islands do not generate full maritime jurisdiction zones (continental shelf and/or exclusive economic zone) when they are competing against continental land areas" (United Nations 2016). Arguing that this interpretation is in line with international jurisprudence and state practices, Turkey asserted that delimitation should "be effected by agreement of *all the related parties* on the basis of the *principle of equity* so as not to prejudice the sovereign rights and jurisdiction of other interested States/entities" (United Nations

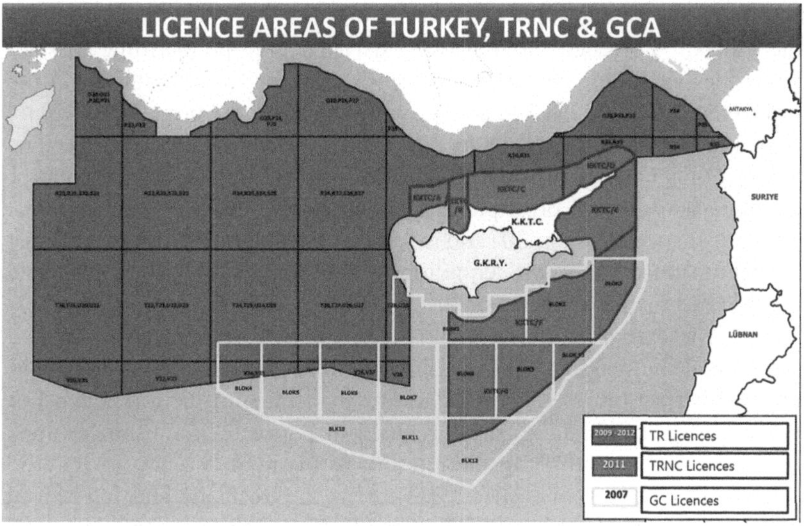

Fig. 4.4 Turkey's continental shelf according to Turkey and licensed areas. (Explanation: Red areas: Turkey's continental shelf and areas where Turkish Petroleum has licenses. Pink areas: Areas where Turkish Republic of Northern Cyprus issued off-shore licenses. Yellow bordered blocks: Licenses issued by Greek Cypriot government. Source: Erciyes 2019, p. 2. Reprinted with permission)

2016) (emphasis by the author). Since no such agreement with the consent of all parties exists, Turkey considered the Greek Cypriot's policy of concluding delimitation agreements with other countries and issuing licenses to international companies a challenge to its own maritime jurisdiction areas and its sovereign rights. Accordingly, Turkey sent a letter to the UN outlining its objections to the delimitation agreement with Egypt on the grounds that it overlapped with its own continental shelf. In this letter, Turkey declared the international oil companies` explorations in the region unacceptable and argued that these explorations aimed "creating de facto situations" (United Nations 2007).

From a legal point of view, the principle of equity is in line with customary law as well as Articles 74 and 83 of the UN Convention on the Law of the Sea (UNCLOS), which refer to the achieving of equitable solutions in delimiting maritime jurisdiction zones.[10] While Turkey is not a signatory of the UNCLOS, it should be remembered that reaching an agreement on delimitation of maritime jurisdiction zones does not necessitate Turkey to be a signatory to the UNCLOS, which has not signed by Israel, the US and others.[11] Three legal frameworks exist on delimiting maritime jurisdiction zones, including the 1958 Convention on the Continental Shelf, the 1982 UNCLOS and customary law, which all share the principle of equity in delimitation (Evans M.D. p. 20 cited in Baseren 2013, 286). The International Court of Justice (ICJ) ruled in 1982 that "the legal concept of equity is a general principle directly applicable as law" (International Court of Justice 1985, p. 30) and in 1985 that "under existing law, it must be demonstrated that the equidistance method leads to an equitable result" (International Court of Justice 1985, p. 38). Regarding the question on the extent to which islands have exclusive economic zones and continental shelves, the ICJ's decisions demonstrate that islands may have a reduced effect or no effect in delimiting maritime jurisdiction zones. For example, in a 1993 ruling, the ICJ ruled that special circumstances must be taken into account considering the "striking difference in length" (International Court of Justice 1993) between Greenland and Jan Mayen Island (Denmark vs. Norway). The Court adjusted the median line, which caused Jan Mayen Island to have a reduced effect in delimitation.[12] Therefore, the Turkish emphasis on the principle of equitable solution and the argument on the effect of islands on maritime jurisdiction zones have legal ground according to narrators. Furthermore, when there is no agreement on delimitation of maritime jurisdiction zones among states, Turkey's position on the consideration of Cyprus' bilateral delimitation agreements and hydrocarbon explorations/drillings relies on the established case-law. The established case-law derives from Articles 74 and 83 of the UN Convention, which foresee states "…to enter into *provisional arrangements* of a practical nature and, during this transitional period, *not to jeopardize or hamper* the reaching of the final agreement" (United Nations Convention of the Law of the Sea 1982) (author's emphasis).

There are two main implications of Turkey's positions in the Eastern Mediterranean. First, bearing in mind the legal considerations, Turkey has been consistent in not allowing any explorations or drillings by international companies in its maritime jurisdiction zone and perceives them as a "challenge to Turkey's jurisdiction areas in the Mediterranean in the west of the Island [Cyprus]" (Ministry of Foreign Affairs n.d.). No offshore activity by international oil companies has occurred in these areas as of June 2019. While TOTAL/ENI holds a license for Block 6, which overlaps with the Turkish continental shelf, ENI's undertaken drilling in this Block was limited to the areas outside Turkey's continental shelf (Fig. 4.5)

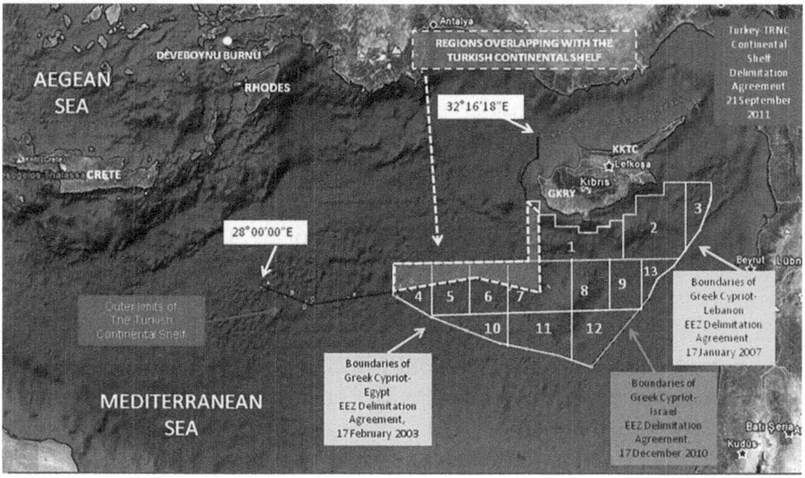

Fig. 4.5 Overlapping fields. (Source: Erciyes 2019, p. 20. Reprinted with permission)

(Karbuz 2018b). Furthermore, Turkey declared that Turkish Petroleum, the Turkish upstream company, would continue its explorations and drilling in Turkey's maritime jurisdiction areas (Fig. 4.4, red areas) in which the company was granted licenses by Turkey in 2009 and 2012. As a reply to the General Affairs Council's declaration asking the Commission to prepare "appropriate measures" (European Council 2019) in its June 2019 meeting, Turkey drew attention to the EU's position acting as a court and "attempting to render a judgement on bilateral disputes related to sovereignty" (Ministry of Foreign Affairs 2019a).

The second implication of Turkey's position in the Eastern Mediterranean concerns the EastMed pipeline. This pipeline is on the EU's list of common interests and aims to transport Eastern Mediterranean gas to Greece via Cyprus and Crete. Although according to Article 79 of UNCLOS coastal states may not impede the construction of pipelines, the same Article also stipulates the consent of the coastal state for laying of such pipelines and the right to "establish conditions for cables or pipelines entering its territory" (United Nations Convention 1982). Therefore, Turkey's position on maritime jurisdiction areas necessitates the Project Company to obtain consent from Turkey in order to be able to cross its territorial waters as the planned route of the EastMed passes through its continental shelf. This may lead to additional requirements made by Turkey which may cause further delays for the EastMed's construction in addition to economic reasons (Tsafos 2019; Tagliapietra 2017).

Drawing from legal considerations, Turkey's position on the delimitation of maritime jurisdiction zones was supported by all actors. References to Turkey's "sovereign rights over its continental shelf" (Erciyes 2019, p. 3) can be found in the declarations of Mevlut Cavusoglu, the Minister of Foreign Affairs, President Erdogan (Turkey plans 2018; Cumhurbaskani Erdogan 2019; Erdogan wishes 2018) and Devlet Bahceli, the Chairman of the AKP-aligned MHP (MHP lideri Devlet Bahceli 2019). Similarly, CHP MP Ali Mahir Basarir expressed concern about sovereign rights, saying "Why do not we, as Turkey, conduct oil and natural gas explorations in our exclusive economic zones for the sake of protecting our rights?" (Basarir 2019). In a reply to the EU sanctions on Turkey's activities in the Eastern Mediterranean, CHP Chairman Kemal Kilicdaroglu declared that they would protect the rights of Turkey in the Eastern Mediterranean and that "as long as the EU does not stop applying double standards, the EU does not have any value in this land" (Kilicdaroglu'ndan 2019).

Other narrators also highlighted the significance of Turkey's sovereign rights. In their common declaration, all parties in the Grand National Assembly, the AKP, the CHP, the HDP and the MHP, declared that they deemed the Turkish State's activities in the Eastern Mediterranean right and proper. Furthermore, they considered the EU's sanctions on Turkey due to its activities in the Eastern Mediterranean to be contrary to international law and unacceptable (AKP, CHP, MHP ve Iyi Parti'den 2019). However, despite this agreement, some actors raised objections to the government's methods of pursuing their foreign policy. For example, the CHP criticised the AKP's foreign policy on the grounds that it resulted in Turkey's loneliness in the Eastern Mediterranean and recommended the prioritisation of energy diplomacy and improving of relations with Israel and Egypt (Turkiye'nin 2018; CHP Genel Baskan Yardimcisi 2018). Underlining the increasing concern about international oil companies` explorations with the Greek Cypriots` permission, CHP Vice-Chairman Unal Cevikoz stated the Party's position as follows: "It has been thought that although one of those companies belong to Qatar, the only country with which Turkey has been continuing to have good relations, the AKP has not reacted in the way that is needed" (Tosun 2018).

The Good Party's narrative on the Eastern Mediterranean was also critical of the AKP foreign policy and emphasised the need to clearly underline that "Turkey will not give up its interests in the Eastern Mediterranean" (Ozdag 2019) in all international platforms. Similarly, the Chamber of Mechanical Engineers asked the AKP to openly declare that Turkey would not recognise any decision or action violating its sovereign rights (Makina Muhendisleri Odasi 2019, p. 17).

The second problem in the Eastern Mediterranean relates to the Cyprus conflict. Recalling that the Turkish Cypriots were an "equal partner in the 1960 Republic of Cyprus and thus have equal rights and say over the natural resources of the island and the maritime areas of Cyprus" (United Nations 2014), the Turkish government argued that the Greek Cypriots` delimitation agreements with other countries and granting of licenses to international oil companies were illegal as the Turkish Cypriots were not represented in the administration and do not participate in the decision-making process. Furthermore, the government highlighted the common understanding in the Cyprus negotiations that issues regarding the delimitation of maritime jurisdiction areas and exploration should be left to a partnership government in which Turkish and Greek Cypriots would share power (Erciyes 2012). In response to the Greek Cypriots` delimitation agreements with other countries and exploration and drillings by international oil companies, the Turkish Republic of Northern Cyprus (TRNC) signed a delimitation agreement with Turkey and issued licenses to the Turkish Petroleum Corporation(TPAO) in September 2011. Dervis Eroglu, then President of the TRNC, declared that the agreement was a preventive measure to convince the Greek Cypriots. Prime Minister Erdogan also stated that Turkey would step back if the Greek Cypriots would do the same. Eroglu later suggested simultaneous termination of all activities until a solution to the conflict was found or a technical committee was established consisting of representatives from both sides to decide on offshore activities, revenue sharing and expenditures needed to solve the conflict. Dimitris Christofias, then President of Cyprus, declared that the delimitation agreement between Turkey and the TRNC was illegal and rejected the suggestions (Baseren 2013, pp. 293–295). A similar suggestion came in July 2019 when the Turkish Cypriot leader proposed the establishment of a joint committee to cooperate on revenue sharing and to "benefit from hydrocarbon resources simultaneously" (Ministry of Foreign Affairs 2019c).

There are two areas in which Turkey's position has an impact. The first area includes the Greek Cypriots` Blocks numbered 2, 3, 9 and 13, most of Block 8 and some parts of Blocks 1 and 12, which overlap with the

TPAOs licenses given by the Turkish Cypriots (Fig. 4.5). The Turkish survey vessel Barbaros conducted surveys in November and December 2018 in the areas overlapping with Blocks 8 and 9. ENI's drillings in Block 3 were stopped by Turkish warships in 2018 (Turkish warships stop 2018) while TPAO's drilling ship Yavuz moved to the eastern part of the Island in July 2019 to begin drilling operations. The second area consists of the Greek Cypriot blocks (Blocks 10 and 11 and some parts of Block 12) which do not overlap with either Turkey's own continental shelf or the fields in which TPAO holds licenses given by the Turkish Cypriots. However, since the Turkish Cypriots are co-owners of the island and "the natural resources … belong to all Cypriots" (United Nations 2012), any drillings by international oil companies will most likely instigate reactions from Turkey and/or the Turkish Cypriots. A recent example occurred just after the signing of the Production Agreement for Block 12 (Aphrodite gas field) between Cyprus, Noble Energy, Delek and Shell in June 2019. George Lakkotrypis, the Minister of Energy of Southern Cyprus, estimated a revenue of "over $ 9 billion during 18 years of the well's lifespan" for Cyprus (Cyprus $9 Billion 2019) while Turkey remarked that "the agreement does not make any reference to Turkish Cypriots and that the Turkish Cypriots are not given any share from the revenues" (Ministry of Foreign Affairs 2019b). Almost two weeks after this declaration, the Turkish Cypriot government decided to "carry out an inventory work" (Turkish Cypriot Gov't 2019) in Maras (Turkish)/Varosha (Greek), which used to be a major tourist location abandoned by the Greek Cypriots in 1974.[13] According to Mustafa Lakadamyali, the Turkish Cypriot Ambassador in Washington D.C., it is expected that such kinds of steps from the Turkish side "could facilitate a process, which could help overcome the existing status quo" (Sofuoglu 2019) that is believed to benefit the Greek Cypriots. Therefore, the Turkish and the Turkish Cypriot governments showed their determination to react to any explorations or drillings by international companies in the areas overlapping with TPAO's licenses issued by the Turkish Cypriot government. However, the motivation of these reactions was based on "reciprocity" and aimed to force a change in the status quo and find a solution that would allow for equality (Turkish Cypriot Gov't 2019).

Similar to the position on the maritime jurisdiction zones in the Eastern Mediterranean, other narrators also showed support for the position on hydrocarbons around Cyprus. In their common declaration, the political parties in the Grand National Assembly declared their full support for the

Turkish State's policies based on fair and equitable solutions for sharing the hydrocarbons in the Eastern Mediterranean. They stated that the unilateral activities of the Greek Cypriots in cooperation with international oil companies and some other countries were against the international law and in contradiction with the societal and political realities (AKP, CHP, MHP ve Iyi Parti'den 2019). However, in domestic discussions, there were also criticisms on the method pursued by the AKP. Criticising the declaration inviting Turkey to act accordingly to the international law and good neighbourly relations made by the EU Mediterranean countries of France, Italy, Spain, Malta, Portugal, Greece and Cyprus, Cevikoz from the CHP argued that this declaration was a consequence of bad AKP policies. Claiming that Turkey and the Turkish Cypriots held rightful positions, he highlighted the significance of prioritising energy diplomacy rather than using the Eastern Mediterranean as a tool for gaining public support in domestic politics (Ocak 2019).

Ownership of natural gas pipelines is the second issue in which modern sovereignty prevails. In natural gas pipeline projects, foreign companies are shareholders, such as SOCAR in the TANAP or Gazprom in the TurkStream pipelines. Some narrators advocated for the transportation of energy resources from neighbour countries via BOTAS' national network with re-export rights. For example, the Chamber of Mechanical Engineers argued that international projects, even those with which BOTAS is a part of, weaken BOTAS' transmission monopoly and abolish Turkey's sovereign rights. The Chamber registered its opposition to granting rights to national or multinational institutions of a foreign country or transnational companies for the construction or operation of pipelines. According to the Chamber, Turkey should have the right to buy the whole or a significant amount of the gas or oil in preferential terms with re-export rights (Turkyilmaz and Aytac 2018, p. 593). Similarly, modern sovereignty functions in some other narratives on the grounds that Turkey would lose its control in the pipelines, which would become "pipelines whose control are in the hands of foreigners" (Simsek 2015) or "projects that are not in the control of Turkey" (Ozdemir 2017, p. 190).

An automatic consequence of these concerns on modern sovereignty is the opposition against articles of IGAs in favour of protecting the investors or applying international rules in the case of disputes. For example, the CHP lodged a statement of opposition to the TurkStream, arguing that Article 3 of the IGA, which forbids the nationalisation and expropriation (or any other operation with similar results) of infrastructure and facilities of the Project or of assets gained within the scope of the Project, is against Turkey's sovereignty (Turkiye Buyuk Millet Meclisi 2016a, p. 7). A similar position was taken by Ozdemir (2017, p. 191) regarding TANAP's dispute settlement mechanism, which utilises the United Nations Commission on International Trade Law (UNCITRAL) arbitration rules.

4.5 Conclusion

The analysis of the Turkish narratives on pipelines showed that security of supply is considered to be one of Turkey's energy goals (Table 4.1). All narrators agreed on the need to diversify suppliers in view of Turkey's geographic location close to energy suppliers and considered natural gas pipelines as means to achieve the goal of ensuring continuous energy supply. While security of supply was the primary institution constituting all narratives, the AKP's narrative differed in that they placed an emphasis on the interaction between being a transit state and an energy hub and on increasing Turkey's role in the current distribution of power. The

Table 4.1 Summary of the analysis in the chapter

Turkish narratives	*Narrators*	*Primary institutions*	*Goals*
Transit state and energy hub	The AKP	Security of supply (foundational, supportive) Balance of power (foundational) Modern sovereignty (foundational)	Securing supplies, establishing an energy hub/terminal, being an energy corridor/transit state, protecting national interests in the Eastern Mediterranean
No transit, yes energy terminal	The union of Petrol-Is, the Union of Chambers of Turkish Engineers and Architects	Security of supply (foundational, supportive) Modern sovereignty (foundational)	Securing supplies, protecting national interests in the Eastern Mediterranean
No transit, yes energy hub but as a success of liberalisation	Private sector, the Competition Authority, some think-tanks, the CHP	Security of supply	Securing supplies, protecting national interests in the Eastern Mediterranean

consideration of the pipelines crossing Turkey and establishment of a trading natural gas hub as tools to strengthen Turkey's position in the region was a common narrative in both Davutoglu and post-Davutoglu periods in Turkish foreign policy. To achieve its goal of joining other rising powers in re-designing the global structure, particularly after the 2008 financial crisis, the AKP considered the pipelines crossing Turkey and the creation of Turkey as an energy hub to be within the scope of the material tools to increase Turkey's power. The emphasis on the linkage between increasing Turkey's significance and the goal of establishing an energy hub was so great that the AKP's narrative on pipelines overshadowed its narrative on liberalisation regarding the energy hub. Furthermore, the AKP narrative placed an emphasis on creating mutual interdependencies via pipelines and argued that it would increase Turkey's significance in return. In this narrative, the growing mutual interdependency with a great power, Russia, via the TurkStream would increase Turkey's leverage and prevent concerns of security of supply thanks to the absence of third parties. From a theoretical point of view as shown in the narrative on TurkStream, we witness a positive interaction between balance of power, great power management and security of supply.

The security of supply as a primary institution factored prominently in the narratives criticising the AKP's pipeline politics. Narrators questioned the extent to which natural gas pipelines contributed to Turkey's security of supply or helped achieve the goal of establishing an energy hub/terminal and took positions against the idea of being a transit state. Rather than considering pipelines as tools to increase Turkey's power, they questioned whether the specific pipeline project furthered the aim of being an energy hub/terminal and facilitated the supply of cheaper gas. However, there were differences, which showed operation of different primary institutions, among them. While the Competition Authority and the private sector used the concept of energy hub but considered it a consequence of success in liberalisation policies rather than a goal, the Chamber of Mechanical Engineers' narrative drew attention to any foreign involvement in pipelines. The Chamber underlined the transportation of energy sources via a national network, after getting permission, with preferential conditions with re-export rights. Therefore, while the market, as will be examined in the next chapter, functioned in the narratives of the Competition Authority and some representatives from the private sector, modern sovereignty functioned in the narrative of the Chamber.

In the Eastern Mediterranean, while Turkey's position on the maritime jurisdiction zones was derived from concerns on sovereignty, her reactions, together with the Turkish Cypriots, on the Greek Cypriots' activities regarding hydrocarbons and international oil companies' operations in the region arose from the intention to force the related parties to change the status quo. Turkey's position on the maritime jurisdiction zones and its rights and obligations in Cyprus as a guarantor state stemming from the Treaty of Guarantee were shared by other Turkish actors, although they differed in their methods. Since Turkey's position on the maritime jurisdiction zones relies on international jurisprudence, it does not seem likely to change this position after the EU sanctions. Rather than imposing sanctions, steps towards co-operation could contribute to the image of the EU as a peace project and hopefully prevent an opportunity to achieve a solution to the Cyprus conflict such as the one in 2004[14] from being missed. Therefore, as long as all related parties in the region do not aim for bilateral/multilateral agreements based on equitable solution, increasing tension will create conflict.

As delimitation of maritime jurisdiction zones between Turkey and Cyprus would be unlikely without a comprehensive settlement of the Cyprus conflict, negotiations on bilateral/multilateral agreements between Turkey, Greece and Egypt could be considered a good start. The 2011 and 2019 proposals by the Turkish Cypriots to establish a joint committee on hydrocarbon resources in the region, including revenue sharing, can be seen as a positive step towards co-operation.

From a theoretical point of view, this chapter allows us to discuss what type of integration the Turkish actors desire to have with the EU. As argued in the theoretical chapter, co-operative energy security societies are based on shared values. When we examine the Turkish narratives on pipelines mindful of the EU's narrative on diversification, it appears that security of supply and diversification were significant for both the EU and Turkey. Whereas the Turkish government's narratives mentioned the Russian great power as a fact in Turkish energy policy, some other Turkish narrators deemed Russia an obstacle for achieving its goals. Although security of supply and diversification were underlined in all Turkish narratives, this does not necessitate automatic co-operation between the EU and Turkey based on securing supply as a shared value. Furthermore, increasing tension in the Eastern Mediterranean has the great potential to turn the relationship into a conflicting one. Therefore, understanding the extent to which common references to diversification and security of supply allow co-operation with the EU necessitates examination of the other component, namely competitiveness, in the EU's definition of energy security in the sphere of natural gas. Comprehension of the Turkish narratives on energy security vis-à-vis integration with the EU can be best achieved by examination of the Turkish narratives on how to achieve competitive/low-cost natural gas, which is related to how to restructure the market. These questions will be analysed in the next chapter.

Notes

1. When referring to the private sector, the book does not include the Independent Industrialists' and Businessmen's Association (MUSIAD), which claims to represent the Islamic identity in economic terms and is thus an alternative to the secular Turkish Industry and Business Association. MUSIAD has received the support of the AKP for the rise of the new middle class. Due to linkage between the AKP and MUSIAD (Koyuncu Lorasdagi 2010) the narrative of the private sector does not include the narrative of the MUSIAD in the book.
2. Liquefied natural gas and natural gas via pipelines.
3. Net energy = energy imports - energy exports.
4. Transit refers to the transportation from eastern, northern or southern energy sources to consumers, mainly to Europe. In this case, Turkey cannot re-export energy passing through its lands and prioritise its own security of supply, and thus is satisfied with transit terms and conditions (Bilgin 2010, p. 114).
5. Different scholars examine the AKP's foreign policy in different periods. For example, Keyman (2017) analyses the foreign policy in three periods: Davutoglu era (2002–2010), transition (2010–2014/2015) and post-Davutoglu era (2014/2015-present). Oguzlu (2018) analyses in three periods which he describes as pro-Western realism (2002–2008), liberal optimism in search for a strategic autonomy (2008–2015) and realism redux in the emerging multipolar world order (2015–2018). The periodisation in this chapter is made based on the extent to which Davutoglu's impact is apparent.
6. Davutoglu's foreign policy was called "zero problems with neighbours" which turned into "zero neighbours without problems" (Oguzlu 2018, p. 10) as Turkey faced problems with Israel, Egypt, Russia, Libya, Iran and Syria in this period. The struggles in foreign policy was justified with the term "precious loneliness", showing an acceptance of being alone and underlying that it was actually valuable. The Davutoglu era ended when Binali Yildirim became the Prime Minister of Turkey in 2016. Yildirim's

first foreign policy declaration highlighted the goal of gaining more friends, which symbolised a return from Davutoglu's policies. Although the perceptions of proactive foreign policy and the pivotal state remained in the post-Davutoglu period, Turkey preferred to be more selective and focused in its foreign policy by setting priorities rather than a multi-dimensional foreign policy with a general activeness as in the Davutoglu period. There was a shift from soft power to hard power as Turkey was engaged militarily in Syria and Iraq. While the EU was considered the anchor for Turkey to become a pivotal state in the Davutoglu era, particularly during the 2002 to 2008 period, no anchor has been mentioned in the post-Davutoglu era (Keyman 2017, pp. 62–66).

7. The identity related capacity has three components, the first of which regards domestic policies to re-organise relations between the state and the society. The second component is regional policies in which the AKP aims to re-define its relations with its neighbours, by putting itself into a central position with the help of its cultural and historical ties. The third component is on global policies, symbolised with Erdogan's speech on "the World is bigger than Five" (Aslan 2018, pp. 20, 31–39). Regarding the latter, Burhanettin Duran, a member of the Board of Security and Foreign Policies under the Presidency in the new Turkish political system, articulates this understanding by underlining that Turkey aims to participate in the existing distribution of power by being influential in the generation of new global norms along with other rising powers (Duran 2018).
8. Transit gas is not re-exported gas.
9. Median line refers to a "line connecting points which are located at equal distance from both coastal states" (Methodology n.d.).
10. The Articles 74 and 83 of the UN Convention foresee "The delimitation of the exclusive economic zone between States with opposite or adjacent coasts shall be effected by agreement *on the basis of international law*, as referred to in Article 38 of the Statute of the International Court of Justice, in order to *achieve an equitable solution*." (United Nations Convention on the Law of the Sea 1982) (author's emphases).
11. UNCLOS had 168 signatory parties as of July 2019 (United Nations 2019b).
12. For an example of islands' having no effect on the delimitation, see the International Court of Justice 2009.
13. Since then, there has not been any settlement, except buildings owned by the UN and the Turkish military, and a female dormitory. Maras/Varosha was one of the main topics in the 2004 Annan Plan, which determined the handover of the territory to Greek Cypriots. However, as the Greek Cypriots rejected the Plan in the referendum dated 2004 with a vote of 76 per cent, there has not been any progress (KKTC'deki Maras Neden

Kapali? 2019; United Nations Security Council 1984; Cyprus 'Spurns Historic Chance' 2004).

14. In 2004, the Greek Cypriots rejected the Annan Plan, which was a UN Peace Plan for the reunification of the Island, in the 2004 referendum by 76 per cent, while the Turkish Cypriots accepted by 65 per cent. Despite this result, Cyprus, as a divided island, became the member of the EU. Therefore, the historic opportunity to use the referendum as a "carrot", which could have ended the conflict and contributed to the EU's asserted image as a "peace project", was not utilised. This was also mentioned by the European Commission: "A unique opportunity to bring about a solution to the long-lasting Cyprus issue has been missed" (Cyprus 'Spurns Historic Chance' 2004, April 25). Gunter Verheugen, the then Commissioner for Enlargement, clearly summarised the awkward situation: "There is a shadow now over the accession of Cyprus" (Cyprus 'Spurns Historic Chance' 2004).

Bibliography

Abakan, M. (2018, February 2). Bakan Cavusoglu: Biz Fransa Degiliz, Turkiye Cumhuriyeti'yiz. *Hurriyet.* Retrieved from http://www.hurriyet.com.tr/bakan-cavusoglu-biz-fransa-degiliz-turkiye-cu-40729497.

AK Parti. (2018). *Cumhurbaskanligi Secimleri ve Genel Secimler Secim Beyannamesi 2018.* Ankara.

AK Parti. (n.d.-a). *Parti programi.* Retrieved from http://www.akparti.org.tr/site/akparti/parti-programi#bolum_.

AK Parti. (n.d.-b). *2023 siyasi vizyonu.* Retrieved from http://akparti.org.tr/parti/2023-siyasi-vizyon.

AKP, CHP, MHP ve Iyi Parti'den ortak 'Dogu Akdeniz' bildirisi. (2019, July 18). *T24.* Retrieved from https://t24.com.tr/haber/akp-chp-mhp-ve-iyi-parti-den-ortak-dogu-akdeniz-bildirisi,831209.

Akturk, A. (2009a). *Nabucco mu? One minute mi? Hangisi daha iyi bir marka olabilir?* Retrieved from http://www.akturk.org/akturk.org/Makaleler_Articles/Entries/2009/7/13_Nabucco_mu_One_minute_m i_Hangisi_Daha_Iyi_Bir_Marka_Olabilir.html.

Akturk, A. (2009b, May 13). *Transitten ticarete donusum; ticaret merkezi kucaklamak.* Ankara.

Akturk, A. (2010). *Transit mi, hub mi yoksa transit hub mi?* Retrieved from http://www.akturk.org/akturk.org/Makaleler_Articles/Entries/2010/11/5_Transit_mi%2C_Hub_m_Yok sa_Transit_Hub_m.html.

Albayrak: Rusya ile Yürütülen Tahkim Süreci için Anlaşmaya Vardık. (2018, May 27). *Sputniknews.* Retrieved from https://tr.sputniknews.com/turkiye/201805271033608811-albayrak-rusya-tahkim-sureci-anlasma/.

Alpour, A. (2015). Turkey's stance towards the main developments in the South Caucasus. *Insight Turkey, 17*(1), 191–211.

Altan, H. (2010). Kamu, piyasa oyuncusu olmaktan cikmali. *Energy Report, 1*(8), 58–67.

Altun, F. (2016, May). Cumhurbaskani Erdogan: 'Kriterimizi yerlilik ve millilik olmali'. *Kriter, 1*(1). Retrieved from https://kriterdergi.com/soylesi/cumhurbaskani-erdogan-kriterimiz-yerlilik-ve-millilik-olmali.

Aras, B., & Akpinar, P. (2011). The relations between Turkey and the Caucasus. *Perceptions, XVI*(3), 53–68.

Aslan, A. (2018). Turk Dis Politikasini Anlamak icin Kavramsal bir Cerceve: Otonomi Arayisi. In K. Inat, B. Duran, & A. Aslan (Eds.), *AK Parti'nin 15 Yili Dis Politika* (pp. 17–40). Istanbul: SETA Yayinlari.

Atesoglu Guney, N. (2018). Turk-Rus Iliskilerinde Ikinci Bahar Kalici Mi? In B. Duran, K. Inat, & M. Caner (Eds.), *Turk Dis Politikasi Yilligi 2017* (pp. 45–52). Istanbul: SETA Yayinlari.

Aydilek, O. (2008). *Dogalgazda zam cikmazi? Indirim mumkun mu?* Retrieved from http://www.globalenerji.com.tr/dergide-bu-sayi/2008/11/11/dogalgazda-zam-cikmazi%2D%2Dindirim-mumkun-mu-.

Bacık, G. (2006). Turkey and pipeline politics. *Turkish Studies, 7*(2), 293–306.

Bakan Albayrak: Dunya ve Avrupa Enerji Arz Guvenligi Acisindan TANAP Tarihi Bir Projedir. (2017, November 2). *Aksam*. Retrieved from https://www.aksam.com.tr/ekonomi/bakan-albayrak-dunya-ve-avrupa-enerji-arz-guvenligi-acisindan-tanap-tarihi-bir-projedir/haber-675477.

Basa, N., & Pamir, N. (2014). *Enerji ve Hukuk Sempozyumu sonuç bildirgesi, temel saptamalar ve sorunlar, cozum onerileri*. Ankara.

Basarir, A. M. (2019, March 4). Soru Onergesi. *Turkiye Buyuk Millet Meclisi*. Retrieved from https://www2.tbmm.gov.tr/d27/7/7-10315s.pdf.

Baseren, S. H. (2013). Dogu Akdeniz Deniz Yetki Alanlari Sinirlandirmasi Sorunu: Taraflarin Gorusleri. In S. H. Baseren (Ed.), *Dogu Akdenizde Hukuk ve Siyaset* (pp. 253–306). Ankara: Ankara Universitesi Siyasal Bilgiler Fakultesi, Yayin No: 608.

Berat Albayraktan Turk Akim Aciklamasi. (2016, October 26). *NTV*. Retrieved from https://www.ntv.com.tr/ekonomi/beratalbayraktan-turk-akimi-aciklamasi,ezXK0go_j0efRsxk7zyIAQ.

Bilgin, M. (2010). *Turkey's energy strategy: What difference does it make to become an energy transit corridor, hub or center?* UNISCI Discussion Paper, 23. Retrieved from: http://www.redalyc.org/pdf/767/76715004007.pdf.

Bilici, A. (2008). Enerji diplomasisi. *Cerceve, 16*(45), 30–33.

BOTAS. (n.d.). *BOTAS stratejik plani 2010–2014*. Ankara.

BP. (2019). *Statistical review of world energy*. Retrieved from https://www.bp.com/content/dam/bp/business-sites/en/global/corporate/pdfs/energy-economics/statistical-review/bp-stats-review-2019-full-report.pdf.

Central Bank of the Republic of Turkey. (n.d.). *Balance of payments and related statistics*. Retrieved from http://tcmb.gov.tr/wps/wcm/connect/EN/TCMB+EN/Main+Menu/Statistics/Balance+of+Payments+and+Related+Statistics.

CHP Genel Bakan Yardimcisi Unal Cevikoz'un 2019 butcesi üzerine dis politika konusmasi. (2018, December 20). *CHP*. Retrieved from https://www.chp.org.tr/haberler/chp-genel-baskan-yardimcisi-unal-cevikozun-2019-butcesi-uzerine-dis-politika-konusmasi.

Cumhurbaskani Erdogan: Doğu Akdeniz'de petrol aramalarini durdurmayacagiz. (2019, February 20). *Anadolu Ajansi*. Retrieved from https://www.aa.com.tr/tr/gunun-basliklari/cumhurbaskani-erdogan-dogu-akdenizde-petrol-aramalarini-durdurmayacagiz/1398226.

Cumhurbaskanligi. (2018). *2019 Yili Cumhurbaskanligi Yillik Programi. Karar Sayisi, 256*. Retrieved from https://www.sbb.gov.tr/wp-content/uploads/2018/11/2019_Yili_Cumhurbaskanligi_Yillik_Programi.pdf.

Cumhurbaskanligi Strateji ve Butce Baskanligi. (2019). Onbirinci Kalkinma Plani (2019–2023). Retrieved from http://www.sbb.gov.tr/wp-content/uploads/2019/07/OnbirinciKalkinmaPlani.pdf.

Cumhuriyet Halk Partisi. (2011a). *CHP 2011 secim bildirgesi* [online]. [viewed 9 January 2013]. Retrieved from http://www.chp.org.tr/wp-content/uploads/Se%C3%A7im_Bildirgesi-.pdf.

Cumhuriyet Halk Partisi. (2011b). *Cumhuriyet Halk Partisi programi* [online]. [viewed 7 January 2013]. Retrieved from http://www.chp.org.tr/wp-content/uploads/chpprogram.pdf.

Cumhuriyet Halk Partisi. (2016). *Turkiye'de elektrik enerjisi ve enerji kooperatifçiliği*. Ankara.

Cumhuriyet Halk Partisi. (2017). *Enerji ve Tabii Kaynaklar Politikasi*. Ankara.

Cumhuriyet Halk Partisi. (n.d.). *CHP 2011 secim bildirgesi*. Retrieved from http://www.chp.org.tr/wp-content/uploads/Se%C3%A7im_Bildirgesi-.pdf.

Cyprus $9 Billion Gas Production Deal Includes Israel's Delek. (2019, June 5). *The Times of Israel.*. Retrieved from https://www.timesofisrael.com/cyprus-9-billion-gas-production-deal-includes-israels-delek/.

Cyprus 'Spurns Historic Chance'. (2004, April 25). *BBCNews*. Retrieved from http://news.bbc.co.uk/1/hi/world/europe/3656753.stm.

Dastan, S. (2018). Negotiation of a cross-border natural gas pipeline: An analytical contribution to the discussions on TurkStream. *Energy Policy, 120*, 749–760.

Davutoglu, A. (2001). *Stratejik derinlik*. Istanbul: Kure Yayinlari.

Davutoglu, A. (2008). Turkey's foreign policy vision: An assessment of 2007. *Insight Turkey, 10*(1), 77–96.

Devlet Planlama Teskilati Mustesarligi. (2006). *IX. Kalkinma Plani Enerji Ozel Ihtisas Komisyonu raporu*. Ankara.

Disisleri Bakanligi. (2011). Turkiye'nin enerji stratejisi. ESGY-I. Ankara.

Disisleri Bakanligi. (n.d.). Guney Kafkasya ulkeleri ile iliskiler. Retrieved from http://www.mfa.gov.tr/turkiye_nin-guney-kafkasya-ulkeleriyle-iliskileri.tr.mfa.

Dunya Enerji Kongresi Turk Milli Komitesi. (2012). *Enerji raporu 2012*. Ankara.

Duran, B. (2018). Turkiye kuresel krizden guclenerek cikacak. *Kriter, 3*(27) Retrieved from https://kriterdergi.com/cerceve/turkiye-kuresel-krizden-guclenerek-cikacak.

Enerji Isleri Genel Mudurlugu. (n.d.). *Denge tablolari*. Retrieved from https://eigm.gov.tr/tr-TR/Denge-Tablolari/Denge-Tablolari.

Enerji Piyasasi Duzenleme Kurumu. (2010). *2009 Yili Dogal gaz piyasasi sektor raporu*. Ankara: EPDK.

Enerji Piyasasi Duzenleme Kurumu. (2019a). *Dogal Gaz Piyasasi 2018 Yili Sektor Raporu*. Ankara: EPDK.

Enerji Piyasasi Duzenleme Kurumu. (2019b). *Elektrik Piyasasi 2018 Yili Piyasa Gelisim Raporu*. Ankara: EPDK.

Enerji Ticaret Dernegi ve Petform. (n.d.). *Turkiye'de gaz piyasasinin liberalleşmesi*. Retrieved from http://www.etd.org.tr/media/files/2012.09.27_Gas_market_story_line_building_the_Turkish_Energy_hub_final_TR.pdf.

Enerji ve Tabii Kaynaklar Bakanligi. (2017a). *Enerji ve Tabii Kaynaklar Bakanligi 2010–2014 stratejik plani*. Ankara.

Enerji ve Tabii Kaynaklar Bakanligi. (2017b). *2018 Yili Butce Sunumu*. Ankara.

Enerjide Turkiye de Rusya'ya Bagimli. (2015). *Turkiye*. Retrieved from http://www.turkiyegazetesi.com.tr/ekonomi/327961.aspx.

Engur, E. (2010). There might be surprises regarding Iraqi gas. *Gazbir, 8*, 24–29.

Erciyes, C. (2012, March 21). Maritime delimitation & offshore activities in the Eastern Mediterranean legal and political perspectives and recent developments. *Ministry of Foreign Affairs*. Retrieved from http://www.mfa.gov.tr/site_media/html/maritime_delimitation.pdf.

Erciyes, C. (2019, May 23). Maritime issues maritime boundary delimitation, & Turkey's off-shore activities in the Eastern Mediterranean. *Ministry of Foreign Affairs*. Retrieved from http://www.mfa.gov.tr/site_media/html/maritime-delimitation-10-5-2019-presentation.pdf.

Erdil, M. (2015, September 11). Turkey, Russia 'Freeze Turkish Stream Talks'. *Hurriyet Daily News*. Retrieved from http://www.hurriyetdailynews.com/turkey-russia-freeze-turkish-stream-talks-88349.

Erdogan wishes peace, stability across globe in 2019. (2018, December 31). *Anadolu Agency*. Retrieved from https://www.aa.com.tr/en/todays-headlines/erdogan-wishes-peace-stability-across-globe-in-2019/1352795.

Ertem, C. (2016, June 22). Turk Akimi ve darbe yuruyuslerinin ekonomi-politigi. *Milliyet*. Retrieved from http://www.milliyet.com.tr/yazarlar/cemil-ertem/turk-akimi-ve-darbe-yuruyuslerinin-2472666/.

Ertem, C. (2017, March 21). Enerjide devrim … *Milliyet*. Retrieved from http://www.milliyet.com.tr/yazarlar/cemil-ertem/enerjide-devrim%2D%2D2417340/.

European Council. (2019, June 20). *European Council meeting (20 June 2019) conclusions*. Brussels. Retrieved from https://www.consilium.europa.eu/media/39922/20-21-euco-final-conclusions-en.pdf.

European Union External Action Service. (2019, May 4). *Statement by High Representative/Vice President Federica Mogherini on Turkey's intended drilling activities within the exclusive economic zone of Cyprus*. Brussels. Retireved from https://eeas.europa.eu/headquarters/headquarters-Homepage/61836/statement-high-representativevice-president-federica-mogherini-turkeys-intended-drilling_en.

Furuncu, Y. (2018a). Mega projelerle Turkiye'nin 2023 vizyonu. *Kriter, 3*(26). Retrieved from https://kriterdergi.com/ekonomi/mega-projelerle-turkiyenin-2023-vizyonu.

Furuncu, Y. (2018b). Enerji Guvenligi ve Karsilikli Bagimlilik Penceresinden Turk Akimi Projesi. *SETA Perspektif, 216*. Ankara.

Gazprom Export. (n.d.). *Gas supplies to Europe*. Retrieved April 5, 2019, from http://www.gazpromexport.ru/en/statistics/.

Girgic. C. (2012). Pamir: 'Enerjide Rusya'ya bagimlilik artiyor'. *Euractiv*. Retrieved from http://www.euractiv.com.tr/enerji/interview/pamir-enerjide-rusyaya-bagimlilik-artiyor-023318.

Gotev, G. (2019, July 26). Russia says second leg of Turkish Stream will go via Bulgaria not Greece. *Euractiv*. Retrieved from https://www.euractiv.com/section/energy/news/russia-says-second-leg-of-turkish-stream-will-go-via-bulgaria-not-greece/.

Guler, H. (2008). Enerji guvenligimiz icin disa bagimliligi makul seviyede tutmaliyiz. *Cerceve, 16*(45), 15–25.

Gur, A. (2017). Turkiye Turk Akimi ile Merkez Ulke Olacak. In *Turkiyede Iktidar Dergisi*. Retrieved from http://turkiyedeiktidardergisi.com/ekopolitik/turkiye-turk-akimi-ile-merkez-ulke-olacak/.

Halkların Demokratik Partisi. (n.d.). Halklarin Demokratik Partisi Programi. Retrieved from https://www.hdp.org.tr/tr/parti/parti-programi/8.

IEA. (2018). *Key world energy statistics 2018*. France: IEA Publications.

International Court of Justice. (1985). *Case concerning the Continental Shelf (Libyan Arab Jamahiriya/Malta) Judgement of 3 June 1985*. Retrieved from https://www.icj-cij.org/files/case-related/68/068-19850603-JUD-01-00-EN.pdf.

International Court of Justice. (1993). *Case concerning maritime delimitation in the area between Greenland and Jan Mayen (Denmark v. Norway) Judgement of 14 June 1993.*. Retrieved from https://www.icj-cij.org/files/case-related/78/6745.pdf.

International Court of Justice. (2009). *Reports of judgements, advisory opinions and orders maritime delimitation in the Black Sea (Romania v. Ukraine) Judgement of 3 February 2009.*. Retrieved from https://www.icj-cij.org/files/case-related/132/132-20090203-JUD-01-00-EN.pdf.

International Crisis Group. (2013, March 22). *Can gas save Cyprus? The long-term cost of frozen conflicts.* Retrieved from https://www.crisisgroup.org/europe-central-asia/western-europemediterranean/cyprus/can-gas-save-cyprus-long-term-cost-frozen-conflicts.

Interviews. (2011). Ankara and Istanbul.

Interviews. (2012). Ankara and Istanbul.

Interviews. (2018). Ankara and Istanbul.

Iyi Parti. (n.d.). *Iyi Parti Programi.* Retrieved from https://iyiparti.org.tr/Assets/pdf/iyi_parti_programi.pdf.

Kalkinma Bakanligi. (2013). *Onuncu Kalkinma Plani (2014–2018).* Ankara.

Karagol, E. T. (2016a). 23. Dunya Enerji Kongresinin yansimalari. *Kriter*, *1*(7). Retrieved from https://kriterdergi.com/yazar/erdaltanaskaragol/23-dunya-enerji-kongresinin-yansimalari.

Karagol, E. T. (2016b). Turkiye enerji merkezi olabilir mi? *Kriter*, *1*(3) Retrieved fromhttps://kriterdergi.com/yazar/erdaltanaskaragol/turkiye-enerji-merkezi-olabilir-mi.

Karagol, E. T. (2016c). Turkiye Enerji Merkezi Olma Kapisini Araliyor. In *SETA*. Retrieved from https://www.setav.org/turkiye-enerji-merkezi-olma-kapisini-araliyor.

Karagol, E. T. (2017). Dogu Akdeniz'de enerji karti. *Kriter*, *2*, 18. Retrieved from https://kriterdergi.com/yazar/erdaltanaskaragol/dogu-akdenizde-enerji-karti.

Karagol, E. T., & Kaya, S. (2014). Enerji arz guvenligi ve Guney Gaz Koridoru (GGK). *SETA*, *108*. Ankara.

Karbuz, S. (2018a, December 7). Rus gaziyla rekabeti daima Rusya kazanir. *Petrotuk.* Retrieved from http://petroturk.com/makale/rus-gaziyla-rekabeti-daima-rusya-kazanir.

Karbuz, S. (2018b, February 16). Dogu Akdeniz Jeopolitiginde Dogal Gazin Dayanilmaz Agirligi. *Petroturk.* Retrieved from http://petroturk.com/makale/dogu-akdeniz-jeopolitiginde-dogal-gazin-dayanilmaz-agirligi.

Kavaz, I. (2018, June 14). TANAP: Kuresel enerji denkleminde yeni donem. *SETA.* Retrieved from https://www.setav.org/tanap-kuresel-enerji-denkleminde-yeni-donem/.

Keyman, F. (2017). A new Turkish foreign policy: Towards proactive moral realism. *Insight Turkey*, *19*(1), 55–69.

Kilavuzoglu, B. A. (2016a). Kerem Alkin: Enerji koridoru ve darbe girisimi. *Turkiye'de Iktidar Dergisi.* Retrieved from http://turkiyedeiktidardergisi.com/ekopolitik/enerji-koridoru-ve-darbe-girisimi/.

Kilavuzoglu, B. A. (2016b). Dunya'nin enerjisi Turkiye'den geciyor. *Turkiye'de Iktidar Dergisi.*. Retrieved from http://turkiyedeiktidardergisi.com/ekopolitik/dunyanin-enerjisi-turkiyeden-geciyor/.

Kilicdaroglu'ndan AB'ye Dogu Akdeniz tepkisi. (2019, July 16). *Cnnturk*. Retrieved from https://www.cnnturk.com/turkiye/kilicdaroglundan-abye-dogu-akdeniz-tepkisi.

Kilinckiran, E. (2015, November 27). Transit tariffs and other charges: Principles and methodologies for their calculation. *International Meetings of Experts*. Beijing. Retrieved from https://energycharter.org/fileadmin/DocumentsMedia/Events/20151127-S2_Ercan_Kilinckiran.pdf.

Kirisci, K., & Toygur, I. (2019). *Turkey's new presidential and a changing west: Implications for Turkish foreign policy and Turkey-West relations*. Turkey Project Policy Paper, 15. Washington, DC: Brookings.

KKTC'deki Maras Neden Kapali? Sadece Askerler Giriyor! Iste Maras'in Konumu. (2019, June 19). *Cnnturk.*. Retrieved from https://www.cnnturk.com/turkiye/kktcdeki-maras-neden-kapali-sadece-askerler-giriyor-iste-marasin-konumu.

Kocak, C. (2018). Enerji sektorunde talep tahminleri ve Turkiye genel enerji degerlerinin irdelenmesi. In Makina Muhendisleri Odasi, *Turkiye'nin enerji gorunumu 2018*, Yayin no: MMO/691 (pp. 11–32). Ankara.

Kostem, S. (2018). The political economy of Turkish-Russian relations: Dynamics of asymmetric interdependence. *Perceptions, XXIII*(2), 10–32.

Koyuncu, L. B. (2010). The relationship between Islam and globalization in Turkey in the post-1990 period: The case of MUSIAD. *Bilig, 52*(Winter), 105–128.

Makina Muhendisleri Odasi. (2012a). *Turkiye'nin enerji gorunumu*. Yayin No: MMO/588. Ankara: Makina Muhendisleri Odasi.

Makina Muhendisleri Odasi. (2012b). *Orta vadeli program (2012–2014) ve 61. Hukumet programının ekonomi, sanayi, KOBI, AR-GE, enerji, altyapı ve ulasim, isci sagligi ve is guvenligi bolumlerinin degerlendirilmesi*. Yayin No: MMO/582. Ankara: Makina Muhendisleri Odasi.

Makina Muhendisleri Odasi. (2014). *Turkiye'nin enerji gorunumu*. Yayin No: MMO/616. Ankara: Makina Muhendisleri Odasi.

Makina Muhendisleri Odasi. (2018). *Turkiye'nin enerji gorunumu 2018*. Yayin No: MMO/691. Ankara: Makina Muhendisleri Odasi.

Makina Muhendisleri Odasi. (2019). *2019 Temmuz itibari ile elektrik ve dogal gaz fiyatlari, tarife uygulamalari, maliyetleri artıran etkenler ve yapilmasi gerekenler uzerine Oda raporu.*. Retrieved from https://www.mmo.org.tr/sites/default/files/temmuz2019_enerjizamlari_odaraporu.pdf.

Makina Muhendisleri Odasi, Enerji Calisma Grubu. (2017). *Turkiye enerji gorunumu 2017 sunumu*. Retrieved from https://www.mmo.org.tr/sites/default/files/TURKIYE%20ENERJ%C4%B0%20G%C3%96R%C3%9CN%C3%9CM%C3%9C_EYL%C3%9CL%202017%20%281%29.pdf.

Makina Muhendisleri Odasi, Enerji Calisma Grubu. (2018). *Turkiye enerji gorunumu 2018 Sunumu*. Retrieved from https://enerji.mmo.org.tr/wp-content/uploads/2019/03/T%C3%BCrkiyeEnerjiG%C3%B6r%C3%BCn%C3%BCm%C3%BC_2018_Sunumu_12.04.2018.pdf.

Methodology for the Creation of the Maritime Boundaries. (n.d.). *Marine regions*. Retrieved from http://www.marineregions.org/eezmethodology.php.

MHP. (2019). lideri Devlet Bahceli, Dogu Akdeniz'de sabirlarimizi zorlayan gelişmeler yasanmaktadir. *Ihlas Haber Ajansi*. Retrieved from http://www.iha.com.tr/ankara-haberleri/mhp-lideri-devlet-bahceli-dogu-akdenizde-sabirlarimizi-zorlayan-gelismeler-yasanmaktadir-egemenlik-haklarimizla-oynamanin-agir-bedeli-olacagini-cok-iyi-bilmelidirler-turkiyeyi-dislayarak-akdenizde-asla-hakimiyet-kurulamaz-dedi-2148712/.

Milliyetci Hareket Partisi. (2011). 2011 Secim Beyannamesi. 2023'e dogru yukselen ulke Turkiye sozlesmesi. Retrieved from https://www.mhp.org.tr/htmldocs/mhp/beyanname/mhp/mhp_beyannamesi.html.

Ministry of Energy and Natural Resources. (n.d.). Strategic plan 2015–2019. Retrieved from https://enerji.gov.tr/File/?path=ROOT%2f1%2fDocuments%2fStrategic%20Plan%2fStrategicPlan2015-2019.pdf.

Ministry of Foreign Affairs. (2009). *Agreement among the Republic of Austria, the Republic of Bulgaria, the Republic of Hungary, Romania and the Republic of Turkey regarding the Nabucco project*. Retrieved from http://www.mfa.gov.hu/NR/rdonlyres/1C1C5D2A-DC4E-425F-9D56- 056B0DB09D8F/0/090714_nabucco_agreement.pdf.

Ministry of Foreign Affairs. (2019a, June 18). *Press release regarding the EU general affairs council conclusions on Turkey*, No 178. Retrieved from http://www.mfa.gov.tr/no_178_-ab-nin-ulkemiz-ile-ilgili-kararlari-hk.en.mfa.

Ministry of Foreign Affairs. (2019b). *Statement of the spokesperson of the Ministry of Foreign Affairs, Mr. Hami Aksoy, in response to a question regarding the Greek Cypriot Administration's recent agreement on natural gas revenue sharing with certain international oil companies*, QA-41, dated June 7. Retrieved from http://www.mfa.gov.tr/sc_-41_-gkry-nin-dogu-akdenizde-bazi-petrol-sirketleri-ile-yaptigi-anlasma-hk-sc.en.mfa.

Ministry of Foreign Affairs. (2019c, July 13). *Press release regarding the new cooperation proposal of TRNC on hydrocarbon resources*, No: 203. Retrieved from http://www.mfa.gov.tr/no_203_-kktc-nin-hidrokarbon-kaynaklarina-iliskin-yeni-isbirligi-onerisi-hk.en.mfa.

Ministry of Foreign Affairs. (n.d.). Greek Cypriots' unilateral activities in the Eastern Mediterranean. Retrieved from http://www.mfa.gov.tr/greek-cypriot_s-unilateral-activities-in-the-eastern-mediterranean.en.mfa.

Moscow and Ankara agree 10.25% gas discount for Turkey. (2015, March 18). *Reuters*. Retrieved from https://www.rt.com/business/241949-russia-turkey-gas-discount/.

News conference following state visit to Turkey. (2014, December 1). *President of Russia*. Retrieved from http://en.kremlin.ru/events/president/news/47126.
Ocak, G. (2019, June 17). CHP Genel Baskan Yardimcisi Cevikoz: Kahire, Sam ve Tel Aviv buyukelcileri ile Kudus baskonsolusu gorev yerine donmeli. *Sputniknews*. Retrieved from https://tr.sputniknews.com/columnists/201906171039389631-chp-genel-baskan-yardimcisi-cevikoz-kahire-sam-ve-tel-aviv-buyukelcileri-ile-kudus-baskonsolusu/.
Ogutcu, M. (2009). Gecikmeksizin yeni enerji ekonomisine gecilmeli. *Finans Dunyasi*. Mart, pp. 26–30.
Ogutcu, M. (2011). Dunya enerjisindeki "oyun degistirici" donusumler ve Turkiye'nin 2023 enerji vizyonu. *Cerceve, 19*(55), 28–36.
Oguzlu, T. (2018). Turkish foreign policy in a changing world order. *All Azimuth* 0(0): 1–13. https://doi.org/10.20991/allazimuth.464076.
Ovunc, K. (2016, September 22). Turkey should focus on its strategic region: Energy minister. *Anadolu Agency*. Retrieved from https://www.aa.com.tr/en/americas/turkey-should-focus-on-its-strategic-region-energy-min/650303.
Ozalp, G. (2009, July 14). Nabucco'ya ruya diyenler BTC'ye de ruya diyorlardi. *Milliyet*. Retrieved from http://www.milliyet.com.tr/nabucco-ya-ruya-diyenler-btc-ye-de-ruya-diyorlardi-ekonomi-1117232/.
Ozdag, U. (2019, April 30). *Turkiye Buyuk Millet Meclisi Genel Kurul Tutanagi*. 27. Donem, 2. Yasama Yili, 72. Birlesim. Retrieved from https://www.tbmm.gov.tr/develop/owa/Tutanak_B_SD.birlesim_baslangic?P4=23263&P5=H&page1=29&page2=29.
Ozdemir, V. (2015). Turk dis enerji politikasi (TANAP ornegi): koridor olamazsin demedik Merkez Olamazsin Dedik. *EPPEN*. Retrieved from http://www.eppen.org/index.php?sayfa=Yorumlar&link=&makale=183.
Ozdemir, V. (2017). The political economy of the Turkey's gas geopolitics. In M. Schroder, M. O. Bettzuge, & W. Wessels (Eds.), *Turkey as an rnergy hub? Contributions on Turkey's role in EU energy supply* (pp. 111–122). Baden-Baden: Nomos Verlagsgesellschaft.
Ozdemir, V., Yavuz, B., & Tokgoz, E. (2015). The Trans-Anatolian Pipeline (TANAP) as a unique project in the Eurasian gas network: A comparative analysis. *Utilities Policy, 37*, 97–103.
Ozel, S. (2019). *At the end of the day, where will Turkey stand?* IAI Papers, 19/04.
Ozen, E. (2012). *Turkiye dogal gaz piyasasi beklentiler, gelismeler 2012*. Ankara: Deloitte.
Pamir, N. (2007, March). Enerji arz guvenligi ve Turkiye. *Stratejik Analiz*, 14–24.
Pamir, N. (2016a). Putin-Erdogan valsi. In *Karabakh Today*. Retrieved from http://tr.karabakh.today/news/environment/8495-putin-erdoan-valsi.
Pamir, N. (2016b). *Enerjinin iktidari* (2nd ed.). Ankara: B. Hayy Kitap.

Petrol-Is. (2007). *Boru hatlari ile ham petrol ve dogalgaz tasimaciligi: BOTAS*. Yayin No: 102. Ankara: Petrol-Is.

Petrol-Is. (2008, November 28). *BOTAS ozellestirilemez*. 28 Kasim tarihli basin aciklamasi. Ankara.

Petrol-Is. (2009). *BOTAS ozellestirilmemeli, guclendirilmelidir*. Retrieved from https://www.petrol-is.org.tr/haber/botas-ozellestirilmemeli-guclendirilmelidir-798.

Presidency of the Republic of Turkey. (2017). *The Baku-Tbilisi-Kars railway is one of the links of the New Silk Road*. Retrieved from https://www.tccb.gov.tr/en/news/542/86168/the-baku-tbilisi-kars-railway-is-one-of-the-links-of-the-new-silk-road.

Rzayeva, G. (2018). Gas supply changes in Turkey. *OIES Energy Insight, 24*.

Simsek, G. (2015, March 17). TANAP ne getirip ne goturecek? *Bloomberg*. Retrieved from https://www.bloomberght.com/ht-yazarlar/guntay-simsek/1742827-tanap-ne-getirip-ne-goturecek.

Simsek, G. (2018, June 14). TANAP guzel, ama bakalim fiyati nasil degisecek? *Haberturk*. Retrieved from https://www.haberturk.com/yazarlar/guntay-simsek-1019/2015296-tanap-guzel-ama-bakalim-fiyati-nasil-degisecek.

Sofuoglu, M. (2019, June 21). Cypriot Turks open a ghost town to tourism to increase stake in Cyprus. *TRT World*. Retrieved from https://www.trtworld.com/turkey/cypriot-turks-open-a-ghost-town-to-tourism-to-increase-stake-in-cyprus-27679.

Sonmez, M. (2018). 2018'e girerken Turkiye'de kirilgan ekonomi ve enerji. In Makina Muhendisleri Odasi, *Turkiye'nin enerji gorunumu 2018*, Yayin no: MMO/691 (pp. 33–48). Ankara.

Soysal, C., Yucel, C. O., Koyuncu, T., & Tokgoz, E. (2012). *Dogalgaz sektor arastirmasi raporu*. Ankara: Rekabet Kurumu.

Tagliapietra, S. (2017, May 10). Is the EastMed gas pipeline just another EU pipe dream? *Bruegel*. Retrieved from http://bruegel.org/2017/05/is-the-eastmed-gas-pipeline-just-another-eu-pipe-dream/.

TANAP. (n.d.). Retrieved from https://www.tanap.com/.

Tatliyer, M., & Ozkir, Y. (2018). AK Parti Genel Baskan Yardimcisi Cevdet Yilmaz: 'Ekonomik saldiri 15 Temmuz'un devami'. *Kriter, 3*(28). Retrieved from https://kriterdergi.com/soylesi/ak-parti-genel-baskan-yardimcisi-cevdet-yilmaz-ekonomik-saldiri-15-temmuzun-devami.

TEIAS. (n.d.). *Turkiye elektrik uretim-iletim 2017 yili istatistikleri*. Retrieved from https://www.teias.gov.tr/tr/turkiye-elektrik-uretim-iletim-2017-yili-istatistikleri.

Tosun, M. (2018, December 10). CHP'den 'Kilicdaroglu KKTC ziyaretine' iliskin aciklama. *Anadolu Ajansi*. Retrieved from https://www.aa.com.tr/tr/politika/chpden-kilicdaroglunun-kktc-ziyaretine-iliskin-aciklama/1334258.

Tsafos, N. (2019). Can the East Med pipeline work? *CSIS*. Retrieved from https://www.csis.org/analysis/can-east-med-pipeline-work.

Turk Akim Turkiye'yi Rus gazinda 'ara kullanici' konumuna getirecek. (2018, December 6). *Anadolu Ajansi*. Retrieved from https://www.aa.com.tr/tr/ekonomi/turkakim-turkiyeyi-rus-gazinda-ara-kullanici-konumuna-getirecek-/1331254.

Turkey plans to explore resources in eastern Mediterranean: FM Cavusoglu. (2018, February 5). *Hurriyet Daily News*. Retrieved from http://www.hurriyetdailynews.com/turkey-plans-to-explore-resources-in-eastern-mediterranean-fm-cavusoglu-126795.

Turkey to Chair 2017 Energy Club of Shanghai Cooperation Organisation. (2016, November 24). *Daily Sabah*. Retrieved from https://www.dailysabah.com/energy/2016/11/23/turkey-to-chair-2017-energy-club-of-shanghai-cooperation-organization.

Turkish 'warships' stop Italy's ENI rig in waters off Famagusta: Greek Cypriot reports. (2018, February 20). *Hurriyet Daily News*. Retrieved from http://www.hurriyetdailynews.com/turkish-warships-stop-italys-eni-rig-in-waters-off-famagusta-greek-cypriot-reports-127107.

Turkish Cypriot Gov't says Varosha not open for settlement, Pres. Akinci says wasn't consulted. (2019, June 22). *Daily Sabah*. Retrieved from https://www.dailysabah.com/politics/2019/06/21/turkish-cypriot-govt-says-varosha-not-open-for-settlement-pres-akinci-says-wasnt-consulted.

Turkiye Buyuk Millet Meclisi. (2009). *Avusturya Cumhuriyeti, Bulgaristan Cumhuriyeti, Macaristan Cumhuriyeti, Romanya ve Turkiye Cumhuriyeti Arasında Nabucco Projesi Hakkinda Anlasmanin Onaylanmasinin Uygun Bulunduguna dair Kanun Tasarisi ve Disisleri Komisyonu Raporu (1/783)*. 23. Donem, Yasama Yili 4, Sira Sayisi 447. Ankara.

Turkiye Buyuk Millet Meclisi. (2010, March 4). Avusturya Cumhuriyeti, Bulgaristan Cumhuriyeti, Macaristan Cumhuriyeti, Romanya ve Turkiye Cumhuriyeti Arasında Nabucco Projesi Hakkinda Anlasmanin Onaylanmasinin Uygun Bulunduguna dair Kanun Tasarisi ve Disisleri Komisyonu Raporu (1/783). *Turkiye Buyuk Millet Meclisi Tutanak Dergisi, Cilt 63*, 23. Donem, 4. Yasama Yili, 69'uncu birlesim.

Turkiye Buyuk Millet Meclisi. (2012). *Turkiye Cumhuriyeti Hukumeti ile Azerbaycan Cumhuriyeti Hukumeti Arasinda Turkiye Cumhuriyetine Dogal Gaz Satisina ve Azerbaycan Cumhuriyeti Kaynakli Dogal Gazin Turkiye Cumhuriyeti Topraklari Uzerinden Transit Gecisine ve Dogal Gazin Turkiye Cumhuriyeti Topraklari Uzerinden Tasinmasi icin Munhasir Boru Hattinin Gelistirilmesine Iliskin Anlasmanin Onaylanmasinin Uygun Bulundugu Hakkinda Kanun Tasarisi ile Disisleri Komisyonu Raporu (1/615)*. Yasama Donemi 24, Yasama Yili 2, Sira Sayisi 298. Ankara.

Turkiye Buyuk Millet Meclisi Disisleri Komisyonu. (2012, June 20). *Tutanak Dergisi*. 24. Donem, 2. Yasama Yili. Retrieved from https://www.tbmm.gov.tr/develop/owa/komisyon_tutanaklari.goruntule?pTutanakId=420.

Turkiye Buyuk Millet Meclisi Disisleri Komisyonu. (2016a). *Turkiye Cumhuriyeti Hukumeti ve Rusya Federasyonu Hukumeti Arasinda TurkAkim Gaz Boru Hatti Projesine Iliskin Anlasmanin Onaylanmasinin Uygun Bulunduguna Dair Kanun Tasarisi (1/788) ve Disisleri Komisyonu Raporu*. Yasama Donemi 26, Yasama Yili 2, Sira Sayisi 441.

Turkiye Buyuk Millet Meclisi Disisleri Komisyonu. (2016b, November 29). *Tutanak Dergisi*. 26. Donem, 2. Yasama Yili. Retrieved from https://www.tbmm.gov.tr/develop/owa/komisyon_tutanaklari.goruntule?pTutanakId=1803.

Turkiye Cumhuriyeti Hukumeti ve The Trans Anatolian gas pipeline company B.V. arasinda Trans-Anadolu dogal gaz boru Hatti sistemi hakkinda Ev Sahibi Hukumet Anlasmasi. (2012). *TANAP*. Retrieved from https://www.tanap.com/content/file/TANAP_Ev_Sahibi_Hukumet_Anlasma.pdf.

Turkiye secime giderken enerji politikalari nasil sekilleniyor? (2007, Haziran). *Ekoenerji Dergisi, 6*, 18–66.

Turkiye'nin Dogu Akdeniz'deki yalnizligini ortadan kaldiracak sekilde yurutulmeli. (2018, December 10). *Birgun*. Retrieved from https://www.birgun.net/haber-detay/turkiye-nin-dogu-akdeniz-deki-yalnizligini-ortadan-kaldiracak-sekilde-yurutulmeli-239668.html.

Turkyilmaz, O., & Aytac, O. (2018). Sonuc ve oneriler. In Makina Muhendisleri Odasi, *Turkiye'nin enerji gorunumu 2018*, Yayin no: MMO/691 (pp. 587–614). Ankara.

Ucar, R. (2017). Turkiye dogal gaz piyasasinda arz, talep ve fiyat dinamiklerinin gelecegi. *Petform*. Retrieved from http://docs.petform.org.tr/docs/ridvan_ucar_ie%C3%BC_altinci_enerji_yonetimi_ve_politikalari_calistayi_11052017.pdf.

Umbach, F. (2017). *Turkey's energy dilemma: Brussels or Moscow?* Geopolitical Intelligence Service. Retrieved from https://www.gisreportsonline.com/turkeys-energy-dilemma-brussels-or-moscow,energy,2416.html#.

Unay, S. (2016). Turkiye-Rusya yakinlasmasi: jeo-ekonomik boyut. *Kriter, 1*(5) Retrieved from https://kriterdergi.com/suriye-idlib/turkiye-rusya-yakinlasmasi-jeo-ekonomik-boyut.

United Nations. (2007, July 26). *Letter dated 23 July 2007 from the Permanent Representative of Turkey to the United Nations addressed to the Secretary-General*. A/61/1011–S/2007/456. Retrieved from https://digitallibrary.un.org/record/604095/files/A_61_1011_S_2007_456-EN.pdf.

United Nations. (2012, June). *Report of the secretary-general on the United Nations operation in Cyprus*. S/2012/507. Retrieved from http://www.cyprusun.org/?p=3056.

United Nations. (2014, June 5). *Letter dated 30 May 2014 from the Chargé d'affaires a.i. of the Permanent Mission of Turkey to the United Nations addressed to the Secretary-General.* A 68–902. Retrieved from https://undocs.org/a/68/902.

United Nations. (2016, June 17). *Letter dated 15 June 2016 from the Chargé d'affaires a.i. of the Permanent Mission of Turkey to the United Nations addressed to the Secretary-General.* A 70-945-S/2016/541. Retrieved from https://undocs.org/A/70/945.

United Nations. (2019a, April 30). *Letter dated 25 April 2019 from the Chargé d'affaires a.i. of the Permanent Mission of Greece to the United Nations addressed to the Secretary-General.* A 73-850-S/2019/344. Retrieved from https://undocs.org/en/A/73/850.

United Nations. (2019b, April 8). *Chronological lists of ratifications of, accessions, and successions to the convention and the related agreements.*. Retrieved from https://www.un.org/depts/los/reference_files/chronological_lists_of_ratifications.htm.

United Nations Convention on the Law of the Sea. (1982). Retrieved from https://www.un.org/depts/los/convention_agreements/texts/unclos/unclos_e.pdf.

United Nations Security Council. (1984). *Resolution 550 (1984) of 11 May 1984.* Retrieved from https://undocs.org/S/RES/550(1984).

Why Invest in Turkish Energy Sector. (n.d.). *Invest in Turkey.* Retrieved from http://www.invest.gov.tr/en-US/infocenter/publications/Documents/ENERGY.INDUSTRY.pdf.

Yesiltas, M., & Balci, A. (2011). AK parti donemi Turk dıs politikasi sozlugu: kavramsal bir harita. *Bilgi, 23*, 9–34.

Yildiz, T. (2010a). Regional and global cooperation in the context of Turkey's energy corridor and terminal concept. *Eurasiacritic.* Retrieved from http://eurasiacritic.blogspot.com.tr/2010/02/regional-and-global-cooperation-in.html

Yildiz, T. (2010b). Enerji isbirligi icin aktif dis politika. *Gorus* (Agustos), pp. 36–37.

Yildiz, T. (2011). Turkiye'nin enerji stratejisi ve 2023 hedefleri; enerji yatirimlarinin boyutu ve tesvikler. *Cerceve, 19*(56), 8–10.

Yivciger, G. (2017). Turk Akimi hattinin kazanani Rusya. *Deutsche Welle.* Retrieved from https://www.dw.com/tr/t%C3%BCrk-ak%C4%B1m%C4%B1-hatt%C4%B1n%C4%B1n-kazanan%C4%B1-rusya/a-38774193.

CHAPTER 5

Turkey's Energy Security and the Natural Gas Market

An examination of the Turkish narratives on the natural gas market is essential for understanding not only the internal discussions but also the type of integration with the EU that Turkish actors favour in the sphere of natural gas. Different narratives on how to accomplish a re-structuring of the market demonstrate the preferred level of harmonisation with the EU's *acquis communautaire*. Therefore, an analysis of different narratives on the natural gas market reveal Turkish actors' answers to the EU's narratives on extending its market values and helps us to determine the type of integration between the EU and Turkey in the field of energy.

Differences among the Turkish narrators on liberalisation are apparent in their positions on the 2001 Natural Gas Law (hereinafter the Natural Gas Law) and the Law on Transit of Petroleum through Pipelines (hereinafter the Transit Law). The Natural Gas Law focuses on importing, transmitting, distributing, storing, trading and exporting natural gas in Turkey and the Transit Law covers the transit of petroleum, which includes natural gas. The Natural Gas Law intends to establish a stable, transparent and financially strong natural gas market and ensure the independent regulation and supervision of the market via liberalisation. The goal is to supply natural gas to consumers in a high quality, continuous, competitive and environmentally friendly manner (Dogal Gaz Piyasasi Kanunu 2001; Enerji ve Tabii Kaynaklar Bakanligi 2012a). The Natural Gas Law provides for third party access, market openness, unbundling and the establishment of a regulatory agency. It envisages the transition from a BOTAS

D. Korkmaz, *Turkey and the EU in an Energy Security Society*,
https://doi.org/10.1007/978-3-030-45774-7_5

monopoly to the liberalisation of market activities with competitive elements and the regulation and supervision of market activities that do not. An attempt was made to amend the Natural Gas Law in 2014. Although the Draft Law is invalid and was not discussed in the Grand National Assembly as of 2019, the chapter also includes the positions of the narrators on the Draft Law to exemplify their perspectives.

The analysis of the Turkish narrators on the Natural Gas Law, the Draft Law and the Transit Law shows how the methods to achieve secure and affordable supplies differ among narrators, despite their agreement on the need to ensure security of supply. While some narrators believed that liberalisation of the natural gas market brings competitive prices and provides secure supplies, others argued that the state should be the leading actor in the market to ensure security of supply. Therefore, the Turkish narratives on the natural gas market revolve around the questions of the extent to which the market should be liberalised and in what manner the state should be involved in the market. From a theoretical perspective, the market and state capitalism function as foundational primary institutions in these narratives.

In line with this main difference, this chapter begins with the market-oriented narrative and follows with the state capitalist one. These sections elaborate on the main differences between liberal and state capitalist narrators as well as among those narrators in favour of liberalisation. In addition to the analysis of the foundational primary institutions, the chapter exemplifies the functioning of the supportive primary institutions, such as great power management, balance of power and sovereignty. Identifying the roles of the market and state capitalism in the Turkish narratives and understanding the functioning of other supportive institutions enable us to complete the picture and determine the nature of the integration between the EU and Turkey.

5.1 The Market-Oriented Narrative: Liberalisation of the Natural Gas Market

The need for investments in the energy sector was the main concern in the AKP narrative, which placed a special emphasis on Turkey's economic growth and increasing population. The AKP named the establishment of a competitive market and development of favourable circumstances for investments as the key strategies for meeting the growing energy demand.

Furthermore, the expectation was that the competitive market would decrease risks and enable efficient production and consumption of energy (Enerji ve Tabii Kaynaklar Bakanligi 2017, p. 2), as stated by the Ministry of Energy:

> The main goal of the liberalisation of the energy sector is to create the investment environment that will allow necessary and adequate investments for security of supply, and to reflect advantages, which will be gained with the increase in efficiency ensured by the competitive environment, to consumers. (Enerji ve Tabii Kaynaklar Bakanligi n.d., p. 32)

Liberalisation of the natural gas market was considered necessary not only to meet the investment needs of the growing economy but also to harmonise with the EU's legislation and integrate with the global economy (Enerji Piyasasi Duzenleme Kurumu 2011, p. 22). This was stated in the Ninth Development Plan (2007–2013): "Turkey has been in the processes of restructuring its energy markets based on competition as a necessity for economic development and integration with the global economy and in particular with the European Union norms" (Devlet Planlama Teskilati Mustesarligi 2006, p. 95). However, it also should be underlined that relations with the EU were not the main reason for liberalising energy markets. The goal of liberalising energy markets began in 2001, before the AKP came to power, as a condition of International Monetary Fund (IMF) loans. As described by Mete Goknel, former Director-General of BOTAS, "the demands were the IMF's and the World Bank's. The EU was not interfering so much in those years" (Dogalgaz piyasasinda yanlisliklar 2008, p. 69). Nevertheless, the establishment of a competitive energy market was considered within the framework of the harmonisation of the legislation after Turkey's EU candidacy in 2004. Accordingly, the Ministry of Development declared that "Turkey attaches utmost importance and gives priority to realising energy market reforms and adapting the national energy legislation fully with the EU energy legislation" (Ministry of Development 2012, p. 80) (original language).

The private sector's narrative also included the goal of the liberalisation of the natural gas markets (Altan 2010). Bearing in mind that the electricity and natural gas sectors contributed 4 per cent of the GDP in 2016 and provided employment for 820,000 people in 2017, the private sector emphasised the significance of market based pricing mechanisms for the effective usage of energy sources and predictability for investments to meet the energy demand in a secure and cost-effective manner. Overall, these measures, along with protection of the environment, broad infrastructure and long-term policies and strategies focusing on competitiveness, technology and efficiency were expected to minimise risks in the Turkish energy sector and efficiently manage the sector (Sandalkhan et al. 2018, p. 11). The Competition Authority's narrative also referenced efficiency, claiming that it would "increase consumer wealth and societal wealth in general" (Soysal et al. 2012, p. 13).

Similarly, the 2011 CHP Manifesto included language on the establishment of a competitive market. The Party highlighted the significance of competitive markets in encouraging investments and reducing prices: "creating a favourable investment climate by means of establishing a competitive market ... by implementing an effective competition policy, prices of energy sources sold to industry will be decreased" (Cumhuriyet Halk Partisi 2011, p. 196). Overall, the Party emphasised the aim of increasing societal wealth in energy markets and considered competitiveness a tool to do so (Cumhuriyet Halk Partisi 2011, p. 243; 2017, p. 23). However, the Party cautioned that if policies to develop competition were implemented without consideration of international developments, security of supply and the conditions of the country, liberalisation would result in private monopolies instead of public ones. The main opposition party argued that the government had no idea about the future of natural gas markets and did not have a strong desire to establish competition and claimed that the main aim of the government was to transfer all public assets and exclusive rights to the private sector without considering consumers' wealth (CHP Bilim Kultur Yonetim Platformu 2008, pp. 24–25). Similarly, the Good Party also drew attention to the presence of "private monopolies" as a result of the privatisation process, although the Party did not specify the sector. The Good Party and the MHP stated the significance of establishing competition (Iyi Parti n.d., pp. 46, 51) and the MHP underlined support for the activities of both the public and private sectors in the field of energy and mentioned the "utilisation of the potential of private sector in all stages ranging from energy production to consumption" (Milliyetci Hareket Partisi n.d., p. 98).

Although these market-oriented narrators shared the goal of establishing a competitive market, there were also differences in their positions on the extent to which energy was a commodity and/or public service, the role and the structure of the state company in the market and the Transit Law. The next sub-sections analyse these differences.

5.1.1 *Public Service*

The first difference among narrators can be seen in their views on the nature of energy and the scope of public service. This difference arose from divergent understandings of the developments in the global political economy since the 1980s. The market-oriented narratives also showed slight variations on this issue. In line with the neo-liberal policies, the AKP pursued policies for de-regulation and decreasing the role of the state. Accordingly, in the Preamble of the Draft Law on Public Administration in 2003, the Party argued that Turkey could not make the necessary changes to adapt itself to the global changes and thus needed to re-define the state's role. The AKP supported the policy of allowing the private sector to gain access to sectors under the state's control, which are considered natural monopolies. As a result, within the scope of public-private partnership, energy projects in the form of build-operate, build-operate-transfer and transfer of operating rights accounted for 90 out of 238 projects between 1986 and September 2018 (Cumhurbaskanligi 2018, p. 26). According to then Minister of Energy Albayrak, improving the public-private sector partnership was expected to increase the quality of the service provided to citizens (Bakan Albayrak 2018).

There was a general understanding in the AKP narrative that the private sector could fulfil the tasks of public service in the field of energy, no matter if it was electricity or natural gas. The perception of energy as a commodity that can be traded was pointed out by a member of Parliament: "There is no inconvenience when energy becomes a commodity which can be bought and sold by everyone freely" (Turkiye secime giderken 2007, p. 36). Then Energy Minister Yildiz's declaration on the privatisation of electricity distribution markets exemplified this approach: "This [privatisation of electricity distribution] means performing public service via the private sector. However, we do not leave the private sector alone. The public sector has the task of monitoring" (Enerji ve Tabii Kaynaklar Bakani 2013). He mentioned that they did not sell the network but transferred the operation rights: "We privatised all distribution companies but we did not sell their assets. We have been maintaining the public service via the private sector. The transmission network still belongs to the state" (Elektrik ozellestirmesi 2010). Accordingly, privatisation of the distribution segment of natural gas and the Articles envisaging privatisation of IGDAS, Istanbul's distribution company, in the Draft Law (Basbakanlik 2014) demonstrated the AKP's preference for having private companies carry out public service. However, the lack of progress in unbundling BOTAS and transforming the company into a competitive culture, the continuation of subsidies, which causes the BOTAS price to be set as the benchmark in wholesale market, and the dominance of BOTAS in the market together raise questions as to the extent of which the AKP pursues the target of establishing a competitive market.

The private sector's narrative stressed the necessity of moving beyond the classical understanding of public service as a service performed by the state. Two different but interrelated approaches to this issue emerged in their narratives. Defining the public interest as a set of values benefiting society rather than as a service provided by the state, Altan Kolbay (2010a), representative of PETFORM, claimed that energy is a strategic sector which does not necessarily have to be run by the state. He emphasised that public interest is a concept that has to be decided case by case. Rejecting the opinion that only a public company could safeguard the public interest and secure supplies, Kolbay suggested a "change in the mentality":

> If we have a problem of security of supply, views such as 'only a public company ensures public benefit' and 'only BOTAS ensures security of supply', which are located at the back of our minds and discredit any discourse of private sector, are only responsible for this. (Kolbay 2012a)

Similarly, Arif Akturk, a representative from the private sector, also discussed the changing scope of the concept of "public service" and advocated for the private sector to perform public service functions in addition to state organisations:

> It has been admitted that public services can be conducted not only by classical administrative institutions but also private institutions. …, in today's understanding of the law, all human activities are appropriate to be public service, no matter what its qualification; as long as political bodies, initially the legislative body, accept that activity as public service. (Akturk 2010)

In contrast to this broad consideration, the second perception on public service limited it to the construction of transmission lines (interview, December 2011). However, this narrow definition did not falsify the first conceptualisation. By limiting the scope of public service to the construction of transmission lines, this approach leaves space for the private sector in other segments:

> Before, gas flowing inside a pipeline used to be a public service. Namely, gas flowing from there to consumers here used to be a public service. However, this is no longer public service. Public service is transporting gas to consumers by constructing a transmission line. Whether gas flows from this pipeline or not, those supplying the gas are not public services. (interview, December 2011)

This understanding was based on policies dividing the energy market into segments and considering transmission lines to be within the responsibility of the state.

As for the other market-oriented narrators, the narratives of the Competition Authority resembled those of the private sector's while the CHP's narratives highlighted the significance of public service provided by the state. The Competition Authority referred to the "commercial enterprise" and "competitive culture" of the state company rather than the performance of "public service": "transformation [of the state company BOTAS] from an institutional identity operating as a public service to the identity of a commercial enterprise by eliminating concessions and obligations as far as possible" (Soysal et al. 2012, p. 151). Similarly, Akturk also referred to competitive culture and argued that "BOTAS should learn competition and should not be afraid of competition" (2011).

The CHP portrayed energy as a public service in its Party Manifesto as follows: "As a necessity for our understanding of social state, the character of energy as a public service will be reflected in regulations and implementations" (Cumhuriyet Halk Partisi 2011, p. 242). The Party's definition of public service included services provided by state organisations: "the state will be responsible for ensuring effective, efficient and high-quality public service, and access of all citizens to these public services, no matter their income" (Cumhuriyet Halk Partisi 2011, p. 147). Within this context, the government's privatisation policies in the energy field were criticised in the CHP's narrative. Underlining the strategic character of energy, the Party argued that energy is considered to be a commercial commodity in the government's narrative. According to Pamir, President of the Energy Commission, "... the government's energy policy is based only on privatisation. According to them, the energy issue is not a strategic but a commercial issue. I think this is totally wrong and constitutes a big risk for our country" (Girgic 2012). Considering the Party's references to the establishment of competition and the prevention of abuse of the dominant position in the market (Cumhuriyet Halk Partisi 2017, pp. 22–23), the

Party's narratives on public services does not reject competitiveness. Instead, in addition to economic and technological effectiveness, the Party included public interest as a priority in the regulation of the domestic market (Cumhuriyet Halk Partisi 2017, p. 22). Thus, the market rather than state capitalism functions in the CHP's narrative.

5.1.2 *The Role and Structure of the State Company in the Market*

The determination of the role and the structure of the state in the market in different narratives is important owing to two reasons. First, it provides an understanding of the positions of the narrators on both de-regulation and privatisation and the unbundling of the incumbent company. This, in turn, affords insight into the extent to which the Turkish narratives co-operate and/or converge with the EU narratives on exporting liberal values to Turkey.

Although the Natural Gas Law was enacted before the beginning of the AKP period, we must first understand how the Natural Gas Law envisages the role of the state in the market and the unbundling of BOTAS. The Law stipulates a gradual decrease in the role of the state company. According to the Law, BOTAS was not allowed to form new natural gas import contracts, with the exception of LNG contracts, until its share of imports decreased to 20 per cent of national consumption by 2009. The Law also provided for the restructuring of the vertically integrated structure of BOTAS (excluding distribution) by 2009 and the privatisation of new companies (except transmission). From a theoretical point of view, the wording of the Natural Gas Law shows the functioning of the pure market as a primary institution with the role of the state company limited to transmission. As elaborated in the theoretical framework, the difference between the market and the pure market as a primary institution is that when the pure market functions as a primary institution the state plays a regulatory role and also acts only in the transmission segment.

AKP Narratives and Practices

Although privatisation of the distribution segment was accomplished with the exception of IGDAS, no significant progress was made in decreasing the dominance of BOTAS and the unbundling of the company. The share of BOTAS in total supplies was 84.12 per cent in 2018 (Enerji Piyasasi Duzenleme Kurumu 2019, p. 25). With the help of a contract release in

2005 and the renewal of Russian gas contracts in 2012, the private sector had contracts for 10 bcm/y gas as of 2019. The success of volume release was even more limited with only 1.2 bcm/y gas transferred to SOCAR Turkey. As an explanation for not meeting targets in the Natural Gas Law, the former Minister of Energy Yildiz stated that a transition period was needed when establishing a competitive market (Enerji ve Tabii Kaynaklar Bakanligi 2012b).

While the Ninth[1] and Tenth[2] Development Plans in 2006 and 2013 emphasised the regulatory and supervisory roles of the state and the investor role in the event of a risk to security of supply (State Planning Organization 2006, pp. 35, 82; Kalkinma Bakanligi 2013, p. 118), the Draft Law of 2014 made references to public entities. Accordingly, the Draft Law referred to a state-owned company in the import and wholesale markets. The Preamble mentioned that, if concerns arose about the security of supply, public entities could be exempted from the limitation that importing and wholesale private companies import and/or sell no more than 20 per cent of the national consumption estimations (Basbakanlik 2014, pp. 23, 24, 26). Therefore, from a theoretical perspective, there has been a move from the operation of the pure market, as elaborated in the Development Plans, towards the functioning of the market as a primary institution in the AKP narrative.

The provisions in favour of ownership unbundling in the Natural Gas Law has not been met. In this type of unbundling, "no supply or production company is allowed to hold a majority share or interfere in the work of a transmission system operator" (European Commission n.d.). Privatisation via share sales, which may pave the way for the state to retain a majority of the shares in the company, was also declared as a possible method for the unbundling of BOTAS. Already in 2010, the Energy Minister Yildiz stated that "We have made our preparations for public offerings. We will offer 49 per cent of TPAO to the public in stages. As a next step, this can gradually come to the agenda for BOTAS as well" (Nayir 2010). In 2012, he referred to Turkish Airlines, of which 49.12 per cent belongs to the state, as a model for the privatisation of TPAO and mentioned BOTAS within the scope of public offerings:

> We don't have any plans for the privatisation of BOTAS or TPAO, however, we have been working on public offerings with the Treasury, we have been thinking of TPAO first. Primarily TPAO should gain a structure like THY

> [Turkish Airlines] composed of the dynamism of the private sector and the seriousness of the public sector. (Turkiye Irak'ta 2012)

Similarly, Mehmet Simsek, the then Minister of Economy, discussed public offerings for the transmission network of BOTAS in 2014 (Demir 2004). Yildiz's declarations in 2012 and 2013 on the restructuring of BOTAS by unbundling the company into two or three smaller companies under the scope of BOTAS Holding to retain its power abroad but divide its domestic tasks made it possible to think of a legally unbundled vertically integrated company, in which "the ownership must be legally separate from other activities of the group" (Talus 2011, p. 114):

> Restructuring BOTAS by dividing it into two or three ... is on the agenda. Actually, I should say that it would be under the BOTAS Holding. Namely, it is required for BOTAS not to wane abroad but unbundle its tasks inside Turkey. (Ataman Ozel and Yildirim 2012)

> We want BOTAS to wane in natural gas sales, share some of its contracts with private sector in order to establish a competitive market. ... There are so many projects worth billions of dollars in the international arena. BOTAS will be involved in these. (Yildiz: BOTAS dogalgaz satisinda 2013)

On the other hand, the 2013 Annual Program included the goal of preventing vertical and horizontal integration in the energy markets (Bakanlar Kurulu Karari 2012, p. 112). Furthermore, the 2014 Draft Law referred to the restructuring of BOTAS by dissolving its vertically integrated structure. The Draft Law proscribed the unbundling of the company into three legal entities which would oversee transmission, management and storage of LNG facilities, and others including imports, exports and wholesale. While details on the shareholders, location and personnel of each entity were to be determined at a later date with co-operation among BOTAS, the Treasury and the State Personnel Administration, only one company would be responsible for imports, exports and wholesale under the name BOTAS. Therefore, the AKP governments' positions on the vertically integrated structure seemed to differ from one another.

An interviewee from BOTAS also articulated scenarios for the state company focusing on imports and leaving the trade segment to private actors:

> The plans to further diminish its [BOTAS'] market share (either via contract or volume transfers) are no longer on the agenda of BOTAS given the current political landscape in and around the country. Due to reasons based on past experience, the political situation of Turkey's gas suppliers and the national priorities which currently outweigh the overall gains to be obtained from the gas market liberalisation BOTAS is re-considering being the single competent authority to handle gas importation as before and by drawing back from trade segment of the industry completely it plans to ensure that liquidity of the market is secured by the private sector only. (Demir 2016, p. 251)

In the same year, Minister of Energy Albayrak reported that work was in progress to transform BOTAS and TPAO into regional actors capable of competing in liberal markets, although it was not determined whether 'the THY model' or a different method would be pursued. Albayrak referred to "holding strategic lists" (Turkiye Buyuk Millet Meclisi Plan ve Butce Komisyonu 2016), showing a willingness to retain the state's shares in these companies. Furthermore, the company was one of the state companies transferred to the Turkey Wealth Fund in 2017. The Wealth Fund aims to "provide resource for ... [the] country's primary investments" (Turkiye Wealth Fund n.d.) and is overseen by Erdogan as the President of the Fund. From a theoretical standpoint, the transfer of the ownership of BOTAS to the Wealth Fund is a clear sign of the operation of the market rather than a pure market.

For the aims of this book, it is also significant to examine AKP practices in addition to their narratives. Despite the dominance of establishing a competitive market and a trading natural gas hub in AKP narratives, no significant progress has been made in reducing the market share of BOTAS and unbundling the company. Three main reasons can be observed for the market concentration. First, the contract release was to only 4 bcm/y in Russian contracts in 2005 due to difficulties in getting prior consent from suppliers. The Russian contracts of 6 bcm/y natural gas were renewed with the private sector in 2012. There has not been any progress on volume release, which was limited to 1.2 bcm. The second reason behind the market concentration is legal restrictions. The Natural Gas Law does not allow private companies to import from suppliers with whom BOTAS has contracts. In other words, private importers are not allowed to import from Russia, Azerbaijan or Iran. Due to some amendments in 2005 and 2018, LNG, CNG and spot pipeline imports are exempted from this rule. The main reason for this kind of restriction was the fact that the volume of contracted gas in 2001, when the Natural Gas Law was enacted, was more than consumption (Fig. 5.1). Furthermore, approval from BOTAS and the Ministry of Energy are required for imports from suppliers with whom BOTAS does not have contracts. These legal restrictions form barriers to new entries.

The third reason for the market concentration relates to BOTAS' pricing policy. Changes in oil prices and exchange rates are significant for BOTAS because long-term natural gas contracts are oil indexed with a 6 to 9-month time lag in the formula and gas imports are paid in US dollars but sold in Turkish lira. When the changes are not reflected in natural gas prices, it is difficult to compete with BOTAS prices as the company's prices become the indicator for wholesale prices. In Turkey, cost-reflective

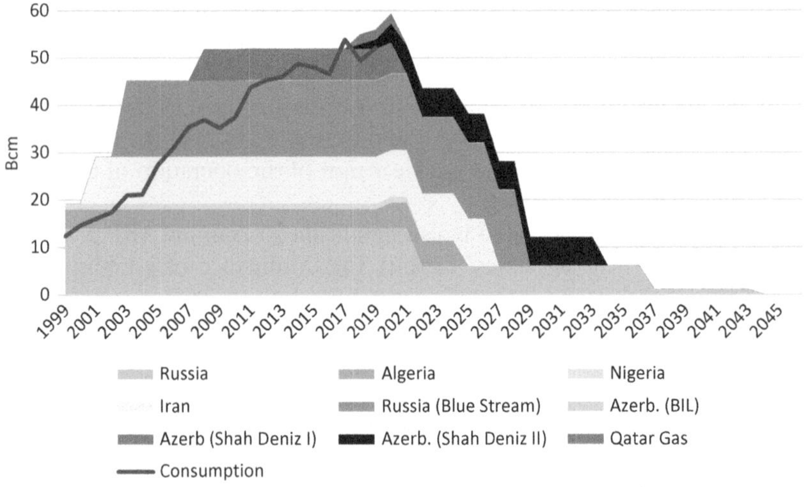

Fig. 5.1 Turkey's gas contracts and gas consumption. (Source: Adopted from Soysal et al. 2012, 146. Data from: Turkiye Dogal Gaz Piyasasi n.d. Data for 2019 is estimation of EMRA (Turkiye bu yil 2019)

pricing, which refers to the reflection of changes in oil prices and exchange rates to the final price, was implemented during 2008 and 2009 after a Decision of the High Planning Board on "Principles and Procedures on Cost Based Pricing to be implemented by Energy Public Economic Enterprises", but was soon terminated. Afterwards, BOTAS declared that it would charge a reduced price for some consumers meeting certain criteria, starting from January 2010. This decision was taken due to low LNG prices, BOTAS' consumers' transfer to private firms and excess gas due to take-or-pay contracts (Ozen 2012, p. 40). Accordingly, BOTAS' price in the wholesale markets was the same between May 2009 and October 2011, despite increases in oil prices (Dilli and Nyman 2015, p. 142) (Fig. 5.2). BOTAS compensated for the gap by selling expensive gas to the state-owned thermal power plant (Electricity Generation Company) and thermal power plants with Build-Operate-Transfer (BOT) and/or Build-Operate (BO) contracts with the state, and cheap gas to eligible consumers and independent electricity power plants. Between 2011 and 2014,

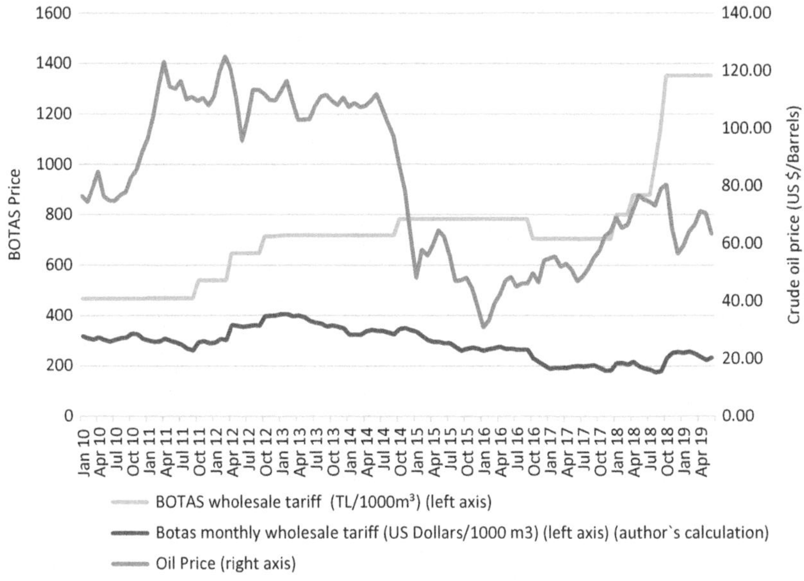

Fig. 5.2 A comparison of BOTAS price for eligible consumers (TL and $) and oil price. (Source: Adopted from Dilli and Nyman 2015, p. 142. Data from Argus Media 2019b; Commodity Markets n.d.)

BOTAS prices increased four times. After a 10 per cent decrease in 2016, prices remained the same in 2017 (Dilli and Nyman 2015, p. 142; Makina Muhendisleri Odasi Enerji Calisma Grubu 2018, p. 26). Drawing attention to the increase in the oil prices and exchange rate since 2016, BOTAS asserted that increases in prices were inevitable, and did so in 2018 (Gazda maliyet 2018). Although subsidies continued for households and industrial consumers throughout 2018 (Fig. 5.3), estimated import prices[3] stood below the domestic price for utilities beginning in September 2018 and remained slightly below the price given to industry players with annual consumption greater than 300,001 m^3 in November and December 2018 (Taranto and Saygin 2019, p. 38). Bearing in mind the two-tier price system for utilities since January 2019,[4] the average price of TL 1550.00/'000m^3 between April and June 2019 was lower than the Russian import price of TL 1699.32/'000m^3.[5] The second tier stood at TL 1700.00/'000 m^3 and was nearly identical to the Russian import price.

Drawing attention to the timing of price increases, other narrators, such as the TMMOB, indicated that the AKP used BOTAS` pricing policy as a tool for its political goals. Price increases occurred following the general elections in 2011, twice in 2012 when there were no elections, after the local elections and elections for the Presidency in 2014 and after the

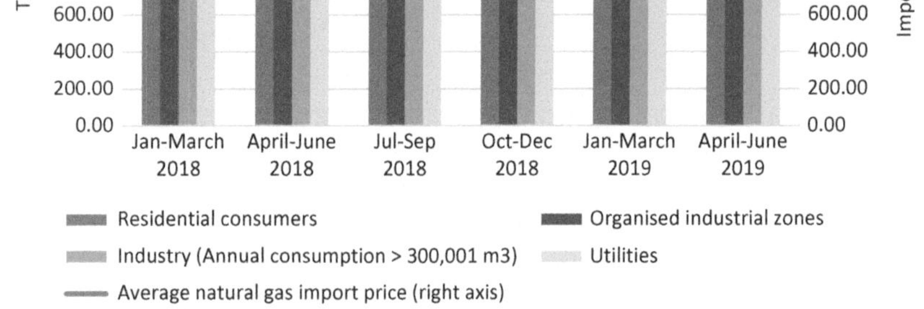

Fig. 5.3 Estimated import price and domestic prices. (Source: Data from Argus Media 2019b)

Presidency and general elections in 2018 (Makina Muhendisleri Odasi Enerji Calisma Gurubu 2018, pp. 26–27). Increases in natural gas prices have both direct and indirect effects on inflation owing to consumption of energy for producing goods and services. For example, according to TUSIAD's 2018 report, a 10 per cent increase in natural gas would cause an increase in inflation of 0.34 points. With the subsidised prices, the share of average natural gas consumption was 2.2 per cent of the minimum wage, lower than in European countries (Sandalkhan et al. 2018, p. 12). The view that BOTAS` pricing policy is a result of the government's policy to provide inexpensive gas to industry and households (Ozen 2012, p. 41) was articulated clearly by individuals from the EMRA interviewed by Demir: "the political will sets natural gas prices in Turkey" (Demir 2016, pp. 261–262).

It should be also underlined that lack of cost-reflective prices may also cause relatively higher prices and have a negative impact on competitiveness when the oil price decreases but is not reflected in the wholesale price. As illustrated in Fig. 5.2, decreases in oil prices starting in 2014 July was not reflected in the BOTAS tariff. Accordingly, the absence of changes in BOTAS prices in 2015 and 2016, at a time when global gas prices were in decline due to decreases in oil prices, raised complaints from the private sector on how to compete with other countries (Demir 2016, pp. 261–262). Together with the arbitration decision, which allowed for a retrospective 15 per cent discount in Iranian gas, this pricing policy contributed to the increase in BOTAS` income and the state company's being in the first rank of corporate taxpayers in 2016 (BOTAS 2016'da 2018; BOTAS vergi 2018).

The continuation of a lack of a cost-reflective pricing policy together with dragging progress in amending the Natural Gas Law and volume release beg the question of whether there is political will to liberalise the market, despite the focus of the AKP's narratives on establishing a trading natural gas hub. This concern was articulated by one narrator: "it is known what to do for liberalisation, but it is a political decision" (interview, October 2018). Individuals from the EMRA, BOTAS and the private sector explained the reason for the failure in liberalising the market as "the general reluctance to reduce BOTAS market dominance and its restructuring" (Demir 2016, p. 249). Furthermore, failure in unbundling BOTAS and decreasing its share was considered "the explicit outcomes of political manoeuvrings in the country" (Demir 2016, p. 249). However, as shown in Fig. 5.1, most of the long-term gas contracts will terminate beginning in 2021, providing opportunity for the Ministry of Energy to decrease BOTAS' market share. Nevertheless, whether private actors will be willing to import more gas is a significant question as the difficulties in competing with BOTAS' prices forced them to sell imported gas to BOTAS in 2018. According to Alpaslan Bayraktar, Deputy Minister of Energy, Turkey expects to gain more flexibility in its contracts at a time when there is an increase in global LNG supplies, which necessitates "more flexible contracts, durations and pricing mechanism" (Turkiye dogal gazda 2019). Furthermore, TurkStream has a spare capacity of 1.75 bcm/y as Turkey's contracts for 14 bcm/y via the Western Line will be replaced by the Turk Stream when its construction is finished. No new contract has been made as of June 2019. If contracted by BOTAS, this will also increase the market concentration. Bearing in mind the deterioration in foreign exchange rates and contraction in the Turkish economy in the last quarter of 2018 and the first quarter of 2019, it may be more realistic to pay attention to the extent to which changes in oil prices and foreign exchange rate will be reflected to the gas price for utilities,[6] rather than expecting the subsidies for industries to be removed.

The Private Sector's Narrative

While the AKP expected liberalisation of the market to boost energy investments to meet growing demand, private sector representatives included a decrease in state involvement[7] as a condition for investments. According to Batu Aksoy, Member of the Executive Board of PETFORM, "investments by the private sector will not take place as long as share of public ownership is not reduced in the markets" (Dogalgazda fiyati 2011). Viewpoints on the extent to which the state should be a market player changed from one representative to another and at different times. Therefore, the market in its purest form and the market as a primary institution alternate in the private sector's narratives. On the one hand, some narrators represented a pure market approach in which the state's role is limited to regulation and supervision whereas elsewhere the state was considered to be an equal player in the market along with the private sector. For example, Kolbay's suggestion of an ownership unbundling without a public institution recalled the market in its purest form: "The method should not be legal/functional, but ownership unbundling. We all know and witness how public institutions function in this country. This is not the Netherlands" (Kolbay 2012b). Similarly, the market also existed in its purest form in the argument of Hale Altan, a representative of the Turkish Industry and Business Association: "the public [public sector] needs to stop being a market player and perform its regulating and supervision duties in an effective way" (Altan 2010, p. 62), (original language). In its opinion on the Draft Law, the Association recommended that the transmission company be autonomous and the transfer to the private sector of the unbundled company's contracted natural gas, excluding LNG, storage and transmission (TUSIAD n.d., p. 25), similar to ownership unbundling.

On the other hand, on another occasion, Kolbay highlighted the lack of private sector investments due to the exclusive dominance of the state in contrast to the dynamism of the energy sector when the state is an arbitrator or plays an equal role in the market: "When the state leaves the field or takes the role of an arbitrator telling its player in the field 'you will also play equally', dynamism enters the sector. This is that simple" (Kolbay 2010a). Likewise, a private sector interviewee mentioned that the state could be a player as long as it played competitively in the market (interview, October 2018). Thus, although the primary institution in operation seemed to change from the market to pure market and vice versa, it can be argued that representatives of the private sector considered it acceptable for the state company to play a role in the market, even though for some of them a pure market would have been the ideal solution.

Similarly, the existence of a vertically integrated structure was deemed acceptable for the private sector on the condition that it is subject to competition. In its 2018 report, TUSIAD proposed the restructuring of BOTAS through the establishment of two companies named BOTAS transmission and BOTAS trade (Sandalkhan et al. 2018, p. 27). Similarly, there were also suggestions for the creation of different transmission and trade companies affiliated with the Ministry of Energy in order to provide independence and a lower workload. Proponents believed that this model would prevent the disadvantages of ownership unbundling and the existence of an independent transmission operator in which the network is operated by a subsidiary of the vertically integrated company with strict supervision. While transmission and trade companies are affiliated with two different public institutions, which would not be usual in the Turkish bureaucracy, in ownership unbundling, the administrative workload increases in systems with an independent transmission operator (interview, November 2018). The creation of a national champion, which refers to a powerful national company competing in the international arena, was recommended by some of the representatives for the sake of securing supplies and participating in the current distribution of power. While the balance of power functioned in the AKP narrative on pipelines with an emphasis on the importance of transit pipelines in increasing Turkey's significance in the region, balance of power appeared in the private sector's narrative on the market in their emphasis on the necessity of creating a national champion. Rather than considering pipelines to contribute to Turkey's significance in the region, the institution of balance of power functioned in the private sector narratives on creating a national champion as a supporting primary institution. For example, Akturk argued that Turkey needed a national energy giant active in the exploration and production segments to secure supplies: "A national champion is in the advantage [interests] of Turkey. For Turkey's security of supply, it is necessary that our national champions take part in exploration and production wherever in the world. Oil and natural gas games are games of giants" (Akturk 2012). Similarly, Chairman of the Petroleum Platform Association Nusret Comert said that "there is no concern on creating national champions, on the contrary we have supporting discourses" (Petroturk 2010).

Representatives of the private sector criticised the perception that a national champion must be a state company and emphasised that private companies also have the potential to be national champions. According to Kolbay, public companies are the first that "comes to the minds of some of our friends when the national champion is mentioned. The reason underpinning this view is the idea that everything which is national has to belong to the state. From where shall we start to criticise this archaic opinion?" (Kolbay 2011a). Similarly, Comert explained that "the important thing is creating national companies, not state companies" (Petroturk 2010). Nevertheless, this does not mean neglecting the state company. Akturk claimed that Turkey needed at least one national champion, either public, private or public-private and that the presence of a public company as a national champion would be considered acceptable by the private sector. This also showed the relevance of balance of power as a primary institution in this narrative: "We need to have one or more public, private or public-private giants in oil-gas-electricity. … This is a game of giants, if you stay as dwarf next to giants, you cannot play this game" (Akturk 2011).

The existence of a vertically integrated company was acceptable as long as competition was established, and the state company was willing and able to compete with the private sector. The private sector called for the prevention of the abuse of dominance in the domestic markets in which import restrictions for the private sector were removed (Kolbay 2010b; Comert 2011). The private sector preferred a predictable market in which there was competition among all players and long-term projections were possible:

> The biggest fear of Turkish private sector is the concern that national champion "kills off in the domestic league with the power of the state". It is the most important thing for the political power to make positive discrimination to the private investors playing in the domestic league and send the national champion to the league of champions. ... It does not matter whether the national champion is state or private company. (Akturk 2012)

> If more players enter the market, a predictable market environment, which supplies reasonable income ... and in which all players including BOTAS can make long term projections, is established, private sector players afford capital intensive investments and support our state with regard to security of supply. No one accepts work in which (s)he knows that (s)he will lose money, by funding one billion USD in an unpredictable market. Kolbay (2012a)

Within this context, a merger between BOTAS and TPAO was not regarded to be a problem if the relevant circumstances were met:

> BOTAS, which is ready to compete with the private sector and has a decreased market share of 20-30 per cent, can co-operate with the TPAO if it wishes. If it wants to co-operate via merger, it can merge. There is no obstacle to this. What is not preferred here is this: If we add a monopolistic BOTAS next to TPAO, then a cumbersome organisation emerges. When you have an organisation not open to the private sector even inside Turkey, this benefits neither BOTAS nor TPAO. (Petroturk 2010)

Similarly, Akturk (2012) stated that the legal unbundling of BOTAS and the merging of the company with TPAO was in the interests of Turkey: "...we can turn some of BOTAS' activities into legal entities. Establishing a national champion by even adding legal entities created as a result of restructuration of TPAO is an advantage also for Turkey" (Akturk 2012). Within the context of restructuring BOTAS, representatives of the private sector also made recommendations on how to decrease its market concentration. While both contract and volume release were mentioned in earlier declarations (TUSIAD n.d.; Comert 2011), TUSIAD's 2018 report referred to successful cases in Europe and recommended volume release (Sandalkhan et al. 2018, p. 27).

Representatives of the private sector considered BOTAS subsidies an obstacle to establishing a liberal market and an energy hub (Ucar 2017, pp. 16–18). Arguing that it was impossible to participate in different activities of the natural gas market and to behave fairly to competitors, Kolbay highlighted the significance of unbundling of BOTAS and competing fairly in the market using the metaphor of a football game:

> Just as you cannot be a player and a referee in a football game, you cannot be an importer, seller and responsible for storage and transmission in the natural gas market. You cannot cover the loss in one of your pockets with the profit you had in other pocket, you cannot behave fairly to your rival company. (Kolbay 2010b)

When the dominant company subsidises the price, it is difficult for the private sector to enter the market, which harms competitiveness and prevents investments. This was explained by Metin Sen, member of the Executive Board of PETFORM: "[l]ack of cost-reflective pricing is the biggest obstacle for increasing the number of importers" (Dogalgazda fiyati 2011). BOTAS' dominance and its subsidies cause other companies to consider the BOTAS price as a benchmark (Dilli and Nyman 2015, p. 142), therefore having a negative impact on the efforts to establish competitiveness:

> None of the companies could sell at the real price when BOTAS sells natural gas at a price lower than its costs. Therefore, all companies sell their gas lower than BOTAS price. This is called competition. (Kolbay 2011b)

BOTAS' subsidised prices coupled with weaker demand caused private importers to sell their gas to BOTAS most months in 2018. An additional problem for private importers occurred due to the fact that some had applied for a 10.25 per cent discount to their contracts with domestic companies on the grounds that they had received the discount from Gazprom in 2016. However, the price disputes in arbitration court ended in favour of Gazprom. Accordingly, the volume of private sector imports from Russia decreased to 7.9 mcm/d in January 2019 from 33 mcm/d in January 2018, increasing the take-or-pay obligation risk. Furthermore, the loss of value in TL created an additional burden for wholesalers, which have purchase contracts based on dollars (Suphi 2018, pp. 22–23; Gazda Maliyet 2018; Ozen 2019; Argus Media 2019a). Other representatives drew attention to the "take or pay risk" for the private sector if BOTAS does not continue to buy gas from private importers (Suphi 2018, p. 33).

The price hikes raised complaints from utilities and industrial consumers. The President of TUSIAD Erol Bilecik pinpointed the immediate sharp increase in prices instead of a gradual one as the main criticism (TUSIAD'dan 2018). Referring to BOTAS as a significant partner of producers in the field of energy, Erdal Bahcivan, President of the Istanbul Chamber of Industry, stated that the shocking price increase should not have been done without consulting other players in the game (ISO Baskani 2018). Despite the positive view of the price increases in the medium and long term, Tamer Calisir, the President of the Energy Trade Association, drew attention to the negative impact on short-term predictability of the last-minute comprehensive changes in pricing. He also argued that energy prices should increase when the costs are high and decrease when they are low (Gazda maliyet bazli 2018).

As Calisir highlighted, pricing policy does not always cause cheaper prices. When oil prices began to decline in July 2014, the decrease was not reflected for a long time in prices (Fig. 5.2), which helped BOTAS compensate for its loss at the time of subsidies (Buyuk mujde 2015). This caused industrial consumers to consume more expensive gas and increased criticism, some of which was articulated by a representative of the private sector:

> Everybody complains about BOTAS' cheap subsidised prices but not many are aware that the situation is now exactly the opposite. As known, gas prices are globally on the decline depending on decreasing oil prices but the sales prices of BOTAS are still the same with those of three years ago. Currently, Turkish consumers are using the world's most expensive gas and this arises the question of how, then, will industrial companies survive if their most important competitive advantage lies in the input of energy? Nonetheless, when these companies were heavily manufacturing, say, iron/steel in furnaces with cheap gas and electricity (also ultimately subsidised by the Turkish tax-payers) and exported to countries like Libya, Iraq and Iran between 2010–2014, this issue was not worthy of attention. Actually, those manufacturing companies seriously thought that they were competing with China. This is where we are with subsidies in Turkey and sadly the same is true with the GFPPs [gas-fired power plants]. They were those who bought cheap BOTAS gas when gas purchase prices were expensive elsewhere and now

due to higher prices look for ways to sell their plants to African countries like Ghana. So in sum, interventions into a liberal market always erupt if not today then does tomorrow or ten years later. And then the market's reaction to it—or its losses—can be much more than its gains in the past. (Demir 2016, pp. 261–262)

The narratives of different individuals interviewed by the researchers drew attention to the AKP governments' reluctance "to lose their control over BOTAS" (Oner and Schröder 2017, p. 191) and the willingness of the governments to "use BOTAS as an instrument to intervene in the gas market" (Demir 2016, p. 249). Similarly, there are also complaints on BOTAS' unwillingness "to abandon its historical monopolistic position for the years to come" (Demir 2016, p. 268).

In addition to the impact of subsidies on achieving the goal of establishing a competitive market, its effect on Turkey's budgetary balance was also raised in the private sector's narrative (Kolbay 2012e). As demonstrated in Fig. 5.4, the difference between the average import price and average selling price has caused losses, with the exception of the second half of 2016 and the first half of 2017. Due to loss of value in TL, the difference between the average import price in US dollars and selling price in Turkish lira increased.

BOTAS' pricing policy created entry barriers for private sector LNG imports. Turkey is mainly dependent on pipe gas despite the increasing share of LNG, which accounted for almost 23 per cent of total imports in

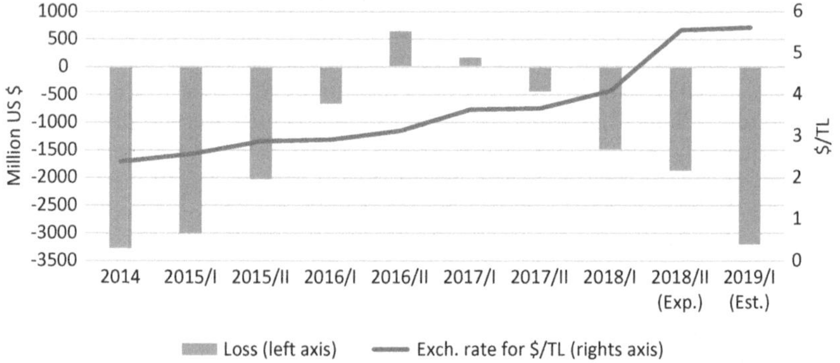

Fig. 5.4 Total loss due to subsidies. (Source: Data from Taranto and Saygin 2019, p. 30; Turkiye Cumhuriyeti Merkez Bankasi n.d.)

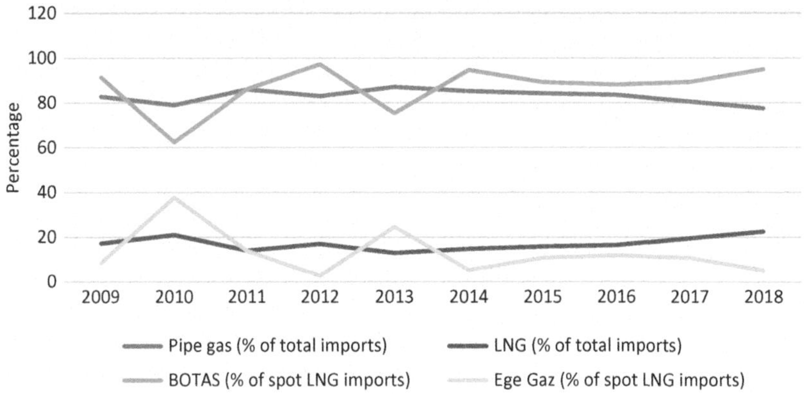

Fig. 5.5 Shares of pipe gas and LNG imports, and BOTAS and Ege Gaz in spot LNG imports. (Source: Data from Enerji Piyasasi Duzenleme Kurumu 2019, pp. 8, 13, 18)

2018 (Fig. 5.5). Furthermore, spot LNG contracts accounted for 10.21 per cent of total LNG imports. Although 47 companies held spot LNG import licences as of 2018, only two companies, including BOTAS with a share of 95 per cent in LNG imports in 2018, are active importers (Enerji Piyasasi Duzenleme Kurumu 2019, pp. 14, 17, 18).

One of the reasons for the low share of the private sector in spot LNG imports is BOTAS' pricing policy. The pricing level creates uncertainties about the market and places an obstacle for the establishment of a competitive market (Soysal et al. 2012, pp. 126–127). The lack of cost-reflective prices carries the risk of preventing new entries in the event that the spot LNG price is lower than the long-term contracted price but higher than BOTAS' subsidised prices. Although LNG prices were lower than BOTAS' prices in 2019, private sector imports were restricted by warmer weather, weaker demand and BOTAS' supplies of LNG. Private importers may face take-or-pay risk in 2019, bearing in mind their low level of imports compared to the previous years due to price disputes with Gazprom and their inability to compete with BOTAS' lower prices. The requirement to offtake a minimum of 80 per cent of the contracted Russian gas prevents these companies benefit from competitive LNG prices. The extent to which BOTAS will continue purchasing natural gas from private importers is questionable bearing in mind BOTAS' increasing amount of spot LNG imports and minimum off-take requirements for the company (LNG Imports 2019). Furthermore, BOTAS' announcement of its monthly prices at the last day of the previous month create an uncertainty for LNG importers (Topuz 2019, p. 15).

Other Market-Oriented Actors' Narratives

The main difference among the narratives of the AKP, the private sector and other market-oriented actors was the latter's emphasis on the role of a state company in the market, which could be either a pure state company or a private-public partnership. The method of liberalising the market without destroying the state company was highlighted by the other market-oriented actors: "there are many economic and political/strategic benefits of keeping BOTAS' presence and even strengthening it" (Gokdemir 2009, p. 154). Likewise, the Competition Authority underlined the role of the state company as a guarantee of continuity in the liberalisation process when the market was at the stage of growth or development, as quoted below:

> It is obvious that the state's role will not be diminished without progressing in liberalisation stages. ... It is possible to evaluate strong existence of the state company in the market as a guarantee of sustainability of liberalisation process in especially *growth* and *development* stages of the market, and not a disadvantage with regard to free and competitive market. (Soysal et al. 2012, pp. 125, 138–139) (emphases in original)

The Competition Authority argued that when the market is at "maturity", the state's role be limited to regulation, transmission and the infrastructure related to establishing an energy trade centre. At the stages of "birth", "growth" and "development" the state is needed as a player. (Soysal et al. 2012, p. ii). The CHP also emphasised the involvement of the state by highlighting that public ownership would "not be an alternative to the market mechanism but a complementary part of it" (Cumhuriyet Halk Partisi 2011, p. 146). Likewise, although one interviewee also signified the importance of a state company for security of supply, (s)he also discussed Turkey's negative experiences:

> ...I also think that for huge buying contracts a state company may be needed, namely I wish there was a dominant company in trade but not dominant in the market. A state company as a backup supplier when needed

is also necessary in my opinion. This can be an interim solution. However, dominance of such a company, as shown in Turkey's case, is used for selling cheap gas, subsidising, thus no space is left for other real players. (interview, December 2011)

To compensate for the inefficiencies of state companies, Bulent Gokdemir, a Competition Expert, suggested public offerings or providing them autonomy (Gokdemir 2009, p. 155). A public offering was also recommended by the Competition Authority (Rekabet Kurumu 2013a) as a method of corporate governance to transform BOTAS into a commercial enterprise. The commonality among these narrators was the willingness to keep the state company while solving the problem of public inefficiency.

Other market-oriented narrators agreed on the need for a legally unbundled vertically integrated company, which would cover all segments and could be solely state-owned or a joint partnership of the state and the private sector. The balance of power institution shaped the arguments in favour of a national champion and/or a vertically integrated company taking part in upstream activities in these market-oriented narratives. The idea was that such a company would participate in the distribution of power in the global markets. For the CHP, the existence of a national champion would "play a more active role in its region" (CHP Bilim Yonetim Kultur Platformu 2008, p. 31). Similarly, as a representative of the private sector, Ogutcu (2011) proposed an energy champion(s) for Turkey, participating in upstream activities, with an eye to the distribution of power in the global energy order, demonstrating the operation of balance of power. He stated that changes in the global energy order and its players affected Turkey and forced it to take measures. Naming the new order 'rising powers/shrinking planet', he argued that power and wealth have moved from energy deficit countries to countries with energy surpluses such as Russia, Saudi Arabia, Venezuela and Kazakhstan. In this context, Ogutcu suggested the creation of an energy company such as Petronas, Petrobras, TOTAL or ENI to conduct exploration and development projects in neighbouring countries with international and local partners (Ogutcu 2009, p. 27). To achieve these aims, he envisaged the merger of the strategic role of the state and the dynamism of the private sector. He stressed that geopolitics also played a role in energy issues and energy was not a commodity to be left totally to market actors (Ogutcu 2009, p. 15; 2011, p. 32). Finally, Ogutcu highlighted the necessity of Turkey creating its "own regional energy giants which will play the game in oil, gas, electricity, coal, wind, geothermal and solar according to international rules" (Ogutcu 2011, p. 32).

The Competition Authority included both geopolitical and economic reasons for the establishment of a vertically integrated body. From a geopolitical perspective, the Authority argued that ownership unbundling of BOTAS and restructuring it into an entity only responsible for pipelines would imperil its strengths of geostrategic location and purchasing power due to growing demand (Soysal et al. 2012, p. 61). The Authority also drew attention to the impact of downsising BOTAS, which has strong purchasing power, on the balance of powers between buyers and sellers (Soysal et al. 2012, pp. 45–46). Given that exporter countries are generally state companies; it was argued by other market-oriented narrators that a state company would have more bargaining power than private undertakings:

> It is not deemed a true strategy that a company with a high purchasing power like BOTAS leaves the market. ... Such a company [state company], bearing in mind the presence of giant energy companies, most of which have been in public ownership, will have better bargaining power than many private undertakings which have relatively limited capacities. (Gokdemir 2009, pp. 144, 154)

> ...bargaining power of a company whose own purchasing power is approximately 90 bcm will be undoubtedly more than that of many local and small-scale importers. (CHP Bilim Yonetim Kultur Platformu 2008, p. 31)

The second reason for the Competition Authority's preference for a strong vertically integrated structure was Turkey's aim of ensuring security of supply in order to establish a liquid[8] wholesale market. Within the framework of international natural gas developments, the Competition Authority advised the creation of a liquid wholesale market with a strong vertically integrated actor rather than a market without strong players and lacking liquidity. Markets with low liquidity and weak players were considered with concern by exporting countries, thereby endangering the security of supply (Rekabet Kurumu 2013a; Soysal et al. 2012, pp. 45, 133–134). The Authority very clearly opposed ownership unbundling, saying "*it is not relevant for BOTAS to be subject to ownership unbundling*" in the Natural Gas Law[9] (Soysal et al. 2012, p. 130) (emphases in original). The provision in the new Draft Law to unbundle BOTAS into three legal entities was also opposed by the Competition Authority: "…BOTAS' being subject to some kind of ownership unbundling within three legal entities is considered an inappropriate preference" (Rekabet Kurumu 2013a). To keep the vertically integrated structure, the Authority suggested restructuring BOTAS to include electricity production on the condition that volume release and legal/functional unbundling for an independent system operator were pursued. Since the lack of a competitive culture in BOTAS was considered the main obstacle in liberalisation of the market, it was expected that this kind of transformation of BOTAS into an energy holding company would contribute to a change from a monopoly to a competitive culture (Soysal et al. 2012, pp. viii, 140, 143). Furthermore, in order to create a vertically integrated structure covering exploration, production, transmission, refinery, distribution and sale, a merger of BOTAS and TPAO was proposed by some actors (Gokdemir 2009, p. 154; Bulbul 2010, p. 29), including the CHP (Cumhuriyet Halk Partisi 2017, p. 32). Thus, from a theoretical perspective, balance of power functioned in the narratives as a supporting primary institution since such a company was expected to strengthen the position of Turkey in its efforts to use the geopolitical location in an efficient way.

The market-oriented narrators heavily criticised the goal of the Natural Gas Law to decrease the market share of BOTAS to 20 per cent by restricting its imports and making contract/volume release, which was kept in the Draft Law. This was best exemplified by the Competition Authority, which drew attention to the target of decreasing the share of the incumbent firm to 50 per cent in the best practices:

> ….aiming to decrease BOTAS' share to 20 per cent in the Natural Gas Law, when there are examples which aim to decrease the incumbent firm's share to a maximum 50 per cent in the best practices, … illustrates the sharp and edged approach of the Natural Gas Law within the framework of target of competitive market. (Soysal et al. 2012, p. 22)

Regarding decreasing BOTAS' market share, volume release rather than contract release was supported. One reason was not to destroy the "purchasing power of BOTAS in international markets" (Soysal et al. 2012, p. 151). Furthermore, removal of import restrictions was recommended (Rekabet Kurumu 2013a, pp. 5–6).

The main problems leading to the failure of the contract release to decrease BOTAS' shares were the reluctance of suppliers to give consent for transferring their contracts with BOTAS to private companies and the confidentiality clauses which prevent prospective bidders from analysing contracts (Cetinkaya 2012, p. 38). According to the Competition Authority, "as a result of this necessity [prior consent], it is observed that a situation in which the competitive structure of the national market is designed by suppliers prevails via the method of contract release" (Rekabet Kurumu 2013a, p. 7). The concern was that the provision for prior consent allowed Gazprom's possible vertical integration into and stronger role in the Turkish natural gas markets. Highlighting the risk of other similar cases for other suppliers, Cetinkaya articulated the concern very clearly: "If insistence on contract transfers arises, the number of subsidies of national oil companies in exporter countries [suppliers] such as Gazprom which are willing to be involved in Turkey's domestic market will gradually increase" (Cetinkaya 2012, p. 38). Similarly, the CHP argued that Gazprom had no reason to supply cheaper gas unless it had a subsidiary relationship with the company it gave consent to: "It is impossible for companies who took over contracts to convince supplier for cheaper prices if there are no irrational reasons (for example, organic relationship [subsidiary relationship]) between Bosphorus and Gazprom" (CHP Bilim Yonetim Kultur Platformu 2008, p. 27). The shareholding structures of new importers after contract releases demonstrated Gazprom's increasing role in the Turkish downstream market. GazpromGermania owned 70 per cent of Bosphorus Gas before it transferred all its shares to the Sen Group in September 2018. Although there are uncertainties on the shareholders of other private companies, Gazprombank owned half of the shares of a joint venture called Promak but sold its shares in 2017, according to an ICIS report. Akfel Holding, in which Gazprombank held minority shares, owned the other share of the joint venture. The joint venture held 60 per cent of Enerco Enerji and 60 per cent of Avrasya Gaz while Akfel Gaz was a subsidiary of Akfel Holding, which was confiscated after the coup attempt (Leading 2018) (Table 5.1). While Gazprom sold its shares in these companies in 2017 and 2018, there were allegations concerning the company's involvement in the market through attempts to persuade seven private companies to merge under Bosphorus Gas, which is claimed to keep its indirect linkage with Gazprom (O'Bryne 2018, 2019). Furthermore, there were also complaints regarding Gazprom's pressure on BOTAS to take over the 4 bcm/y contract from the private sector

Table 5.1 Contracts of the private sector as of 2019

Companies	*Annual volume of gas (bcm)*
Enerco energy	2.5
Bosphorus gas	2.5
Avrasya gas	0.5
Shell	0.25
Akfel	2.25
Bati Hatti Dogalgaz	1.0
Kibar gas	1.0
Total	10.00

Source: Turkiye Dogal Gaz Piyasasi (n.d.)

when the contract terminates. The functioning of great power management as a supportive primary institution in these narratives was demonstrated in concerns regarding Russian power in Turkey resulting from Gazprom's supplier status, its subsidiaries active in the Turkish natural gas market and allegations of the company's involvement in the market design.

In addition to the argument that Gazprom allowed for the transferring of the contract to the private sector, mainly to its subsidiaries, the CHP claimed that nested relations prevailed between certain companies and the Turkish government at the time of getting consent from Gazprom. Accordingly, the Party argued that Gazprom was allowed to enter the Turkish wholesale market in return for giving prior consent to companies with close relations to the government:

> The proximity of two other companies [Enerco and Avrasyagaz] to the current government has often been noted in the press. Within this framework, it has inevitably been thought that prior consent was given to companies close to the government in compensation to Gazprom's presence in wholesale market jeopardising competition. (CHP Bilim Yonetim Kultur Platformu 2008, pp. 21, 27)

An example for this kind of news was the claim that Fatih Baltaci, the ex-owner of Enerco (Enerco obtained 2.5 bcm of Russian gas after the contract release) held shares in an energy company with a different name but same address along with Cihan Kamer. Kemal Kilicdaroglu, then the Republican People's Party's candidate for Mayor of Istanbul Metropolitan

Municipality, argued that Cihan Kamer, who also had shares also in Enerco, had a close relationship with the Prime Minister Erdogan's family as Erdogan's son and daughter-in-law were shareholders in Atagold, Kamer's jewellery company (Kilicdaroglu yine Kamer'in Pesinde 2009; Yilmaz 2006). Opposition narrators used such examples to demonstrate the nested relations among certain energy companies and government representatives (Yilmaz 2006).

Although the CHP held a market-oriented narrative, the Party published a report in 2008 which was deemed "radical" by its own writers and included state capitalist features. The report proposed that BOTAS would keep its monopoly in imports, transmission and exports but leave the wholesale market to private firms. This would allow the company to be a national energy champion, in the vein of other international examples such as the state companies of Russia, China, France, Norway and Algeria. This would serve Turkey's national interests and would enable it to play a more active role in its region (CHP Bilim Yonetim Kultur Platformu 2008, pp. 6, 7, 30, 31). The CHP view can be summarised as below:

> The second gain is the emergence of BOTAS as a public monopoly as a result of tasking it with foreign trade, as a giant energy actor serving Turkey's interests in international markets like its counterparts in Russia, France, Norway, Algeria and China. This would enable Turkey as an energy bridge to play a more active role in its region. (CHP Bilim Yonetim Kultur Platformu 2008, p. 31)

A similar suggestion came from Gokdemir (2009, pp. 154–159), who linked BOTAS' responsibility for production and foreign trade and Turkey's political-strategic advantages and national interests. The functioning of the state capitalism as a primary institution is reflected in the view of the state company as the leading actor in foreign trade that efficiently uses its geopolitical location (Gokdemir 2009, p. 159).

As for BOTAS' pricing policy, the Competition Authority argued that although BOTAS was a company with economic activities, its pricing mechanism was a result of state policies on security of supply, social policies and economic policies rather than a decision of an independent undertaking. The Authority offered the example of BOTAS' supplying of gas to nine distribution companies in 2011 when their suppliers had cancelled the contracts and argued that an undertaking that truly sought profit would not have acted in this manner, which supplied gas within the context of public service. However, the Authority considered the pricing mechanism to be the main reason why the market was still at the growth stage. A pricing mechanism that does not reflect real costs not only has a negative effect on the competition in the market but also sends the wrong signals to new entries and investors in infrastructure and trade. This mechanism affected both the demand structure by promoting investments for gas fuelled power plants and the LNG trade by creating entry barriers to LNG (Soysal et al. 2012, pp. 49, 106, 121–127, 147). Similarly, the CHP's narrative on pricing policy was critical. The Party argued that although the pricing policy might be regarded as favourable to consumers in the short term, it was not favourable to the market nor for reaching the target of establishing competition (CHP Bilim Yonetim Kultur Platformu 2008, p. 26).

5.1.3 *The Transit Issue*

A discussion on the positions of the market-oriented narrators on the Transit Law is essential in order to establish the extent to which Turkish actors foresee full harmonisation of legislation with the EU's *acquis communautaire*. The EU legislation makes no distinction between the legal treatment of transit and transmission (Yafimava 2011; Talus 2013). As the aim is to establish a European single energy market, the main principles regarding transmission are third-party access, including that of other transmission system operators, to the transmission network (European Parliament and the Council of the European Union 2009a, p. 118) and co-operation among transmission system operators. The aim is "to minimise any disruption of transmission services to network users and transmission system operators in other areas and in order to ensure equal benefits with respect to security of supply including in relation to transit" (European Parliament and the Council of the European Union 2009b, p. 50). An understanding of the extent to which the Turkish narratives in favour of liberalisation are willing to develop similar legislation is necessary to be able to determine the type of integration between the EU and Turkey in the sphere of natural gas.

Regarding the Turkish legislation on transit, it is crucial to mention first that neither the Natural Gas Law nor the Draft Law includes transit as a market activity. The Natural Gas Law refers to transmission, distribution, wholesale, imports, exports and storage (including storage in LNG facilities) as market activities (Article 2). In contrast to the EU legislation, the

Turkish Natural Gas Law does not include transit gas in the transmission segment. Although the Draft Law referred to LNG terminal operation and LNG and CNG trade in addition to transmission, distribution, wholesale, imports, exports and storage within the scope of market activities, it did not include transit. However, the Natural Gas Law includes references to transit with regard to the definition of system users, transmission, exports and tariffs. In the definition of the system user, the Law includes "a real person or legal entity who ... does transit gas transmission through the system" (Dogal Gaz Piyasasi Kanunu 2001). Additionally, the Law refers to transit in different Articles. Accordingly, Article 4(c)/8 authorises the Board of EMRA to examine and approve "transmission network investment programmes developed by taking into consideration the transit natural gas transmission" (Dogal Gaz Piyasasi Kanunu 2001). Article 4(f)/3 refers to transmission companies operating transit lines. Additionally, Article 11(2) authorises the EMRA "to determine the transit transmission tariffs according to procedures and principles different from those applicable to local transmission tariffs for the purposes of encouraging the transit transmission of the natural gas" (Dogal Gaz Piyasasi Kanunu 2001). All of these references to transit in terms of the definition of system user, transmission and tariffs were eliminated in the Draft Law. This could be considered a step towards abolishing the "grey area" (interview, October 2018) regarding transit in the Natural Gas Law. The Preamble of the Draft Law includes a mention of the many national and international regulations involved in the transit issue.

While neither the Natural Gas Law nor the Draft Law deems transit an activity, the Transit Law aims to regulate the rules and procedures concerning the transit of oil and natural gas through pipelines and to ensure enforcement of the provisions of international agreements on transit pipelines of which Turkey is a part. The need for the Transit Law prevailed during negotiations for transporting Turkmen gas and the Baku-Tbilisi-Ceyhan oil pipeline project. Preparations for a new Draft Transit Law within the Ministry of Energy to establish a transit regime and put an end to separate provisions on transit in different Laws (Cal 2008, p. 117; IEA 2016, p. 117) did not succeed.

Transit pass is defined in the Transit Law as the transportation of oil and/or natural gas, coming from another country or via that country to be transported to another country, via pipelines inside Turkey. It is mentioned that the entrance of oil and/or gas to Turkey via an interconnector does not preclude the transit nature of oil and/or gas. The existence of an international agreement for the transit pass of petroleum, which refers to all hydrocarbons in the form of liquid or gas, is established in the Law as follows:

> The goal of this Law is determining procedures and principles regarding transit pass of petroleum via pipelines and ensuring implementation of provisions of *international agreements*, which Turkey is a part of, regarding each project for transit petroleum pipeline. (4586 Sayili 2000) (author's emphasis)

Therefore, as Sedat Cal (2008, pp. 117–118), a senior expert at the Energy Charter at that time, claimed, the Law does not form a legal background for a transit regime open to everyone but allows for the implementation of provisions of an international agreement with regard to transit projects. Cal also drew attention to the wording of the Law and references to the "international agreements" in the Article 1 and "project agreements", which refer to international agreements and any agreement signed by public institutions and the investor (4586 Sayili 2000) in Articles 5, 7, 10, 11 and 12 of the Law. Therefore, the Transit Law establishes the legal background for intergovernmental agreements on transit pipelines. It also assumes that the Ministry of Energy is competent to execute project agreements related to transit petroleum pipeline projects and to enforce the Law.

In order to fulfil the legal, technical, administrative and financial work related to transit projects, a Transit Petroleum Pipeline Department was also established (4693 Sayili, 2001). However, all tasks of this Department were transferred to the Directorate General of Foreign Relations and International Projects within the Ministry of Energy. According to the new presidential system, which gives the executive power to the Presidency, the President is the leading actor in the determination and execution of all policies, thus minimising the roles of the ministries. Like the other ministries, the focus of the Ministry of Energy will be to implement and supervise policies that are determined by the President (Sobaci et al. 2018, p. 1). Among the Directorates and Boards within the Presidency, the Strategy and Budget Directorate, the Board of Security and Foreign Policy and the Board of Economic Policies are responsible for contributing to the Presidency's institutional capacity to execute energy policies.

Since the AKP lacks a narrative on transit, the AKP governments' practices with regard to transit pipelines must be examined to establish an understanding of the AKP's position on transit. TANAP and Turk Stream pipelines are two examples in which IGAs established the transit framework. In both of these cases, the signatory parties agreed to create transmission companies to own and operate TANAP and the second line of Turk Stream pipeline. Accordingly, BOTAS gained a 30 per cent share in the TANAP transmission company and a 50 per cent share in the Turk Stream transmission company. Rather than the Turkish regulatory legislation such as the third party access, the host government agreements envisage the rights and procedures. Accordingly, the TANAP Project Entity has the exclusive right to decide on the usage of the total capacity, negotiate allocation of capacity to shippers and charge tariffs. The Company is responsible only for informing the Ministry of Energy about the capacity allocation and tariffs (Turkiye Cumhuriyeti Hukumeti 2012, p. 14). Similarly, the IGA on TurkStream vested the total capacity of the second line in Gazprom. In the event that the transmission capacity of the second line exceeds the established 15.75 bcm/y, the joint venture, in which Turkey and Russia each has equal shares, shall agree on the utilisation of the excess capacity with the offshore company. The right to use 100 per cent of the onshore second line of the TurkStream is vested in Russian company and the terms of operation, including tariffs, will be exclusively decided by the joint company (Turkiye Buyuk Millet Meclisi Disisleri Komisyonu 2016). Furthermore, Article 8(10) specifies that the offshore section company, Gazprom, and the joint venture for the onshore second line "shall not be subject to the laws of Republic of Turkey governing the natural gas market, including the requirements to tariff regulation, third party access and unbundling" (Turkiye Buyuk Millet Meclisi Disisleri Komisyonu 2016, p. 27). Therefore, one concrete consequence of considering transit and transmission as different activities is that transit pipelines are not subject to the rules of third-party access or unbundling. The Regulatory Agency does not have any right on these pipelines regarding the third-party access or tariffs.

The second practice on transit pipelines is in the event of the lack of an intergovernmental agreement. Until 2013, the Petroleum Law numbered 6326, which enabled the AKP to grant transit rights to the private sector with a decision of the Council of Ministers in case of lack of an international agreement, had been in operation. The Petroleum Law numbered

6491, which repeals the Petroleum Law numbered 6326, does not contain any provisions on transit pipelines. Therefore, the AKP continues to rely on a legal framework based on intergovernmental agreements. However, there had been two cases, in which AKP had granted the task to private companies without any tender, before 2013. Although there has not been concrete progress in these two pipelines, which are elaborated on below, these have been significant examples to demonstrate the understanding about the transit pipelines, thus the primary institutions from a theoretical perspective.

In 2006, the Council of Ministers decided[10] that Calik Holding, a private company whose then CEO, Berat Albayrak, later became Minister of Finance, would construct the Samsun-Ceyhan oil pipeline. The pipeline would transport Russian oil from the northern point of Turkey to the southern point, while the main plan was to transport Russian oil to Israel via Samsun-Ceyhan in Turkish territory and MedStream in the Mediterranean (Koylu and Isik 2009). Due to the absence of an intergovernmental agreement between Russia and Turkey at that time, the Council of Ministers' decision was based on the legal framework in the Petroleum Law numbered 6326, rather than the Transit Law (Cal 2008, p. 117). The fact that the Council of Ministers made this decision without any bid despite six applicants, three of which were for trans-Thrace route and the rest for Samsun-Ceyhan, raised criticisms. These criticisms increased when the CHP provided evidence of the request made by the Turkish Ministry of Foreign Affairs to the Israeli authorities to grant the right to construct the Ceyhan-Israel pipeline to Calik Holding (Samsun-Ceyhan'da 2006; Yanit Gelmezse 2007). Furthermore, Calik Holding was rewarded the fields, 55 per cent of which belonged to the Treasury, upon which to build a refinery in Ceyhan with no bid (AKP'den Calik'a 2009).

In 2007, the Council of Ministers decided that the Trans Anatolian Pipeline Company, which consisted of Calik Holding and ENI, would construct the pipeline from the town of Unye instead of Samsun (Samsun-Ceyhan 2009; Enerji ve Tabii Kaynaklar Bakanligi 2013a). The Russian decision to supply oil to the Samsun-Ceyhan pipeline came in 2009 at an energy summit between Turkey, Russia and Italy. At the same summit, Turkey announced its decision on its first nuclear power plant to be constructed by Russia, the only applicant. This was published in the newspaper Radikal with the headline: "Russia gave the business of oil to Calik, Turkey gave the business of nuclear power plant to Russia" (Koylu and Isik 2009).

In a second example, private company Turang Transit was granted transit rights for the construction of the Turkish portion of the Iran-Turkey-Europe Gas Pipeline (ITE) carrying Iranian and Turkmen gas to Germany via Turkey. With an approximate length of 5000 km, the Turkish section stretches for 1789 km. The pipeline is planned to carry a maximum of 35 bcm gas (Proje n.d.). This project began in 2008 with the signing of a Memorandum of Understanding (MoU) between Turkey and Iran, granting gas fields numbered 20, 21 and 23, in the South Pars to Turkey and allowing Iran and Turkey to establish a joint venture with a 50 per cent share (Iran ile dogalgaz anlasmasi, 2009; Iran'la dogalgazda anlastik 2008). Although the MoU raised concerns in the USA on the grounds that it would give harm to American and Turkish efforts to develop Caspian resources and transport to global markets via Turkey (ABD elcisi uyardi 2007), the Council of Ministers granted a "Natural Gas Pipeline Document" to Turang Transit in 2010. Owing to some unsuccessful attempts to come to an intergovernmental agreement (Iran'la gaz anlasmasi 2009), Article 83 of the Petroleum Law served as the legal background for the Council of Minister's decision, rather than the Transit Law. On the other hand, the Council of Ministers' decision on Turang Transit Company underlined that the Document does not grant the company with privileges or the right to ask for privileges. Furthermore, the negotiation of a transit fee to be paid to Turkey during its operation was stipulated in the Decision. Additionally, while project activities could not begin without an official declaration by Iran permitting Turkmen gas to be transported to Turkey via Iran (Petrol Isleri Genel Mudurlugu 2010), two project meetings were held in Turkey in 2015 and 2016 and cadastral surveys were initiated (Iran dogalgazinin proje toplantisi 2016; Ekinci 2014), leading to the assumption that an official declaration was given. The company obtained the second largest economic incentive in the history of the Turkish Republic for the ITE pipeline, second only to that given to Calik Holding for the Samsun-Ceyhan pipeline (Ekinci 2014). Although progress on the pipeline was slower than expected, public awareness of the company grew due to claims made by CHP Chair Kemal Kilicdaroglu about the financial relations between President Erdogan and Sitki Ayan, the owner of Turang Transit (Kilicdaroglu 2017).

The AKP governments' position on transit highlights two significant points. First, the AKP narrative on liberalisation changed according to the means in question. In other words, while the AKP's narrative was in favour of the liberalisation of the natural gas market, the narrative and the practice on transit did not involve the motivation for a liberal regime. Second, the AKP governments' positions on transit also explained their lack of interest in the Energy Community, which aimed to establish an integrated regional market in South East Europe tied to the EU's internal market in the future. In addition, other reasons for the reluctance were given and will be analysed in the next sub-section under the umbrella of modern sovereignty. Neither the market nor state capitalism functioned in the AKP's practice on transit. The reluctance to establish a liberal transit regime and the willingness to opt for a state company (in the presence of an intergovernmental agreement) or a private company (in the event that such an agreement was not made) prevents us from identifying either of these primary institutions. The position of the AKP governments on the Samsun-Ceyhan Oil Pipeline, Iran-Turkey-Europe Gas Pipeline, TANAP and Turk Stream demonstrate that the AKP aimed to retain the sovereignty of the state to decide the transit company in pipeline projects. However, the state's leading role on transit did not necessitate that state companies be in operation on transit pipelines. In two of the projects, the state company BOTAS had shares in the transmission companies, whereas private companies were awarded the projects without any tenders in the other two. Therefore, the examination of the AKP's practice on transit[11] shows that the Party's preference for the state's exclusive role to determine the transit issue prevented us from identifying the market as a primary institution.

Rather, modern sovereignty functioned in the AKP governments' narrative on transit as there was a marked emphasis on Turkey's involvement in all stages of the process of transporting Middle Eastern and Caspian oil and natural gas to markets. Turkey's participation in all stages was considered a part of the main energy policies and strategies, as stated by former Energy Minister Guler (2008, p. 15). Similarly, Energy Minister Yildiz confirmed the "continuation of Turkey's geopolitical and strategic leadership in transit oil and natural gas pipelines" (Enerji ve Tabii Kaynaklar Bakanligi 2013b, p. 64) in the context of establishing an energy transit and hub. Reference to necessary measures to "be active in selling gas to Europe" (Devlet Planlama Teskilati Mustesarligi 2006, p. 70) in the Ninth Development Plan demonstrated that Turkey, as a state, sought to be involved in the process of transporting natural gas from exporters to importers. Davutoglu, then adviser to the Minister of Foreign Affairs, made a similar remark when reflecting on European reticence on this issue:

> Turkey's national interest lies in the proper utilisation of its geography. Here, what disappoints and surprises us is the EU's inability to grasp this vision. Some Europeans seem to have this thought in mind: the Turkish state and its people are not European but Turkey's geography is freely open to European use. (Davutoglu 2008, p. 92)

While modern sovereignty characterised the AKP's narrative on transit pipelines, the AKP governments' practices showed that it did not matter whether the transit company was a public or private company. The participation of foreign companies, as in the case of ENI in the Samsun-Ceyhan pipeline, SOCAR in TANAP and the Gazprom in TurkStream, was even accepted. Therefore, the function of modern sovereignty in the AKP governments' practice was different than the one in the state capitalist narrative in which any foreign involvement was rejected, as will be analysed in the coming section.

The position of the private sector on transit was the same as their position on liberalisation of the domestic natural gas market. Accordingly, the Petroleum Platform Association was in favour of liberalisation of the transit regime and included long-term co-operation, non-discrimination, transparency and cost-reflective and objective tariff mechanisms as main principles for the transit regulation, demonstrating the market institution. Within this context, the Association underlined the need for commercial arrangements rather than intergovernmental agreements, well-defined rules for transit tariffs and transit operations, third party access and capacity allocation, specific responsibilities to EMRA to ensure non-discrimination and announcement of the method of calculation for transit tariffs (Kolbay 2012d). Similarly, Akturk (2008) referred to third party access and transparent tariff mechanisms in which EMRA would be involved. TUSIAD referred to the inclusion of transit into the Natural Gas Law (TUSIAD, Sanayi, Hizmetler ve Tarim Komisyonu 2008, p. 6). The discourse of the head of TUSIAD Arzuhan Dogan Yalcindag on Turkey's need to actively participate in the Energy Community encourages the interpretation that the expectation of the private sector was to liberalise the transit legislation without any exceptions and to harmonise with the EU's *acquis communautaire* (TUSIAD 2007).

As for the other market-oriented narrators, a few references were made to the transit issue. Erdinc Ozen (2012, p. 77), a consultant, former executive of TANAP Transmission Company and a retired executive of BOTAS, argued that transit should be considered a market activity and should thus be covered by the Natural Gas Law. He proposed a transitional period in which some capacity in the current transmission system be allocated for transit and continuation of the current legislation based on intergovernmental agreements for new transit pipelines. With a concern for the security of supply, he recommended special provisions to avoid any problems in meeting security of supply in domestic markets. He highlighted the significance of the creation of a regulation on transit and argued that harmonisation of the legislation with the EU's *acquis* could be on the agenda depending on the level of relations between the EU and Turkey. A combination of third-party access for transit in the current transmission system and intergovernmental agreements for new pipelines was a middle way solution between the market and the state capitalism. This kind of middle solution was also supported by some others on the grounds that transit pipelines should be owned by the state (interview, October and November 2018).

5.1.4 Modern Sovereignty: Concerns on the Energy Community

This sub-section explains the positions of the AKP governments and some of the market-oriented actors on the Energy Community but excludes the private sector which expressed narratives in favour of membership to the Energy Community. It is significant to underline that no broad domestic discussion on membership to the Energy Community took place at the time of writing. Therefore, the data in this section relies on interviews, theses of two experts working at related administrations, a written question from the opposition party and the government's reply in the Grand National Assembly.

To the question as to why Turkey did not sign the Treaty despite its support of the Athens process, which provided the basis for the establishment of the Community, the AKP government emphasised that the Energy Community Treaty envisaged the "establishment of a legally-binding Community with a supranational character" (Turkiye Buyuk Millet Meclisi 2005, p. 604) and drew attention to its economic, technical and political consequences for Turkey. The government did not provide any details about the legally binding and supranational character. However, bearing in mind the goal and the spirit of the Treaty, it can be argued that there is a clash of different understandings of sovereignty between Turkey and the EU regarding the Energy Community, as will be elaborated on below.

The Treaty's "legally-binding" character arises from Article 6, which obliges members to "take all appropriate measures, whether general or particular, to ensure fulfilment of the obligations arising out of this Treaty… and abstain from any measure which could jeopardise the attainment of the objectives of this Treaty" (Energy Community 2005, p. 15). The contracting parties are obliged to adopt the EU's legislation on energy, environment, competition, renewables and development plans to comply with the generally applicable standards of the European Community. In line with the evolution of the *acquis*, the contracting parties are to adapt their legislation accordingly. Therefore, being a member of the Community implies an obligation for non-EU members to adopt legislation decided without the participation of all parties in the legislative process. Although amendments to the *acquis* are not adopted automatically and Article 24 refers to "taking into account … the specific situation of each of the Contracting Party" (Energy Community 2005, p. 18), the measures are taken on a proposal from the European Commission and with a majority of the votes cast. Although the Treaty does not designate a supranational body, the provisions for adopting the current EU legislation, adapting the evolution of the *acquis*, the lack of participation in the legislative process and lack of unanimity in the decision making process on the extension of the *acquis communautaire* prevents us from naming the Treaty sovereignty as modern sovereignty. On the other hand, the Energy Community Treaty does not envisage the transfer of competence to an authority in the field of competition, state aid and energy. Therefore, the Contracting Parties of the Treaty also have the right to adopt legally binding acts. For these reasons, from a theoretical perspective, the sovereignty in the Treaty can be considered to be contemporary sovereignty. In addition to the non-EU members' position on the harmonisation of legislation, the European Commission's major roles and privileges in the decision-making process and representativeness demonstrate the functioning of contemporary sovereignty. According to the decision-making process, it is impossible to decide anything without the consent of the European Commission. The Commission is the co-ordinator for the extension of the *acquis communautaire* (Article 4) and has the right to propose, alter or withdraw measures for the extension of the *acquis communautaire* (Article 79). Furthermore, measures establishing a mechanism for the operation of network energy markets and procedural acts can be adopted only with the agreement of the European Commission (Articles 83 and 87). Moreover, since unanimity is needed for provisions for the creation of a single market, Turkey has the right to preclude decisions contrary to its interests only for Articles within the scope of creating an internal market. The European Commission enjoys a privileged position among the Energy Community Institutions and has two representatives in the Ministerial Council and Permanent High Level Group while other parties have only one representative for each Institution (Articles 48 and 54) (Dastan 2008, pp. 130, 131, 163; Energy Community 2005).

For the revision of the Energy Community Treaty, the Secretariat's suggestions for introducing procedural rules on competition and state aid based on the EU models, thus transforming itself into an executive agency with decision making powers, somehow justifies the consideration of supranationality (Energy Community Secretariat n.d., p. 7). Expressing a similar concern on modern sovereignty, the Competition Authority drew attention to the extent to which Turkey was required to commit itself to implementing the EU Competition Law on energy issues when the Secretariat's suggestions envisaged acquiring the power of national competition authorities in energy related competition cases and appointing the European Court of Justice as the Court of Appeal (Rekabet Kurumu 2013b). The Secretariat's suggestions can be considered an attempt to introduce post-modern sovereignty, as it envisioned an upgrade in its role to the Commission's exclusive role in the areas of competition and state aid.

Answering a written question from the CHP in the Grand National Assembly on why Turkey had not yet signed the treaty despite its long-term support, the AKP government responded that the government's "dissenting opinion on the Draft [Energy Community Treaty] are based on the non-commitment of Turkey on issues which are not yet negotiated and would be determined at the end of the negotiations" (Turkiye Buyuk Millet Meclisi 2005, p. 605). As discussed by one of the interviewees, unlike in the "negotiations on the accession process' energy chapter where Turkey can put its national interests at the forefront" (interview, January 2012), being a member of the Energy Community Treaty "would close the case" (interview, January 2012). Therefore, the interviewee stated that "it is not possible for Turkey to sign that Treaty" (interview, January 2012). Other market-oriented narrators, excluding the private sector, also shared this view. One interviewee argued that the EU's desire for Turkey to become a member of the Energy Community rather than opening accession negotiations caused a "dilemma" (interview, December 2011). One of the interviewees made a comparison to the Customs Union and considered participation in the Energy Community to be "against Turkey's interests similarly to its accession to the customs union without full membership of the EU" (interview, January 2012). Another interviewee considered Turkey's inclusion in the Energy Community Treaty without EU membership to be naive (interview, January 2012).

Although according to the Commission the harmonisation of legislation with the Energy Community could be achieved following a timetable set according to Turkey's preferences (Yilmaz, pp. 134–135), membership was not considered attractive. The Turkish actors' cognitive map can be explained by the government's emphases on differences between Turkey and the other contracting countries in terms of the growth of demand, the scale and growth potential of the energy sector, the country's geographical size and location, the significant stages in reforming the markets and the negotiations with the EU (Turkiye Buyuk Millet Meclisi 2005, pp. 604–605). As one of the interviewees mentioned clearly, Turkey already attracted investors and thus did not need the Energy Community as a tool for this (interview, December 2011). By following its own path and pace of liberalisation in different energy sectors, the country could receive the benefits of liberalisation without giving anything in return. One of the interviewees underlined that it was unlikely for Turkey to sacrifice some of its leverage without having any certainty regarding its accession to the EU (interview, December 2011).

The AKP governments' positions on a liberal transit regime demonstrate their unwillingness to harmonise with the EU's rules on transit and establish a single mechanism for the cross-border transmission and/or transportation of electricity and natural gas. According to one interviewee, the main problem for Turkey in the harmonisation with the EU legislation was transit legislation (interview, January 2012). In addition to the equal treatment of transmission and transit in the EU legislation, Article 28 of the Energy Community Treaty enables the Community to "take additional measures establishing a single mechanism for the cross border transmission and/or transportation of Network Energy" (Energy Community 2005, p. 19). Accordingly, Turkey did not accept the Article on the grounds that it would prevent Turkey from being able to prioritise its own security of supply, which is the main goal of energy policy (Yilmaz 2014, pp. 134–135). Echoing this sentiment, one interviewee argued that Turkey should prioritise its own security of supply and thus develop projects before the EU does (interview, December 2011). Furthermore, Turkey objected to the harmonisation of some of the *acquis* on environment and competition, which remained unaddressed in the national competition legislation (Turkiye Buyuk Millet Meclisi 2005, p. 605). Here, Turkey must be referring to the state aid legislation under the scope of competition, which was not addressed in the Turkish Parliament as of June 2019. In response to the reserves placed on harmonisation of legislation on environment and competition and Article 28 on the establishment of a single mechanism, the Commission stated that Turkey could develop its own timetable for the harmonisation of the legislation and adoption of Article 28 (Yilmaz 2014, pp. 134–135). However, no progress was achieved.

Turkey also dissented on Article 43, which envisages an external energy trade policy and the regulation of relations with third countries (Turkiye Buyuk Millet Meclisi 2005, p. 605). One of the interviewees summarised the concerns over Article 43,[12] which refers to possible measures for imports and exports of energy to or from third parties, as follows: "If you develop a project, you will do it according to the EU rules and you will develop the ones approved by the EU. But we are not a member of the EU" (interview, December 2011). The external energy trade policy was also criticised by the market-oriented narrators on the grounds that it "takes away the right to contract energy agreements" (interview, December 2011). The same interviewee argued that Turkey's sovereignty would be limited by Article 43: "Let's say that you signed a contract with Syria to buy gas. If a Chinese compressor is used in the construction of the Syrian part of a pipeline, the EU does not permit this. Can there be something like this?" (interview, December 2011). Another interviewee brought up the role of sovereignty as a primary institution in this instance: "We couldn't agree on the necessity for states' sovereign rights to have priority. This is the reason why we are not a member. … It is seldom articulated but this is the main issue" (interview, January 2012).

Turkey also objected Article 101, which requires the contracting parties "to take all appropriate measures to eliminate the incompatibilities [of agreements concluded by a contracting party before the signature of the Treaty] established, no later than one year after the date of entry into force" (Energy Community 2005, p. 32). The reason given for the reserve was the fact that those agreements were commercial contracts, which could not be renewed before they expired (Yilmaz 2014, pp. 134–135). This Article aroused criticism that Turkey would be "obliged to harmonise all energy agreements with the Treaty provisions" (interview, December 2011).

Briefly, the Commission's proposal to create a timetable for the harmonisation of legislation and establish a single mechanism for cross-border transmission according to Turkey's preferences did not facilitate any progress in the negotiation process. Turkey considered the provision on external energy trade policy and the obligation to eliminate the incompatibilities of energy contracts to be potential interferences to its sovereignty. Therefore, modern sovereignty is the primary institution functioning in these narratives.

5.2 State Capitalist Narrative: The State as the Leading Actor in The Market

Although all Turkish narrators referred to security and sustainability in their definitions of the concept of energy security, competitiveness was not included in all narratives. State capitalist narrators referred to cheap/low-cost supplies in their definitions rather than competitiveness. While the market-oriented narratives considered the liberalisation of the market as sufficient to competitively secure supplies, the state capitalist narrators discarded the linkage between security of supply and liberalisation of the market. Instead, they were in favour of the dominance of the state in the market and the centralisation of energy affairs. The main representatives of this type of narrative included the union Petrol-Is, the Union of Chambers of Turkish Engineers and Architects and the Chambers within the Union such as the Chamber of Mechanical Engineers.

State capitalist narrators supported "public planning and production" and opposed liberalisation, as illustrated in a report of the Chamber of Mechanical Engineers: "...we invite our country's officials. ... to take public planning and production as the basis, not liberalisation and privatisation" (Makina Muhendisleri Odasi 2012a, p. 207). In this context, it is significant to emphasise that some narrators criticised the contemporary economic paradigm as the starting point for privatisation. This was best articulated by the Union of Chambers of Turkish Engineers and Architects: "[d]ominant economic paradigms put forth by the system convenient to the new capital accumulation model are seen as the basis for privatisation/ liberalisation implementations in the sector" (Turk Muhendis ve Mimar Odalari Birligi 2006, p. 124). Criticising the "*dependence on international market rules*" (Turk Muhendis ve Mimar Odalari Birligi 2006, pp. 91) (emphases in original), the Union of Chambers of Turkish Engineers and Architects advised Turkey to "pursue a programme aiming to decrease or eliminate uncertainties/risks arising from "the market" practices" (Turk Muhendis ve Mimar Odalari Birligi 2006, pp. 124). Accordingly, an analysis of what the state capitalist narrators think about the concept of public service, the role and structure of the state company in the market and the Transit Law provides an understanding of the differences and similarities between the state-capitalist and market-oriented narratives.

5.2.1 *Public Service*

The emphasis on the role of the state as the leading actor relies on the conceptions of energy consumption as a "public right", energy as a "public good" and supplying energy as a "public service", which was defined by the narrators as services run by the state (Turkyilmaz 2007, p. 494). Therefore, "using natural gas as a contemporary energy source" is deemed a public right and "urban distribution services, even if provided by the private sector, is a public service" (Makina Muhendisleri Odasi Enerji Calisma Grubu 2018, p. 593). The assumption is that the interests of society can only be met by the state carrying out the public service while the private sector solely seeks profit. Accordingly, in this conceptualisation, public-private partnerships to run public services are also considered to disregard the public interest (Ercan et al. 2018, p. 583). The Chamber of Mechanical Engineers advised that the state companies carrying out the public service be re-organised based on a new understanding of public ownership and public governance. According to the Chamber, democratic participation, accessibility and accountability were the main principles of public ownership and governance (Turkyilmaz and Aytac 2018, p. 590).

In the state capitalist narrators' understanding, public service refers to the whole system consisting of all activities aiming to reach the goal of supplying energy to the society. Rather than dividing the system into activities, such as transmission, import and storage and questioning the extent to which those activities can be regarded as public service, the Chamber considered all activities of the chain as a whole and deemed the whole system to be a public service. Accordingly, the state capitalist narrative relies on the argument that neo-liberal policies marketise the energy field and divide those activities into pieces for privatising. In this narrative, privatisation abolishes the concept of "public service" in the field of network services in favour of the concept of "services of general interest", which transforms the production and supply of network services to the "production of a commodity" belonging to the sphere of private law (Erdogdu 2005, pp. 97–101).

Here it is important to underline that this narrative likened liberalisation to privatisation. One of the interviewees also highlighted this: "…actually liberalisation does not mean privatisation … but that an equal relationship has been established. On behalf of myself and the institutions I have been representing, I don't think this is true" (interview, December 2011). Similarly, representatives of the state capitalist narrative blamed the Energy Market Regulatory Authority and Turkish Industry and Business Association for falsely portraying "liberalisation and privatisation as identical to each other" (Elektrik Muhendisleri Odasi 2005, p. 4). However, this equation of privatisation and liberalisation did not signify any opposition to the private sector. The existence of the private sector and the sale of some shares of the state company were acceptable in this narrative (Petrol-Is 2007, pp. 65–67; Makina Muhendisleri Odasi 2012a, p. 219), as will be elaborated on in the sub-sections. Nonetheless, the method with which to unbundle the state company, to whom ownership and management belong and whose interests the company serve were important for them. Accordingly, they highlighted the significance of "public benefit", "the public interest"[13] and the role of the state company in the market, which is examined in the next sub-section.

5.2.2 *The Role and Structure of the State Company in the Market*

The main argument in the state capitalist narratives relied on the necessity of having an integrated and centralised approach on energy and a strong state company. The Chamber of Mechanical Engineers suggested a new paradigm based on decreasing energy consumption, using energy efficiently and consuming indigenous and renewable energy produced using domestic technology. Criticising the current policy of industrialisation based on industries such as cement, textile, iron and steel, which harm the environment, consume lots of energy, create relatively low added-value and have old technology, the Chamber proposed a shift to high technology industries with low energy consumption and domestic production. Within the context of these macro changes, the Chamber was in favour of a centralised public approach based on security of supply, sustainability and decreased external dependency (Turkyilmaz and Aytac 2018, pp. 587–588). Similarly, the Union of Chambers of Turkish Engineers and

Architects deemed "increasing the efficiency level of public institutions and strengthening public management in the sector" priorities (Turk Muhendis ve Mimar Odalari Birligi 2006, p. 125).

The preference for a centralised approach was justified by the need to co-ordinate activities such as regulation, planning, monitoring and the rational use of energy resources with a perspective of protecting the public interest as well as the strategic nature of energy: "There is a need for a centralised public body in terms of ... strategic importance of energy sector..." (Makina Muhendisleri Odasi 2014, p. 207). Similarly, Saltuk Duzyol, the former Director-General of BOTAS and CEO of TANAP Transmission Company at the time of writing, argued in 2009 that all control should not be left to the private sector, either domestic or foreign, in the natural gas and oil sector due to the strategic nature of the energy market and supplier countries' policies of using energy as an economic weapon (Botas'in ozellesmesi 2009). This strategic nature of energy differentiates it from other commodities: "...the claim that 'energy resources do not have a strategic feature and are identical to other ordinary goods in the market' is also unfounded and wrong" (Basa and Pamir 2014, p. 21). Accordingly, the Chamber argued that Turkey needs to have a long-term energy policy to be a player in the energy game rather than a bystander. It proposed the establishment of a "National Energy Platform" which would serve as a meeting and discussion point for different actors and a "National Energy Strategy Centre" affiliated to Ministry of Energy which would work in coordination with the Platform (Turkyilmaz and Aytac 2018, pp. 588–590, 593).

According to the state capitalist narrators, the second role of the state was to be a player in the market with a strong state company. The Chamber of Mechanical Engineers articulated this clearly: "in addition to transmission owned by a public monopoly, it is necessary that the state has a serious weight [role/dominance] in imports and storage" (Turkyilmaz and Aytac 2018, pp. 594). The market and state capitalism narratives on the state company differed in the latter's argument that the state rather than the market should be decisive, which requires the state to be the leading economic actor in the energy market. Here, the main challenge was determining "to whom ownership and management belong and whose interests they serve" (interview, December 2011). The state capitalist narrators criticised the private sector on the grounds that it "puts profit into the centre rather than public benefit" (Petrol-Is 2008, p. 2).

While state capitalist narratives insisted on a strong state company, they also accepted the sale of some shares of the state company at the exchange market on the condition that the state retained a majority holding in the company (TPAO ile BOTAS 2006). The Petrol-Is narrative signified the preference for a company in which the majority of the shares are owned by the state due to the role of state companies as suppliers in the petroleum and natural gas sector:

> Sellers of petroleum and natural gas are generally state companies. When the buyer is a big state company with *a state share in its capital*, rather than many private companies, it provides an environment in which negotiations in buying-selling contracts are conducted state to state … Unbundling/ Privatisation of BOTAS within the framework of restructuration should be abandoned. On the contrary, *its character as a company whose shares mostly belong to the public*, should be preserved. (Petrol-Is 2007, pp. 65–67), (author's emphases)

Therefore, similar to some market-oriented narrators who underlined the need for a state company, the state capitalist narrators also referred to the "purchasing power" of a company whose shares mostly belong to the state. Conducting state-to-state relations was considered more useful when the suppliers were mostly state companies.

With regard to the participation of private actors, which was one of the elements of liberalisation, the state capitalist narrators agreed that the public and private sectors can and should co-exist. For example, the Chamber of Mechanical Engineers argued in favour of removal of all import restrictions, which were considered as one of the main obstacles to a competitive market by the market-oriented narrators, and referred to private companies in addition to BOTAS within this context: "rights for importing and contracting new natural gas agreements should be given to BOTAS and *other organisations* so requesting" (Makina Muhendisleri Odasi 2012a, p. 219), (author's emphases). Similarly, Petrol-Is advocated "the goal of ensuring BOTAS and *other local private companies* to take a more active role in international energy markets" (Petrol-Is 2007, p. 67) (author's emphases), as one of the main elements to be taken into account during regulation. References to other organisations show the acceptance of the presence of other companies in the market.

A critical approach in the state capitalist narrative prevailed regarding the IMF, which launched the liberalisation process, and the EU, with whose legislation Turkey had agreed to harmonise. The state capitalist narrators argued that the liberalisation process was part of the current paradigm and was promoted by international organisations or unions like the EU, as the Union of Chambers of Turkish Engineers and Architects stated: "policies/implementation in this direction [privatisation/liberalisation] are faced via international institutions like the IMF, the World Bank, the unions of developed countries like the EU and organisations of developed countries like the OECD" (Turk Muhendis ve Mimar Odalari Birligi 2006, p. 124). Similarly, Ayfer Egilmez, Petrol-Is representative, argued that Turkey's energy policy "is determined in line with the tendencies of international companies and their partners" (Elektrik Muhendisleri Odasi 2005, p. 4) and could be found "not in Turkey's documents but in the EU's and those of other international institutions" (Elektrik Muhendisleri Odasi 2005, p. 4). Furthermore, citing the example of Nord Stream, she complained about the necessity of harmonising Turkey's energy legislation with the *acquis communautaire* when the presence of a common European policy was generally questioned. The state capitalist narrators claimed that the EU had double standards for promoting liberalisation on the one hand and closing its own market to Gazprom on the other. The Chamber of Mechanical Engineers articulated this opinion clearly: "The EU is on the one hand forcing energy firms like BOTAS to be privatised via liberalisation, on the other hand, fearing that Gazprom would buy their public energy firms, it makes plans on how to close their liberal markets for Gazprom" (Makina Muhendisleri Odasi 2007, p. 172). Therefore, according to the Chamber of Mechanical Engineers' consistent views, Turkey should not pursue competition in the natural gas markets:

> Turkey's persistence on liberalisation and a market-oriented competition policy in an environment where the EU does not want to open its own markets is very wrong. (Makina Muhendisleri Odasi 2008a, p. 1)

> Turkey's persistence on liberalisation and a market-oriented competition policy, which has recently failed, is meaningless in a period when the opening of European markets to foreign competition is hampered by the European Union. ... giving countries such as Russia a reason [referring to the third-party clause]. (Makina Muhendisleri Odasi 2012b, p. 41)

Briefly, the main difference between the narratives of the state capitalist and market-oriented narratives was the state capitalists' consideration of the market and competitiveness as irrelevant for Turkey's interests in energy issues. Therefore, it was argued that the state should lead the market, rather than the market itself.

The state capitalist narrators' insistence on the leading role of the state in the market necessitated the creation of a vertically integrated state company in which the state holds the majority of shares. Although the state capitalist narratives had some commonalities with some of the market-oriented narratives, the emphasis in the latter was on the need for a vertically integrated state company, successful liberalisation of the market successfully and creation of a liquid wholesale market. By contrast, the state capitalist narrators' insistence on the leading role of the state and the necessity of having a vertically integrated body were related to public planning to ensure secure supplies and low-cost/cheap energy. Owing to the integrated structure of the oil and natural gas markets, the interlinked nature of exploration, production, transmission and consumption and the strategic nature of natural gas, the state capitalist narrators proposed an integrationist and centralist approach. Additionally, a vertically integrated body would be the key actor in the market (Turk Muhendis ve Mimar Odalari Birligi 2006, p. 125; Makina Muhendisleri Odasi 2008b, pp. 2–3; Makina Muhendisleri Odasi 2012a, pp. 209, 219). Otherwise, the division of the whole system into different parts and the realisation of activities such as imports, transmission, wholesale, distribution and storage by the private sector would make co-operation and planning difficult. Accordingly, establishment of an "Authority for Natural Gas and Oil" by merging TPAO and BOTAS was recommended in order to create a vertically integrated body covering exploration of oil and natural gas, production, refinery, transmission, distribution and sales (Turkyilmaz and Aytac 2018, pp. 592, 594).

The state capitalist narrators' opposition to the methods for restructuring BOTAS arose from concerns about undermining the role of the state company. Accordingly, the Natural Gas Law was heavily criticised for its aim of ownership unbundling and the privatisation of BOTAS. The provisions of the Draft Law on unbundling BOTAS into three entities were also considered unacceptable (Basa and Pamir 2014, p. 134). The Chamber recommended halting all "[p]olicies and implementations aiming at privatisation, downsizing and disabling public institutions" (Turkyilmaz and Aytac 2018, p. 592). Similarly, Petrol-Is also announced its opposition to privatisation and preference for a high level of state ownership in the company: "The initiative for breaking up/privatising BOTAS in the name of restructuring should be abandoned. On the contrary, its character as a company whose shares mostly belong to the public should be maintained" (Petrol-Is 2007, pp. 66–67). Petrol-Is declared its concerns on the transfer of BOTAS to the Turkey Wealth Fund and warned that this restructuring should not end up with privatisation (Petrol-Is 2017). Conversely, Mustafa Sonmez, a journalist and economist, stated that the public companies within the Wealth Fund were those that are not likely to be privatised. By creating a parallel budget, which would not be investigated by the Audit Office, he argued that the AKP aimed to finance the sectors or mega projects that were in financial difficulties without causing a deficit in the general budget (Hayatsever 2017).

While the state capitalist narrators insisted on the need to have a vertically integrated body, this did not mean that they were against legal unbundling. As one of the interviewees also recommended, the establishment of a "state holding" to enable legal unbundling was possible as long as there was a separation from politics:

> For example, a state holding could be an option. Our view is that it should be independent, should not be dependent on the political power, its staff should have the power in governance and monitoring, at least five people representing those working in that sector should be represented on the Executive Committee, which consists of seven people, and should make their own decisions by themselves. However, within that holding, a transmission company, a storage company can be different, this is an organisational problem. (interview, December 2011)

According to the state capitalist narratives, the Authority should be financially autonomous in order to avoid political interference, with its staff participating in the decision-making processes of the management and in supervision. Although this authority would be administratively run by the state, its managers would not be influenced by daily politics (interview, December 2011). Underlining the significance of the development of a new understanding on public administration, the Chamber highlighted the need for transparency, accountability and accessibility to protect the interests of the society and called for a new understanding of public administration (Turkyilmaz and Aytac 2018, pp. 589–590).

In addition to the role of the state in the market and for a preference for the creation of a vertically integrated body, another feature apparent in both the state capitalist and some of the market-oriented narratives was that they expected the vertically integrated structure to increase Turkey's significance in the current distribution of power. Accordingly, it was advised that BOTAS be strengthened as a powerful player in the global markets: "It is impossible for a weak BOTAS, which is unbundled and has transferred its contracts and conducts transmission only, to play an international role in our region in which natural gas production and trade are rapidly increasing" (Petrol-Is 2007, p. 9). Likewise, in 2009, Duzyol proposed that BOTAS "be transformed into a regional player in the short and a global actor in the long term ... [and] compete in the league of giants" (BOTAS'in ozellesmesi 2009) as a powerful player in the distribution of power, showing the functioning of balance of power in the narrative. Similar to the market-oriented narrators in favour of a national energy champion, the arguments given for the creation of an energy giant included the presence of state companies as sellers, the need for state-to-state negotiations and the better purchasing and negotiating power of state companies in negotiations vis-à- vis small private firms:

> Sellers of petroleum and natural gas are generally state companies. ... This [when the negotiations in gas contracts are conducted state to state] will put the buyer which is a state company in an advantageous position not only vis-à-vis natural gas prices but also obligations for purchasing, ... and additional discounts. (Petrol-Is 2007, p. 65)

Furthermore, the Union advised that "the aim of ensuring that BOTAS is more active in international energy markets while regulating markets" (Petrol-Is 2007, p. 126) be kept in mind. Similarly, in their recommendation for a merger between BOTAS and TPAO, the Chamber of Mechanical Engineers argued that a strong public company was needed to secure supply and enjoy the geopolitical superiorities in line with the national interests (Turkyilmaz and Aytac 2018, p. 593). Accordingly, many Chamber reports underlined the need for a vertically integrated company active in exploration and production (Makina Muhendisleri Odasi 2012b, p. 41; Turkyilmaz 2007). From a theoretical perspective, the view that a vertically integrated body active in exploration and production is necessary demonstrates the functioning of balance of power as a primary institution.

In addition to balance of power, great power management and modern sovereignty functioned as supporting primary institutions in the state capitalist narratives. Similar to some market-oriented narrators, there was a concern on the subsidiary relationship between Gazprom and some private companies in the Turkish natural gas market. Accordingly, the Union of Chambers of Turkish Engineers and Architects advised the termination of the practice of contract release on the grounds that it "only favoured companies approved and supervised directly or indirectly by selling companies" (Turk Muhendis ve Mimar Odalari Birligi 2006, p. 36). Concerns about the increasing role of foreign suppliers in the Turkish downstream market were not only related to the great power management institution but also modern sovereignty. Prior consent was considered a way of allowing foreign suppliers to interfere in the Turkish natural gas market. This was best articulated in the narrative of the Union of Petrol-Is: "...prior consent will enable foreign countries and companies to influence Turkey's natural gas distribution and trade" (Petrol-Is 2007, p. 125).

5.2.3 *The Transit Issue*

In the state capitalist narrative, the leading role of the state in the market manifested itself more strongly in the transit issue. In their interpretation, there was no room for private companies in transit activity. Their position was to retain BOTAS as the only company responsible for the transportation of natural gas to meet Turkey's own energy needs and to transport natural gas from third countries to Europe and other regions. In this view, the capacity of the transmission system should be increased while the ownership and management of the transmission system should belong solely to BOTAS.

The Chamber's narrative on transit included two significant points. First, the Chamber announced their support for the projects conducted by BOTAS aiming to transport Caspian and Middle Eastern gas supplies to the EU but underlined that gas should be transported for a transportation fee via the national network on the condition that it was in the national interest and that the Ministry of Energy and BOTAS considered it appropriate. While the Chamber was in favour of transit pipelines, it also stipulated its support for Turkey's right to buy a significant amount of natural gas under preferential trade conditions, consume it for its national needs and re-export it (Makina Muhendisleri Odasi 2012a, pp. 74–75, 218–220; Turkyilmaz and Aytac 2018, p. 593). The difference in comparison to the AKP's narrative is that while the AKP governments' practices allowed the domestic private companies to be involved in the transit of energy, the state capitalist narrators were in favour of a state company being responsible for transit.

The second point the Chamber underlined shows the functioning of modern sovereignty as a primary institution. Drawing attention to the ownership and management of pipelines, the Chamber argued that BOTAS should not only be involved in transporting gas and oil in neighbouring countries but also own and operate the network. Therefore, the Chamber opposed projects that grant construction and operation rights to foreign states and their companies even if BOTAS was a shareholder Accordingly, it recommended revisions of the intergovernmental agreements on transit pipelines, such as the (then) Nabucco, TANAP and Turang projects, on the grounds that the transit regime of these projects would weaken BOTAS' monopoly on transmission. According to the Chamber, construction and operation rights given to transnational companies paved the way for the interference of foreign countries/companies in Turkey's domestic natural gas market and weakened Turkey's sovereign rights (Makina Muhendisleri Odasi 2012a, pp. 74–75, 218–220; Turkyilmaz and Aytac 2018, p. 593). One of the interviewees mentioned this concern very clearly: "We need to check whose interest these pipelines serve. Who is going to be responsible for the operation? To what extent will Turkey have a say? To what extent will it be influential in the decision making?" (interview, January 2012). This position on transit in light of modern sovereignty begs the assumption that the Chamber would be against membership of Turkey into the Energy Community, although no discussion on this issue among the state capitalist narrators could be found.

There was a slight difference in the extent to which modern sovereignty functioned in the narratives on transit of AKP and some market-oriented and state capitalist actors. The difference was that while the AKP and some other market-oriented narrators emphasised the state's involvement in all stages of transporting energy from suppliers to Europe, the inclusion of foreign companies together with the Turkish ones seemed acceptable for them. However, the state capitalist narrators stated that no foreign state, its national or multinational institutions or transnational companies should be involved in constructing and operating pipelines even if BOTAS was a shareholder. Therefore, the state capitalists' understanding was much more limited than the others, who showed concerns about sovereignty but consented to the involvement of foreign companies. For the sake of clarifying the differences among different types of sovereignties, it is important to underline that contemporary sovereignty exists in the narratives when a liberal transit regime is established. In this kind of regime, third party access to transit pipelines, cost-reflective tariffs, non-discrimination and transparency are the main principles. Furthermore, such a regime envisages a licensing process to establish the same legal background for each transit project. However, this type of sovereignty was not apparent in either the AKP or the state capitalist narratives.

5.3 Conclusion

While the market-oriented narrators shared the main goal of the liberalisation of energy markets, the establishment of a competitive market was not the goal in the state capitalist narratives (Table 5.2). Differences within the market-oriented narratives and between the market oriented and the state capitalist narratives manifested in three issues. The first difference was the consideration of the scope of public service. There was a similarity between the narratives of the government and the private sector on public service that allowed the private sector to perform this kind of service. However, the government's reluctance on the unbundling of BOTAS, its transformation into a competitive company and continuation of its dominant position in the market and subsidies raise questions on the extent to which the government truly aims for a competitive market. The Competition Authority suggested the transformation of BOTAS from public service-tasked company to a competitive one and the CHP underlined the necessity for public service to be fulfilled by the state. Although the state capitalist narrative did not oppose the participation of private companies in the market, the narrators argued that a competitive market would not guarantee security of supply. This argument drew upon the consideration that energy was a public commodity and energy was one of the public services provided by the state. Therefore, according to the state capitalist narrative, the state should be decisive in the provision of public services rather than the market.

The second difference was on the role and structure of the state company. There had been references in some AKP documents to both the state company as a player and the limitation of the state's role to regulation and supervision. Although the AKP opposed horizontal and vertical integration in some Government Programs, it endorsed a legally unbundled vertically integrated body in some Energy Minister declarations. Clear opposition persisted to the merger of BOTAS and TPAO in the AKP narrative. However, no progress was made on the re-structuring of the state company. Although the establishment of a natural gas trading hub was prominent in the AKP narrative, BOTAS continues to dominate the

Table 5.2 Summary of the analysis in the chapter

Turkish narratives	*Narrators*	*Primary institutions*	*Goals*
The market without liberalisation in transit	The government	The market (excluding transit) (foundational) Modern sovereignty (supportive)	Establishment of a competitive market
The market with liberalisation in transit	The private sector	The market (foundational) Balance of power (supportive)	Establishment of a competitive market
The market with limited liberalisation in transit	Other market-oriented narrators	The market (foundational) State capitalism (supportive) (The latter is owing to some narrators' recommendations for a dual policy on transit vacillating between the market and state capitalism and some narrators' suggestions for keeping the state monopoly for imports and exports and establishing a competitive market for wholesale) Modern sovereignty (supportive) Contemporary sovereignty (supportive) Great power management (supportive)	Establishment of a competitive market
State capitalist	The union of Petrol-Is, the Union of Chamber of Turkish Engineers and Architects, the Chamber of Mechanical Engineers	State capitalism (foundational) Modern sovereignty (supportive) Balance of power (supportive) Great power management (supportive)	Securing low-cost energy, establishing a leading role for the re-organised state company

market and subsidise the price of natural gas. Similarly, no progress was made on amending the Natural Gas Law even as the Draft Law is currently invalid, despite being sent to the Grand National Assembly in 2014. Due to the inability to compete with BOTAS` subsidised prices coupled with weaker demand and disagreement on a price discount with Gazprom, private importers had to sell their gas to BOTAS for most of 2018. Despite the fact that the termination of long-term contracts in the 2020s will provide a significant opportunity to decrease BOTAS' market share, the continuation of subsidies should be kept in mind when discussing the extent to which the private sector would be willing to take over the contracts.

Although the private sector's position regarding the role of the state and structure of the state company was also interchangeable, it seemed that the state company's vertically integrated structure was acceptable for the private sector as long as the state company played fairly in the market. There was also a reference to at least one national champion, which could be a public, private or public-private undertaking. On the other hand, there was an emphasis on the role of the state as a player in the market in other market-oriented narratives. Accordingly, they prioritised a legally unbundled vertically integrated company covering all segments of the market and owned solely by the state or a joint venture of the state and private sector. It was argued that such a company with state involvement would help Turkey retain its strong elements, which are its purchasing power and geostrategic location. Furthermore, a strong vertically integrated structure would serve to establish a liquid wholesale market. Therefore, a merger of BOTAS and TPAO was possible to the extent that the companies obey the competition rules. Similarly, the state capitalist narrative underlined the role of the state in the market and emphasised the necessity of a vertically integrated structure. However, the state capitalist narrative differed from the market-oriented narrative on the motivation for a vertically integrated structure and the state as a player in the market. The emphases on a strong player in the market in the state capitalist, the private sector and other market-oriented narratives show the functioning of the balance of power institution, as the expectation was to contribute to Turkey's significance in the current distribution of power.

The third difference concerned the Transit Law. Whereas the market institution functioned in the private sector's narrative with the suggestion for third party access and non-discrimination, the AKP's preference was to maintain the current system of intergovernmental agreements. However, it is difficult to argue that state capitalism prevailed in the government's story, bearing in mind the government's practice of granting the task of transit to third parties in some cases without any tendering process. Although there is little data on transit in the market-oriented narratives, support for a middle way solution between the private sector's narrative and the current legislation can be found. The suggestion for the allocation of third-party access in the current transmission system and the continuation of intergovernmental agreements for new transit pipelines had both market and state capitalist features assuming that state companies would be given the transit task for new intergovernmental agreements. The state capitalist narrative was in favour of keeping the state company's monopoly in the transit of natural gas. Not only foreign companies but also Turkish private companies were considered competitors of the state company.

In addition to the market institution and state capitalism as foundational primary institutions in the Turkish narratives on the market, other supportive primary institutions could be found in these narratives, such as great power management, balance of power and modern sovereignty. The state capitalist and some market-oriented narrators underlined the provision for prior consent for contract release to be a tool for Gazprom to achieve vertical integration into the Turkish downstream market, which showed functioning of the great power management as a primary institution. Furthermore, balance of power was present in these narratives as well as the private sector's narratives regarding the suggestion of a vertically integrated structure. Conversely, balance of power constituted the government's story on pipelines, as was elaborated in Chap. 4.

Last but not least, modern sovereignty was articulated in all narratives except the private sector on the Energy Community. The government mentioned the legally binding character of the Treaty, harmonisation of legislation in the competition policy and the provision for a common external energy trade policy as the reasons for their dissenting opinion. These dissenting opinions demonstrated the concerns about modern sovereignty, as there is an obligation to harmonise the transit legislation before Turkey becomes a full member of the EU. Although the Commission gave Turkey the ability to set its own timetable, Turkey did not accept, due to the consideration of differences between Turkey and other contracting parties. Furthermore, there is a risk that a common external energy trade policy could force members of the Energy Community to follow similar rules in their relations with third countries. Moreover, members of the Energy Community are obliged to adopt the EU *acquis communautaire* on energy, environment, renewables and competition policy. This means that the Treaty binds the members to adopt legislation without being involved in the legislative process. Similar concerns manifested themselves in some other market-oriented narratives. Narrators' dual approach towards transit in this narrative demonstrated the struggle between contemporary and modern sovereignties. On the one hand, third-party access to the current transmission system limited modern sovereignty and introduced contemporary sovereignty as third-party access allows the allocation of some capacity in the current network. On the other, the emphasis on the need to keep the current system of having intergovernmental agreements showed the concerns regarding modern sovereignty, as these agreements require state involvement. Furthermore, references to national solutions rather than external ones recalled the presence of modern sovereignty in this narrative.

To what extent were these different positions in line with the EU's energy legislation? These discussions on the Natural Gas Law and the Draft Law demonstrated that the market-oriented narratives in Turkey were in line with the EU legislation on energy. Bearing in mind the EU narrative on extending market values, the market constituted both the EU and Turkish narratives. The differences within the Turkish narratives on the scope of public service and the role and the structure of the state company in the market did not necessarily mean a divergence from the EU legislation. The state as a player in the market and as a legally unbundled vertically integrated company, including other discussions within the market-oriented narratives, were in harmony with the rules of the Third Energy Package. However, some other market-oriented narrators' advice to keep the state monopoly for imports and exports while establishing a competitive wholesale market diverged from the EU rules. Therefore, the extent of the convergence between the EU and the market-oriented narrative in Turkey differed depending on the narrator. Whereas those recommendations can be considered within the scope of a co-operative energy security society as there was competitiveness as a shared value but a restricted one, other market-oriented narratives converged with the EU narrative.

Although it would be possible to speak of a convergence regarding the Natural Gas Law and Draft Law in the market-oriented narratives, the lack of harmonisation prevailed in the narratives on the Transit Law. As previously elaborated, the EU treats transmission and transit equally, which necessitates third-party access in transit. The private sector's narrative on the Transit Law was in harmony with the EU *acquis* with its goal of liberalisation. Given their support for membership of the Energy Community and the provision in the Energy Community Treaty for an external energy trade policy, it can be argued that the private sector was willing to have a converging energy security society. The government's narrative was not in line with the EU legislation as it did not support third-party access in transit. As for market oriented narrators, the suggestion of a capacity allocation for third-party access in the current transmission system was in line with the EU energy *acquis* whereas the proposal for maintaining the current system of intergovernmental agreements for new pipelines was not. Therefore, focus must be placed on the actors and the means to understand the extent of convergence with the EU. Overall, the market-oriented narratives, with the exception of the private sector's, fell short of fulfilling the requirements for a converging energy security society and remained as a co-operative type whereas the private sector's narrative met the conditions for such a convergence type.

The state capitalist narrators` argument in favour of a state company monopoly in the transit segment and opposition to market-oriented policies were not in harmony with the EU *acquis*. Although derogations from market opening and some other provisions such as unbundling are possible in the case of emergent and isolated energy markets as in the case of Finland and the Baltic States, Turkey does not meet the conditions.[14] The state-capitalist argument that the state rather than the market be decisive demonstrates their lack of co-operation in terms of shared values. Therefore, we can argue that the state capitalist narrators prefer a coexistent energy security society with the EU.

Notes

1. "The main elements of the liberalisation efforts are; gradual elimination of the state's role as an investor in electricity and natural gas sectors excluding transmission, and the privatisation of facilities under its ownership, strengthening the regulatory role of the state by ensuring that the private sector makes the necessary investments within a competitive environment and ensuring supply security. ... The state will be adequately equipped in a way to closely monitor the supply security within the framework of its regulatory and supervisory role and to take measures" (State Planning Organization 2006, pp. 35, 82) (original language).
2. "Within the framework of the regulatory and supervisory role of the public sector, formulation of a competitive market and an appropriate investment environment will be supported on the one hand and security of supply will be closely monitored on the other hand. The public sector will contribute to the healthy operation of the market as an investor only if the market is insufficient to ensure security of supply" (Kalkinma Bakanligi 2013, p. 118).

3. Import prices are confidential as they are determined in long-term contracts with the suppliers.
4. Since January 2019, Botas has applied a two-tier price system for utilities and a few industrial firms. While the price is TL 1485.00/000m^3 for consumption up to 70 per cent of monthly contractual quantities, the price rises to TL 1700.00/000m^3 for the remainder, which makes a weighted average of 1550.00/000m^3 (Argus Media 2019b). The average price is more than the estimated import price.
5. The calculation is made based on the average exchange rate for April–June 2019 (1$= 5.88 TL) and $ 289/'000m^3 (Turkiye Cumhuriyeti Merkez Bankasi n.d.; Argus Media 2019c).
6. Since 2018, there have been 4 different pricing methods for utilities. The first method was dependent on a gradual increase of the price, if natural gas power plants were willing to buy all their gas needs from BOTAS. In this case, 50 per cent of their monthly consumption would be charged with a BOTAS tariff, 50–70 per cent of the monthly consumption would be charged by multiplying the tariff by 1.2 and the rest would be charged by multiplying the tariff by 1.25. After the price hikes in August, the second method began with a fixed $ 270.00 tariff for utilities. Due to fluctuations in the exchange rate, a fixed exchange rate of 1$=6.5 TL was set for the period between 8–17 September. The third method was a return to TL in September with a slight price discount (Aplus Enerji n.d., p. 18). The fourth method has been applied since January 2019. As of June 2019, a two-tier price system in which the contractual price is subsidised for consumption up to 70 per cent of the monthly contracts and the price was increased for the rest of the contract (Argus Media 2019a).
7. As of 2018, the share of BOTAS in total gas supplies was 84.12 per cent and 84.65 per cent of imports (Enerji Piyasasi Duzenleme Kurumu 2019, pp. 11, 25).
8. A liquid market is defined as "a market with many bid and ask offers, low spreads and low volatility. In a liquid market, it is easy to execute a trade quickly and at a desirable price because there are numerous buyers and sellers. In a liquid market, changes in supply and demand have a relatively small impact on price" (Investopedia n.d.).
9. According to the Competition Authority (Soysal et al. 2012, p. iii), the main problem of the Natural Gas Law was the fact that the Law stipulated regulations for a "developing" or "advanced" market while the natural gas market in Turkey is at the level of "growth". Thus, it was argued that the Law does not consider steps in between and is far from being a tool for establishing competitive markets.
10. Decision numbered 2006/10342 and dated 10.04.2006.

11. As the Baku-Tbilisi-Ceyhan transit pipeline was signed before the AKP took power, all transit pipelines, no matter gas or oil, after 2002 are taken into account to identify the primary institution in operation.
12. "The Energy Community may take Measures necessary for the regulation of imports and exports of Network Energy to and from third countries with a view to ensuring equivalent access to and from third country markets in respect of basic environmental standards or to ensure the safe operation of the internal energy market" (Energy Community 2005, p. 22).
13. "The welfare of the public as compared to the welfare of a private individual or company" (The Law Dictionary n.d.).
14. Articles 26 and 49 of the Gas Directive allow exemptions in the event of the unbundling of small companies and emergent and isolated gas markets. Accordingly, it is stipulated that "Member States may decide not to apply the unbundling requirements. ... to an integrated electricity or natural gas undertaking serving fewer than 100,000 connected customers. ... [if] a Member State is not directly connected to the interconnected system of any other Member State and has only one main external supplier (meaning that one supplier has more than 75 per cent of the market), it may derogate from certain requirements of the gas market directive, including the unbundling requirements, the market opening requirement and the authorisation procedure for new gas facilities" (Talus 2013, pp. 93–94).

Bibliography

4586 Sayili Petrolun Boru Hatlari ile Transit Gecisine Dair Kanun. (2000, June 20). *Resmi Gazete, 24,093*. Retrieved from http://www.resmigazete.gov.tr/main.aspx?home=http://www.resmigazete.gov.tr/eskiler/2000/06/20000629.htm&main=http://www.resmigazete.gov.tr/eskiler/2000/06/20000629.htm.

4693 Sayili Enerji ve Tabii Kaynaklar Bakanliginin Teskilat ve Gorevleri Hakkında Kanunda Degisiklik Yapilmasina Dair Kanun. (2001, July 5). *Resmi Gazete, 24, 453*. Retrieved from http://www.resmigazete.gov.tr/eskiler/2001/07/20010705.htm#2.

ABD elcisi uyardi: Iran'la anlasirsaniz, Hazar'i vurursunuz. (2007, July 27). *Hurriyet*. Retrieved from http://www.hurriyet.com.tr/gundem/abd-elcisi-uyardi-iran-la-anlasirsaniz-hazar-i-vurursunuz-6969799.

AKP'den Calik'a boru hatti kiyagi. (2009, October 21). *Birgun*. Retrieved from http://www.birgun.net/haber-detay/akp-den-calik-a-boru-hatti-kiyagi-48929.html.

Akturk, A. (2008). *Turkey as a hub for transit projects*. Retrieved from http://www.energycharter.org/fileadmin/DocumentsMedia/Events/20080619-Mashreq_Gas_Initiative_S3_AAAkturk.pdf.

Akturk, A. (2010). *Demokrasi, ongorulebilirlik, seffaflik, kamu hizmeti ve enerji sektoru*. Retrieved from http://www.akturk.org/akturk.org/Makaleler_Articles/Entries/2010/1/12_Demokrasi,_Ongorulebilirlik,_ Seffaflk,_Kamu_Hizmeti_ve_Enerji_Sektoru.html.

Akturk, A. (2011). *Global enerji Nisan 2011 sayisinda roportaj seyl gazi, dogalgaz yatirimlarini etkiledi*. Retrieved from http://www.akturk.org/akturk.org/Makaleler_Articles/Entries/2011/4/8_Global_Enerji_Nisan_2011_Saysnda_RoportajSeyl_gaz%2C_dogal_gaz_yatrmlarn_etkiledi.html.

Akturk, A. (2012). *Kar merkezleri*. Retrieved from http://enerjigunlugu.net/kar-merkezleri_298.html?Pagenum1=5&Pagenum=5&id=298&yid=77#.Vo45SfmLTIU.

Altan, H. (2010). Kamu, piyasa oyuncusu olmaktan cikmali. *Energy Report, 1*(8), 58–67.

Aplus Enerji. (n.d.). *2018 yili enerji piyasasi ozet raporu*. Retrieved from http://www.aplusenerji.com/turkiye-enerji-piyasasi-2018-yili-ozet-raporu-yayimlandi-1/.

Argus Media. (2019a). Turkish exchange prices hold discount to import costs. In *Argus European Natural Gas Report*, January 15, London. Retrieved from www.direct.argusmedia.com.

Argus Media. (2019b, June). BOTAS monthly balancing price. *Argus Data.*. Retrieved from www.direct.argusmedia.com.

Argus Media. (2019c, April 26). Turkish day-ahead gas prices fall. In *Argus European Natural Gas Report,* London. Retrieved from www.direct.argusmedia.com.

Ataman Ozel, L., & Yildirim, O. (2012). Esed elektrik istedi. *Beyaz Gazete*. Retrieved from http://www.beyazgazete.com/video/anahaber/kanal-7-28/2012/11/03/esed-elektrik-istedi- 340410.html.

Bakan Albayrak: Yatirimlarin rahatca yapilabilmesi icin tum adimlari attik. (2018, February 8). *Milliyet*. Retrieved from http://www.milliyet.com.tr/enerji-bakani-albayrak-konusuyor-ekonomi-2606095/.

Bakanlar Kurulu Karari. (2012). *2013 Yili Programi*. Retrieved from http://www.sbb.gov.tr/yillik-programlar/.

Basa, N., & Pamir, N. (2014). *Enerji ve hukuk sempozyumu sonuc bildirgesi temel saptamalar ve sorunlar, cozum onerileri*. Ankara: Barolar Birligi.

Basbakanlik Kanunlar ve Kararlar Genel Mudurlugu. (2014). *Dogalgaz Piyasasi Kanununda Degisiklik Yapilmasina Dair Kanun Tasarisi*. Retrieved from http://www2.tbmm.gov.tr/d24/1/1-0963.pdf.

BOTAS vergi rekortmenligini bu. yil Merkez Bankasi'na kaptirdi, (2018, April 9). *Haberturk*. https://www.haberturk.com/botas-vergi-rekortmenligini-bu-yil-merkez-bankasina-kaptirdi-1911285-ekonomi.

BOTAS 2016'da Kurumlar vergisi rekoru kirdi. (2018, August 9). *Milliyet.* http://www.milliyet.com.tr/botas-2016-da-kurumlar-vergisi-ekonomi-2498829/.
Botas'in ozellesmesi buyuk hata olur. (2009, February 11). *Deniz Haber Ajansi.* Retrieved from http://www.denizhaber.com.tr/botasin-ozellesmesi-buyuk-hata-olur-haber-17573.htm.
Bulbul, M. O. (2010). Liberalization of the Turkish natural gas market. *Rekabet Dergisi, 11*(1), 7–35.
Buyuk mujde! Dogalgaza indirim geliyor. (2015, December 18). *Aksam.* Retrieved from https://www.aksam.com.tr/kobi/buyuk-mujde-dogalgaza-indirim-geliyor/haber-472618.
Cal, S. (2008). Baku-Tiflis-Ceyhan boru hatti projesi kapsamindaki anlasmalarin hukuki yonden degerlendirilmesi. *Ankara Universitesi SBF Dergisi, 63*(4), 89–134.
Cetinkaya, S. (2012). Thrace hub should be considered. *Gazbir, 12*(June), 28–39.
CHP Bilim Yonetim Kultur Platformu. (2008). *Enerji serisi raporlari dogalgaz.* Ankara.
Comert, N. (2011). *Turkiye'nin enerji gorunumu isiginda dogalgaz piyasasinin liberalizasyonu.* Retrieved from http://www.petform.org.tr/images/yayinlar/sunum_ve_konusmalar/steam_13_enerji_arenasi_sunumu_nu sret_comert_08092011.pdf.
Commodity Markets. (n.d.). *World Bank.* Retrieved from http://www.worldbank.org/en/research/commodity-markets.
Cumhurbaskanligi. (2018). *2019 Yili Cumhurbaskanligi Yillik Programi*, Karar Sayisi: 256. Retrieved from https://www.sbb.gov.tr/wp-content/uploads/2018/11/2019_Yili_Cumhurbaskanligi_Yillik_Programi.pdf.
Cumhuriyet Halk Partisi. (2011). *Cumhuriyet Halk Partisi Programi.* Retrieved from http://www.chp.org.tr/wp-content/uploads/chpprogram.pdf
Cumhuriyet Halk Partisi. (2017). *Enerji ve Tabii Kaynaklar Politikasi.* Ankara.
Dastan, D. (2008). *Enerji piyasalarinda yeni bir olusum: Guneydogu Avrupa Enerji Toplulugu.* Uzmanlik Tezi. Ankara: Enerji Piyasasi Duzenleme Kurumu.
Davutoglu, A. (2008). Turkey's foreign policy vision: an assessment of 2007. *Insight Turkey, 10*(1), 77–96.
Demir, R. (2004, October 6). Bakan Simsek ozellestirilecek alanlari acikladi. *Anadolu Ajansi.* Retrieved from https://www.aa.com.tr/tr/ekonomi/bakan-simsek-ozellestirilecek-alanlari-acikladi/113630.
Demir, O. (2016). *Natural gas market reform in Turkey: A critical review of progress toward liberalisation and the gas target model.* PhD diss. Anglia Ruskin University.
Devlet Planlama Teskilati Mustesarligi. (2006). *IX. Kalkinma Plani Enerji Ozel Ihtisas Komisyonu raporu.* Ankara.

Dilli, B., & Nyman, K. (2015). *Turkey's energy transition milestones and challenges.* World Bank, No. ACS14951.

Dogal Gaz Piyasasi Kanunu. (2001). *Enerji Piyasasi Duzenleme Kurumu.* Retrieved from https://www.epdk.org.tr/Detay/Icerik/23-2-1007/mevzuat.

Dogalgaz piyasasinda yanlisliklar, dogalgaz piyasasi sorunlari ve dogalgaz projeleri. (2008, Aralik). *Eko- Enerji Dergisi, 24,* 64–78.

Dogalgazda fiyati piyasa belirlemeli. (2011, Mart 24). *Enerji Enstitusu.* Retrieved from http://enerjienstitusu.de/2011/03/24/dogalgazda-fiyati-piyasa-belirlemeli/.

Ekinci, I. (2014, February 9). Cumhuriyet tarihinin en buyuk ikinci tesvigini alan Turang'in perde arkasi. *Dunya.* Retrieved from https://www.dunya.com/sektorler/enerji/cumhuriyet-tarihinin-en-buyuk-ikinci-tesvigini-alan-turangin-perde-haberi-237344.

Elektrik Muhendisleri Odasi. (2005). *Turkiye'de enerji politikalari ve yasal duzenlemeler paneli.* Retrieved from http://www.emo.org.tr/ekler/707329bece455a4_ek.pdf.

Elektrik ozellestirmesi varlik satisi değil. (2010, August 10). *Memurlar.net.* Retrieved from https://www.memurlar.net/haber/173985/elektrik-ozellestirmesi-varlik-satisi-degil.html.

Energy Community. (2005). *Treaty Establishing the Energy Community. Retrieved from* http://www.energy-community.org/pls/portal/docs/2796177.PDF.

Energy Community Secretariat. (n.d.). *An Energy Community for the future—The Secretariat's view.* Retrieved from http://www.energy- community.org/pls/portal/docs/2806177.PDF.

Enerji Piyasasi Duzenleme Kurumu. (2011). *Dogal gaz piyasasi 2010 yili sektor raporu.* Ankara.

Enerji Piyasasi Duzenleme Kurumu. (2019). *Dogal gaz piyasasi 2018 yili sektor raporu.* Ankara.

Enerji ve Tabii Kaynaklar Bakani Taner Yildiz aciklamasi. (2013, December 27). *Haberler.Com.* Retrieved from https://www.haberler.com/enerji-ve-tabii-kaynaklar-bakani-taner-yildiz-2-5479221-haberi/.

Enerji ve Tabii Kaynaklar Bakanligi. (2012a). *4646 Sayili Dogalgaz Piyasasi Kanununda Degisiklik Yapilmasina Dair Kanun Tasarisi Taslagi.* Retrieved from http://www.enerji.gov.tr/duyurular/4646_Sayili_Kanun_Degisikligi.doc.

Enerji ve Tabii Kaynaklar Bakanligi. (2012b). *2013 yili butce sunumu.* Ankara.

Enerji ve Tabii Kaynaklar Bakanligi. (2013a). *Osmaniye Milletvekili Sayin Hasan Turkoglu'nun yazili soru onergesi ve cevaplari (7/23078).* Retrieved from https://www2.tbmm.gov.tr/d24/7/7-23078c.pdf.

Enerji ve Tabii Kaynaklar Bakanligi. (2013b). *2014 yili butce sunumu.* Ankara.

Enerji ve Tabii Kaynaklar Bakanligi. (2017). *2018 yili butce sunumu.* Ankara.

Enerji ve Tabii Kaynaklar Bakanligi. (n.d.). *Enerji ve Tabii Kaynaklar Bakanligi 2010–2014 Stratejik Plani*. Ankara.

Ercan, N., Turkyilmaz, O., Aytac, O. (2018). Dunyada kamu isletmeciliginin rolu artiyor mu? Kamusal hizmetler tekrar kamuya donebilir, kamu eliyle verilebilir mi? In Makina Muhendisleri Odasi, *Turkiye'nin Enerji Gorunumu 2018*. Yayin No: MMO/691 (pp. 575–586). Ankara: Makine Muhendisleri Odasi.

Erdogdu, S. (2005). Turkiye'de enerji sektorundeki gelismeler ve kamu mulkiyeti. *Turkiye V. Enerji Sempozyumu*. Retrieved from http://www.emo.org.tr/ekler/6b122d4358357d8_ek.pdf.

European Commission. (n.d.). *Market legislation*. Retrieved from https://ec.europa.eu/energy/en/topics/markets-and-consumers/market-legislation.

European Parliament and the Council of the European Union. (2009a). Directive 2009/73/EC of the European Parliament and of the Council of 13 July 2009concenring common rules for the internal market in natural gas and repealing Directive 2003/55/EC. *Official Journal of the European Union*, *L* 211/94, 118. Retrieved from https://eur-lex.europa.eu/LexUriServ/LexUriServ.do?uri=OJ:L:2009:211:0094:0136:en:PDF.

European Parliament and the Council of the European Union. (2009b). *Regulation (EC) No 715/2009 of the European Parliament and of the Council of 13 July 2009 on conditions for access to the natural gas transmission network and repealing Regulation (EC) No 1775/2005*. Retrieved from https://eur-lex.europa.eu/legal-content/EN/TXT/PDF/?uri=CELEX:32009R0715&from=EN.

Gazda maliyet bazli fiyatlamaya geciste DEV ADIM. (2018, August 14). *Elektrik Ureticileri Dernegi*. Retrieved from http://www.eud.org.tr/2018/08/14/gazda-maliyet-bazli-fiyatlamaya-geciste-dev-adim/.

Girgic, C. (2012). Pamir: 'Enerjide Rusya'ya bagimlilik artiyor'. *Euractiv*. Retrieved from http://www.euractiv.com.tr/enerji/interview/pamir-enerjide-rusyaya-bagimlilik-artiyor-023318.

Gokdemir, B. (2009). *Turkiye'de dogalgaz sektorunun yeniden yapilanmasi: sekiz yillik deneyimin arz guvenligi ve rekabet politikasi perspektifinden degerlendirilmesi*. Ankara: TEPAV.

Guler, H. (2008). Enerji guvenligimiz icin disa bagimliligi makul seviyede tutmaliyiz. *Cerceve, 16*(45), 15–25.

Hayatsever, H. (2017, February 6). Varlik Fonu tartismasi: 'Paralel butce' mi, 'kamu kaynaklarinin daha etkin kullanimi' mi? *Sputnik Turkiye*. Retrieved from https://tr.sputniknews.com/columnists/201702061027092432-turkiye-varlik-fonu-ziraat-bankasi-borsa-istanbul-botas-thy/.

IEA. (2016). *Energy policies of IEA countries Turkey review*. Paris.

Interviews. (2011, December). Ankara and Istanbul.

Interviews. (2012, January). Ankara and Istanbul.

Interviews. (2018, October and November). Ankara and Istanbul.

Investopedia. (n.d.) *Liquid market*. Retrieved from http://www.investopedia.com/terms/l/liquidmarket.asp.

Iran dogalgazinin proje toplantisi Trabzon'da yapildi. (2016, October 6). *Milliyet*. Retrieved from http://www.milliyet.com.tr/iran-dogazgazi-nin-proje-toplantisi-trabzon-yerelhaber-1583823/.

Iran ile dogal gaz anlasmasi imzalaniyor. (2009, October 28). *T24*. Retrieved from https://t24.com.tr/haber/iran-ile-dogalgaz-anlasmasi-imzalaniyor,59420.

Iran'la dogalgazda anlastik, Guney Pars boru hatti yapilacak. (2008, November 18). *Sondakika*. Retrieved from https://www.sondakika.com/haber/haber-iran-la-dogalgazda-anlastik-guney-pars-boru-hatti/

Iran'la gaz anlasmasi yine ertelendi. (2009, October 29). *Milliyet*. Retrieved from http://www.milliyet.com.tr/ekonomi/iran-la-gaz-anlasmasi-yine-ertelendi-1155713.

ISO Baskani Bahcivan: BOTAS sanayiciye buyuk bir sok yasatti. (2018, August 1). *Sozcu*. Retrieved from https://www.sozcu.com.tr/2018/ekonomi/iso-baskani-bahcivan-botas-sanayiciye-buyuk-bir-sok-yasatti-2551820/.

Iyi Parti. (n.d.). *Iyi Parti Programi*. Retrieved from https://iyiparti.org.tr/Assets/pdf/iyi_parti_programi.pdf.

Kalkinma Bakanligi. (2013). *Onuncu Kalkinma Plani (2014–2018)*. Ankara.

Kilicdaroglu, 'Man Adasi dekontlarini' gosterdi: Ispat ettim. (2017, November 28). *Gazeteduvar*. Retrieved from https://www.gazeteduvar.com.tr/politika/2017/11/28/kilicdaroglu-erdoganin-istifa-restne-yanit-vriyor/.

Kilicdaroglu yine Kamer'in Pesinde. (2009, February 18). *T24*. Retrieved from http://t24.com.tr/haber/kilicdaroglu-yine-kamerin-pesinde,29842.

Kolbay, A. (2010a). *Ulusal sampiyonluk ve rakiplerle buyumenin erdemi*. Petroturk. Retrieved from http://www.petroturk.com/HaberGoster.aspx?id=3622&haber=Ulusal-şsampiyonluk-ve-rakiplerle-birlikte-buyumenin-erdemi.

Kolbay, A. (2010b). *Dogalgaz Piyasasi Kanunu nasil yenilenmeli-II*. Petroturk. Retrieved from http://www.petroturk.com/HaberGoster.aspx?id=4012&haber=Dogalgaz-Piyasasi-Kanunu-nasil-yenilenmeli.II.

Kolbay, A. (2011a). *TPAO nasil 'milli sampiyon' olur? I*. Petroturk. Retrieved from http://www.petroturk.com/HaberGoster.aspx?id=6144&haber=TPAO-nasil-Milli-sampiyon-olur-I.

Kolbay, A. (2011b). *Arama-uretimde mukayeseli ustunluklerimiz ve zayifliklarimiz II*. Petroturk. Retrieved from http://petroturk.com/HaberGoster.aspx?id=5849&haber=Arama-uretimde-mukayeseli-ustunluk-ve-zayifliklarimiz-II.

Kolbay, A. (2012a). *Yaklasan arz guvenligi sorununa iliskin cozum onerileri II*. Petroturk. Retrieved from http://www.petroturk.com/HaberGoster.aspx?id=6990&haber=Yaklasan-arz-guvenligi-sorununa-iliskin-cozum-onerileri-II.

Kolbay, A. (2012b). *Rekabet Kurumu dogal gaz raporu elestirisi III*. Petroturk. Retrieved from http://petroturk.com/HaberGoster.aspx?id=7818&haber=Rekabet-Kurumu-Dogal-Gaz-Raporu-elestirisi-III.

Kolbay, A. (2012d). *Latest developments in Turkish natural gas market and their impacts on transit pipeline projects*. Petroturk. Retrieved from http://www.petform.org.tr/images/yayinlar/sunum_ve_konusmalar/gas_to_power_turkey_sunumu_altan_kolbay_20062012.pdf.

Kolbay, A. (2012e). *2013 yili programinda enerji II*. Petroturk. Retrieved from http://petroturk.com/HaberGoster.aspx?id=8090&haber=2013-Yili-Programi-nda-Enerji-II.

Koylu, H., & Isik, T. (2009). Rusya'dan Calik'a petrol, Turkiye'den Rusya'ya ihale. *Radikal*. Retrieved from http://www.radikal.com.tr/turkiye/rusyadan-calika-petrol-turkiyeden-rusyaya-ihale- 948508/.

Leading Turkish gas importers in takeover bid by ex Gazprom partner. (2018, December 6). *ICIS*. Retrieved from https://www.icis.com/explore/resources/news/2018/12/06/10291221/leading-turkish-gas-importers-in-takeover-bid-by-ex-gazprom-partner/.

LNG Imports Competitive for Turkey, but Barriers Persist. (2019, January 31). *ICIS*. Retrieved from https://www.icis.com/explore/resources/news/2019/01/31/10313567/lng-imports-competitive-for-turkey-but-barriers-persist.

Makina Muhendisleri Odasi. (2007). Enerji sorununun cozumu dogrultusunda BOTAS ve TPAO birlesmeli, aynı sekilde elektrik üretim, iletim ve dagitim kuruluslari da teklesmelidir. In Makina Muhendisleri Odasi, *Basin aciklamalari, basina verilen demec, makale ve yapilan soylesiler* (p. 172). Ankara: Makina Muhendisleri Odasi.

Makina Muhendisleri Odasi. (2008a, June 20). *Turkiye'nin dogal gaz temin ve tuketim politikalarinin degerlendirilmesi Oda raporu basin aciklamasi*. Ankara: Makina Muhendisleri Odasi.

Makina Muhendisleri Odasi. (2008b). *TMMOB Makina Muhendisleri Odasinin dogal gaz strateji belgesine iliskin gorusleri*. Ankara: Makina Muhendisleri Odasi.

Makina Muhendisleri Odasi. (2012a). *Turkiye'nin enerji gorunumu*. Yayin No: MMO/588. Ankara: Makina Muhendisleri Odasi.

Makina Muhendisleri Odasi. (2012b). *Orta vadeli program (2012–2014) ve 61. Hukumet programının ekonomi, sanayi, KOBI, AR-GE, enerji, altyapı ve ulasim, isci sagligi ve is guvenligi bolumlerinin degerlendirilmesi*. Yayin No: MMO/582. Ankara: Makina Muhendisleri Odasi.

Makina Muhendisleri Odasi. (2014). *Turkiye'nin enerji gorunumu*. Yayin No: MMO/616. Ankara: Makina Muhendisleri Odasi.

Makina Muhendisleri Odasi Enerji Calisma Gurubu. (2018). *Elektrik ve dogal gaz fiyatlarina yapilan son zamlarin analizi*. Retrieved from https://www.mmo.org.tr/sites/default/files/temmuz2019_enerjizamlari_odaraporu.pdf.

Milliyetci Hareket Partisi. (n.d.). *2011 Secim Beyannamesi—2023'e dogru yukselen ulke Turkiye sozlesmesi*. Ankara.

Ministry of Development. (2012). *Pre-accession economic programme 2013–2015*. Retrieved from http://www.mod.gov.tr/Lists/PreAccessionEconomic Programs/Attachments/1/Pre- Accession%20Economic%20Programme%20 2013-2015.pdf.

Nayir, M. (2010). *Enerji ve Tabii Kaynaklar Bakani Yildiz: 'TPAO'nun yüzde 49'nu halka acmayi planliyoruz'*. Global Enerji. Retrieved from http://www.globalenerji.com.tr/dergide-bu-sayi/2010/10/12/enerji-ve-tabii-kaynaklar-bakani-taner-yildiz%2D%2Dtp.

O'Bryne, D. (2018, December 27). Outlook 2019: Turkish natural gas market set for potential 'de-liberalization' in 2019. *Platts*. Retrieved from https://www.spglobal.com/platts/en/market-insights/latest-news/natural-gas/122718-outlook-2019-turkish-natural-gas-market-set-for-potential-de-liberalization-in-2019.

O'Bryne, D. (2019, May 30). Turkey curtails Q1 pipeline imports. *Natural Gas World*.Retrieved from https://www.naturalgasworld.com/turkey-curtails-q1-pipeline-imports-70374.

Ogutcu, M. (2009, Mart). Gecikmeksizin yeni enerji ekonomisine gecilmeli. *Finans Dunyasi*, 26–30.

Ogutcu, M. (2011). *Kuresel enerjide duzen ve oyunculari degisiyor. Gorus, 68*, 30–32.

Oner, N., & Schröder, M. (Eds.). (2017). *Turkey as an energy hub? Contributions on Turkey's role in EU energy supply* (M. Schroder, M. O. Bettzuge, & W. Wessels, Eds.), (pp. 185–202). Baden-Baden: Nomos Verlagsgesellschaft.

Ozen, E. (2012). *Turkiye dogal gaz piyasasi beklentiler, gelismeler 2012*. Ankara: Deloitte.

Ozen, E. (2019, February 7). Serbestlestirme surecinde Turkiye dogal gaz piyasasi. *DEKTMK*. Retrieved from https://www.dunyaenerji.org.tr/wp-content/uploads/2019/02/ErdincOzenSunum.pdf.

Petrol Isleri Genel Mudurlugu. (2010, November 23). Petrol Hakkina Muteallik Karar. *Resmi Gazete, 27*, 764. Retrieved from http://www.resmigazete.gov.tr/ilanlar/eskiilanlar/2010/11/20101123-4.htm#%C3%8702.

Petrol-Is. (2007). *Boru hatlari ile ham petrol ve dogalgaz tasimaciligi: BOTAS*. Yayin No: 102. Ankara: Petrol-Is.

Petrol-Is. (2008). *BOTAS ozellestirilemez*. 28 Kasim tarihli basin aciklamasi. Ankara.

Petrol-Is. (2017, February 14). *28. Donem 5. Olagan Genisletilmis Baskanlar Kurulu Sonuc Bildirgesi yayınlandı*. Retrieved from https://www.petrol-is.org.tr/haber/28-donem-5-olagan-genisletilmis-baskanlar-kurulu-sonuc-bildirgesi-yayinlandi-10783.

Petroturk. (2010). *Ithalat ozel sektor oyuncuları tam olarak serbest birakilmali*. Retrieved from http://www.petroturk.com/HaberGoster.aspx?id=4071 &haber=-ithalat-ozel-sektor-oyunculari-icin-tam-olarak-serbest-birakilmali.

Proje. (n.d.) *Turang Transit Tasimacilik*. Retrieved from http://turangtransit.com.tr/proje.

Rekabet Kurumu. (2013a). *4646 Sayili Doğal Gaz Piyasasi Kanununda Degisiklik Yapilmasina Dair Kanun Tasarisina iliskin Rekabet Kurumu gorusu*. Retrieved from http://www.rekabet.gov.tr/File/?path=ROOT%2fDocuments%2fKurum+G%C3%B6r%C3%BC%C5%9F%C3%BC%2fdogalgazgorus.pdf.

Rekabet Kurumu. (2013b, December 10). *Avrupa Enerji Toplulugu Anlasmasi hakkinda Rekabet Kurumu gorusu*. Retrieved from http://www.rekabet.gov.tr/File/?path=ROOT%2fDocuments%2fKurum+G%C3%B6r%C3%BC%C5%9F%C3%BC%2fAvrupa+Enerji.pdf.

Samsun-Ceyhan diye bir proje yok. (2009, Agustos 7). *Odatv*. Retrieved from https://odatv.com/samsun-ceyhan-boru-hatti-diye-bir-proje-yok-0708091200.html.

Samsun-Ceyhan'da 4–5 imza daha eksik. (2006, February 7). Hurriyet. Retrieved from http://bigpara.hurriyet.com.tr/haberler/genel-haberler/samsun-ceyhan-da-4-5-imza-daha-eksik_ID551316/.

Sandalkhan, B., Bolukbasi, S., & Selcuk, F. (2018). *Surdurulebilir gelecek icin surdurulebilir enerji kisa ve orta vadeli oneriler*. (Bora Sekip Guray, Nursen Numanoglu & Cansu Uttu, Eds. Istanbul: TUSIAD.

Sobaci, M. Z., Mis, N., & Koseoglu, O. (2018). Turkey's new governmental model and the presidential organization. *SETA Perspective, 45*.

Soysal, C., Yucel, C. O., Koyuncu, T., & Tokgoz, E. (2012). *Dogalgaz sektor arastirmasiraporu*. Ankara: Rekabet Kurumu.

State Planning Organization. (2006). *Ninth development plan (2007–2013)*. Ankara.

Suphi, D. (2018, June). Rus dogal Gazinda 'al ya da ode' baskısı suruyor ozel sektor 260 milyon Dolar dogal gaz bedeli odemek zorunda. *Enerji Panorama, 6*(60).

Talus, K. (2011). *Vertical natural gas transportation capacity, upstream commodity contracts and EU competition law*. Alphen aan den Rijn: Wolters Kluwer.

Talus, K. (2013). *EU energy law and policy: A critical account*. Oxford: Oxford University Press.

Taranto, Y., & Saygin, D. (2019). *Turkiye enerji sektorunde fiyatlandirma ve piyasa disi fon akisi*. Istanbul: Shura Donusum Merkezi.

The Law Dictionary. (n.d.). *What is public interest?* 2nd ed. Retrieved from http://thelawdictionary.org/public-interest/.

Topuz, K. (2019). *The missing piece in the Turkey's gas hub ambitions*. IICEC Energy and Climate Research Paper. Retrieved from https://iicec.sabanciuniv.edu/sites/iicec.sabanciuniv.edu/files/iicec_energy_and_climate_research_paper_the_missing_piece_in_the_turkeys_gas_hub_ambitions.pdf.

TPAO ile BOTAS birlestirilmeli. (2006). *Global Enerji, 5* (10).

Turk Muhendis ve Mimar Odalari Birligi. (2006). *TMMOB enerji raporu*. Ankara: Turk Muhendis ve Mimar Odalari Birligi.

Turkiye bu yil 52,1 milyar metrekup dogal gaz tuketecek. (2019, January 26). *Hurriyet*. Retrieved from http://www.hurriyet.com.tr/ekonomi/turkiye-bu-yil-52-1-milyar-metrekup-dogal-gaz-tuketecek-41095300.

Turkiye Buyuk Millet Meclisi. (2005). *TBMM Tutanak Dergisi 93–1, 22. Donem, 3. Yasama Yili, 127. Birlesim*. Retrieved from http://www.tbmm.gov.tr/tutanaklar/TUTANAK/TBMM/d22/c093/tbmm22093127.pdf.

Turkiye Buyuk Millet Meclisi Disisleri Komisyonu. (2016). *Turkiye Cumhuriyeti Hukumeti ve Rusya Federasyonu Hukumeti Arasinda TurkAkim Gaz Boru Hatti Projesine Iliskin Anlasmanin Onaylanmasinin Uygun Bulunduguna Dair Kanun Tasarisi (1/788) ve Disisleri Komisyonu Raporu*. Yasama Donemi 26, Yasama Yili 2, Sira Sayisi 441.

Turkiye Buyuk Millet Meclisi Plan ve Butce Komisyonu. (2016, November 8). 2017 Yılı Merkezi Yonetim Butce Kanunu Tasarisi (1/774) Ile 2015 Yili Merkezi Yonetim Kesin Hesap Kanunu Tasarisi (1/733) ve Sayıstay Tezkereleri. *Turkiye Buyuk Millet Meclisi*. 26. Donem, 2. Yasama Yili. Retrieved from https://www.tbmm.gov.tr/develop/owa/komisyon_tutanaklari.mv_goruntule?pTutanakId=13415.

Turkiye Cumhuriyeti Hukumeti ve The Trans Anatolian Gas Pipeline Company B.V. arasinda Trans-Anadolu Dogal Gaz boru Hatti Sistemi Hakkinda Ev Sahibi Hukumet Anlasmasi. (2012). *TANAP*. Retrieved from https://www.tanap.com/content/file/TANAP_Ev_Sahibi_Hukumet_Anlasma.pdf.

Turkiye Cumhuriyeti Merkez Bankasi. (n.d.). Kurlar. Retrieved from https://evds2.tcmb.gov.tr/index.php?/evds/serieMarket/#collapse_2.

Turkiye Dogal Gaz Piyasasi. (n.d.). *Petform*. Retrieved from https://www.petform.org.tr/dogal-gaz-piyasasi/turkiye-dogal-gaz-piyasasi/#0.

Turkiye doğal gazda onemli doneme giriyor. (2019, February 26). *Hurriyet*. Retrieved from http://www.hurriyet.com.tr/ekonomi/turkiye-dogal-gazda-onemli-doneme-giriyor-41130206.

Turkiye Irak'ta 7 bin petrol kuyusunun pesinde. (2012). *Dunya Bulteni*. Retrieved from http://www.dunyabulteni.net/haber/233352/turkiye-irakta-7-bin-petrol-kuyusunun- pesinde.

Turkiye secime giderken enerji politikalari nasil sekilleniyor? (2007, Haziran). *Ekoenerji Dergisi*, *6*, 18–66.

Turkiye Wealth Fund is there for a stronger Turkey. (n.d.). *Turkiye wealth fund*. Retrieved from http://turkiyevarlikfonu.com.tr/EN/icerik/51/about-us.

Turkyilmaz, O. (2007). Turkiye dogal gaz piyasasinin yeniden yapilandirilmasi. In Makina Muhendisleri Odasi, *Uluslararasi Dogal Gaz Kongresi ve Sergisi*. Yayin No. E/2007/427 (pp. 481–504). Ankara: Makina Muhendisleri Odasi.

Turkyilmaz, O., & Aytac, O. (2018). Sonuc ve oneriler. In Makina Muhendisleri Odasi, *Turkiye'nin enerji gorunumu 2018*, Yayin no: MMO/691 (pp. 587–614). Ankara: Makina Muhendisleri Odasi.

TUSIAD. (n.d.). *4646 Sayili Dogalgaz Piyasasi Kanununda Degisiklik Yapilmasina Dair Kanun Tasarisi Taslagi hakkindaTUSIAD gorusveonerileri.* Retrieved from http://www.tusiad.org.tr/rsc/shared/file/4646-Sayili-Dogalgaz-Piyasasi-Kanununda-Degisiklik-Yapilmasina-Dair-Kanun-Tasarisi-Taslagi%2D%2D-Tusiad-Gorusu.pdf.

TUSIAD, Sanayi, Hizmetler ve Tarim Komisyonu Enerji Calisma Grubu. (2008). *Dogal gaz strateji belgesine Iliskin TUSIAD degerlendirmeleri.* TS/BSN/2008–51.

TUSIAD: Elektrik piyasasinda kamu agirligini koruyor. (2007, June 5). *Hurriyet.* Retrieved from http://www.hurriyet.com.tr/ekonomi/tusiad-elektrik-piyasasinda-kamu-agirligini-koruyor-6650974.

TUSIAD'dan 'dogalgaz zammi geri cekilmeli' cagrisi. (2018, August 1). *Hurriyet.* Retrieved from http://www.hurriyet.com.tr/ekonomi/ekonominin-daha-dengeli-buyumesine-ihtiyacimiz-var-40915188.

Ucar, R. (2017). Turkiye dogal gaz piyasasinda arz, talep ve fiyat dinamiklerinin gelecegi. *Petform.* Retrieved from http://docs.petform.org.tr/docs/ridvan_ucar_ie%C3%BC_altinci_enerji_yonetimi_ve_politikalari_calistayi_11052017.pdf.

Yafimava, K. (2011). *The transit dimension of EU energy security: Russian gas transit across Ukraine, Belarus and Moldova.* Oxford: Oxford University Press.

Yanit gelmezse belgeyi aciklayacagim. (2007, July 10). Haberler. Retrieved from https://www.haberler.com/yanit-gelmezse-belgeyi-aciklayacagim-haberi/

Yildiz: BOTAS dogalgaz satisinda kuculecek. (2013). *Turkiye.* Retrieved from http://www.turkiyegazetesi.com.tr/ekonomiturkiye/32255.aspx.

Yilmaz, S. (2006, January 29). Kamer'in ortagi Baltaci'nin adresinde. *Milliyet.* Retrieved from http://www.milliyet.com.tr/2006/01/29/yazar/yilmaz.html.

Yilmaz, H.M. (2014). *Avrupa Birligi Uyelik Surecinde Stratejik Bir Kaldirac: Siyasi ve Iktisadi Boyutlarıyla Enerji Toplulugu ve Turkiye* (Unpublished expertise dissertation). Ministry of Energy and Natural Resources, Ankara.

CHAPTER 6

Conclusions: What Type of Energy Security Society is Possible in Turkey-EU Relations in the Sphere of Natural Gas?

Utilising the English School theory and narrative policy analysis, the purpose of this book is to discuss the extent to which the positions held by Turkish actors on energy security in the sphere of natural gas constrain and/or enable integration with the EU. This chapter first revisits the starting points of the study and then presents the theoretical and empirical findings. Accordingly, it compares the EU and the Turkish narratives to ascertain how the content and scope of the integration varied in the EU and Turkish narratives between January 2001 and July 2019. Furthermore, based on this analysis, the chapter concludes with the policy implications of these narratives.

For the aims of the book, it must be underlined that the word "integration" is related to the theoretical framework and does not necessarily refer to Turkey's full membership in the EU. Applying Buzan's (2004) structural interpretationist ES approach to Turkey-EU relations in the sphere of natural gas allowed us to broaden our analysis to a variety of actors and their different understandings of energy relations between Turkey and the EU. Other theoretical frameworks would have restricted the study to either co-operation or conflict, allowing for a focus on only one dimension such as territories and pipeline routes or interdependency. Therefore, the book began by drawing the theoretical framework, portraying different types of integrations, defining the concept of primary institutions and identifying how they operate in different integration types.

D. Korkmaz, *Turkey and the EU in an Energy Security Society*,
https://doi.org/10.1007/978-3-030-45774-7_6

Two concepts within the ES permit this broad analysis. First, the concept of the "three traditions" of realism, rationalism and revolutionism allowed the analysis of different types of energy relations within the same framework. This is significant because the consideration of suppliers and transit states is unavoidable when speaking about EU energy policy due to its high external dependence (Aalto and Korkmaz-Temel 2014). Moreover, the book's aim of analysing Turkey's place in the pan-European energy community, which is a common regulatory space around Europe, further creates the need for a broad framework. Buzan's revision of the three traditions and his inclusion of these three traditions as different integration types within interstate societies allowed for the discussion of different types of energy relations between Turkey and the EU. Last but not least, his inclusion of non-state actors in his interpretation of international society enabled an analysis of all actors in the Turkish domestic market and discussion of their preferences regarding their preferred type of integration with the EU.

The second concept of the ES is that of "primary institutions", which represent the basic character and purpose of society (Buzan 2004, p. xviii) and determine the integration type. The multifaceted nature of energy necessitates the simultaneous functioning of different primary institutions, such as the market, security of supply and balance of power. By ascertaining the types of primary institutions that exist in a particular society, it is possible to understand its institutional structure, which constitutes the political, economic and legal frames of that society. The institutional structure of any society provides an understanding of the dynamics of that society, such as how it functions, what is significant for its actors, what to expect from them and whether there is any room for them to manoeuvre. In this way, we are able to comprehend both the main motivations and limitations of actors in decision-making and policy-making processes. Alasuutari's (1995) and Roe's (1994) approaches to narrative analysis allowed for the identification of the primary institutions functioning in the EU and Turkish narratives. Therefore, the methodological and theoretical frameworks were complementary to each other. Accordingly, the theoretical framework allowed for the conceptualisation of the Commission's concept of the pan-European energy community as an energy security society while the examination of the EU and Turkish actors' narratives enabled comprehension of the primary institutions. This made it possible to determine the type of integration the EU and the Turkish actors would prefer to have in Turkey-EU relations in the sphere of natural gas.

In order to discuss the type of integration between the EU and Turkey in the sphere of natural gas, it was vital to identify the pan-European energy community's energy security society type and where Turkey was located in this society according to the EU actors. Analysis of the EU narratives on Turkey's role in European energy security showed that the goals of the EU actors were to diversify energy routes and extend liberal values. The existence of Russia as a great power, showing its capability to influence the securitisation process of the EU with its energy disputes and energy policies, raised concerns in an externally dependent EU in terms of security of supply and prompted EU to accelerate its diversification efforts. Turkey's geographical location close to energy rich regions made the country key to the EU's diversification efforts. Although EU actors agreed on the goal of extending liberal values, they differed on the means that should be used to achieve it. While the narratives of some actors, including some political parties in the EP, some Member States, including the UK, and the Directorate General of Enlargement, considered both the Energy Community and the opening the energy chapter for negotiations within the context of the accession process as means to achieve EU goals, other EU actors addressed only the Energy Community. The common point between their narratives was the emphasis on the necessity for intense cooperation, which would produce mutual benefits for Turkey and the EU.

From a theoretical perspective, while the goal of the diversification of energy routes demonstrates the operation of security of supply as a primary institution, extending liberal values shows the functioning of the market in the EU narratives. The narratives also referred to the impact of Russia in the EU's diversification efforts, which is evidence of the operation of great power management as a primary institution in the EU narratives. Analysis show the interaction between great power management and security of supply, great power management and the market and between the market and security of supply. Accordingly, the establishment of a competitive integrated market is expected to secure supply by creating a well-interconnected market, sending the right signals to investors and attracting exporters. Moreover, a competitive market plays the role of eliminating the capacity of the great powers (such as Russia) to influence the securitisation process. Diversification of energy suppliers and routes is expected to contribute to the forming of energy partnerships through the development of similar rules and principles with energy producers and transit states.

Regarding the type of integration, the fact that the EU has a shared rather than exclusive competence in energy issues and lacks postmodern sovereignty in energy affairs requires the consideration of the EU as a converging energy security society. A converging energy security society necessitates not only shared values but also some kind of convergence on legal and economic forms. The possibility of an external energy trade policy in the Energy Community Treaty entailed the questioning of the likelihood of a confederative energy security society. However, the Member States' concerns about their sovereignty and the requirement of unanimity to take measures to regulate imports and exports from third countries excluded any consideration of a confederative type, which requires supranationality and postmodern sovereignty. This demonstrates that the differences among the EU actors on the means that should be used to achieve the goal of extending market values signify nothing regarding the place of Turkey in the energy security society according to the EU narratives. Therefore, Turkey's place seems to be the same in the eyes of the EU regardless of its accession to the EU membership. However, while Turkey's accession to the EU will not change its desired place in the energy security society, the country would become involved in the legislative process if it was a member of the EU. Accordingly, the agreement among the EU narrators on extending market values demonstrated the EU's preference for a converging energy security society for its integration with Turkey in the sphere of natural gas (Fig. 6.1).

To understand how Turkish narrators perceived the EU's narratives on diversification and extension of market values, the Turkish narratives on pipelines and restructuring the market were analysed. The main discussion in the narratives on pipelines focused on two questions: To what extent do natural gas pipelines ensure Turkey's security of supply and to what extent do they contribute to Turkey's significance in the region? Regarding the narratives on how to restructure the market, two questions preoccupied the narrators: How do we achieve competitive/low-cost energy and what should be the role of the state within this context? Different approaches on these questions also had an impact on the definition of the concept of energy security among different Turkish narrators. These two contexts of Turkish narratives were indeed complementary to each other. While the narratives on pipelines considered natural gas pipelines to be means, the narratives on restructuring the market were related to how to operate those pipelines.

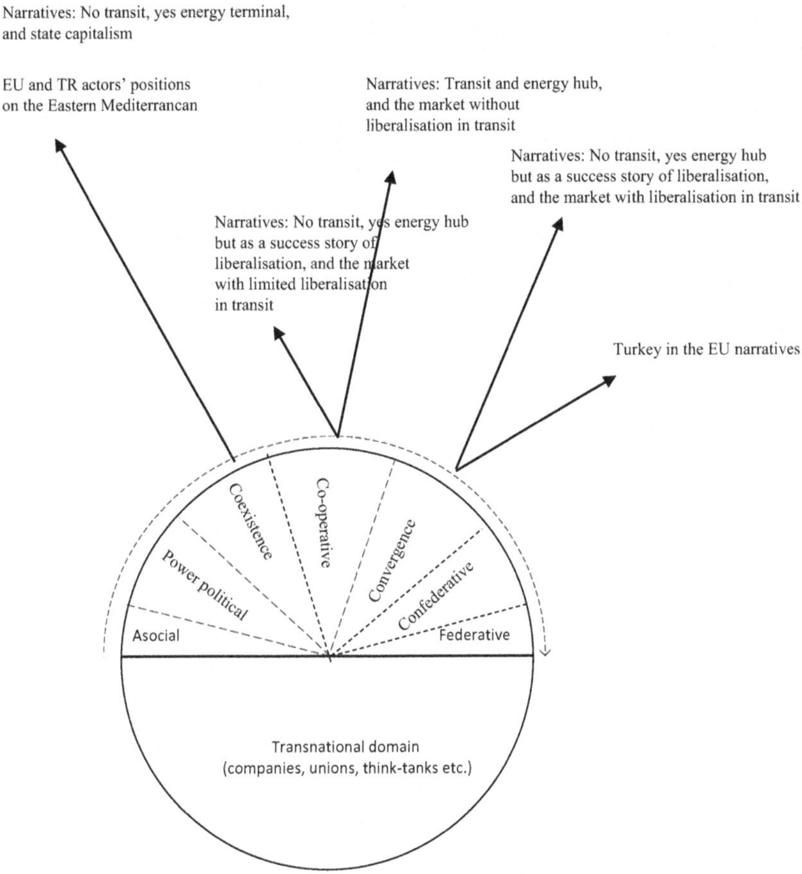

Fig. 6.1 The EU and Turkish narratives in the theoretical framework

Ensuring Turkey's security of supply was the main goal in all Turkish narratives, showing the functioning of security of supply as the foundational primary institution. The narrators were unanimous on the need to diversify suppliers given Turkey's geographical location. Narratives disagreed on the ways by which this could be achieved and on the best method to strengthen Turkey's role in the existing distribution of power. The AKP's emphasis on increasing Turkey's role in the current distribution of power manifested itself in an energy policy with a strong reference to establishing an energy hub. This derived from the AKP's foreign policy based on making Turkey a central country which would influence the transformation of the world order. However, the natural gas pipelines crossing Turkey were also considered to be tools for increasing Turkey's significance in the region and contributing to its transformation into a central country at a time when the East was achieving a greater role in international politics. Therefore, balance of power was present as a foundational primary institution in the AKP's narrative.

Other actors criticised the AKP's narrative on the grounds that being a transit state or an energy corridor would not be sufficient to ensure secure supplies. Some actors, such as the private sector and the Competition Authority, put forward that the establishment of an energy hub can be considered to be a success story of liberalisation. Others, such as the Chamber of Mechanical Engineers, were in favour of an energy terminal in which BOTAS would be the main player. They were the ones who were critical of competitiveness in their definition of the energy security. Although all Turkish narrators' positions on the transportation of natural gas to Europe were co-operative, their methods, which were mainly related to their positions on the EU's narrative on extending market values, differed from each other. On the topic of Eastern Mediterranean hydrocarbons, all Turkish actors underlined Turkey's sovereign rights in its own maritime jurisdiction zones and drew attention to Turkey's responsibilities and obligations in Cyprus as a guarantor state protecting the Turkish Cypriots' rights to benefit fairly from hydrocarbons in the region. However, there were criticisms against the AKP's policies on the Eastern Mediterranean on the grounds that these policies created "Turkey's loneliness" in the region and recommended giving emphasis on energy diplomacy with the coastal countries.

Although all narrators shared the goal of securing supply, bearing in mind Turkey's high external dependence, they differed on how to ensure secure and competitive/low-cost energy. The main dividing line between the different narratives was the state's role in the market. The three market-oriented narratives referred to competitiveness in their definition of energy security and considered the state to be either a player and regulator in a competitive market or solely a regulator. On the contrary, the state capitalist narrators mentioned low-cost energy in their definition of energy security and underlined the state's role as the leading decisive actor in the market. These narratives differed among each other with regard to the concept of public service, the role and structure of the state company in the market and the transit issue.

The analysis of these differences showed that the Turkish actors' positions on liberalising the transit segment was the critical point for being able to determine the type of integration the Turkish actors would prefer to have with the EU in the sphere of natural gas. Although the AKP's narrative on restructuring the market included the establishment of a competitive market, the transit issue was excluded from the liberalisation process. Instead, the AKP practice involved not only the continuation of the current system of intergovernmental agreements but also the granting of the task of transit to some private companies without any tendering process. The state's involvement in all stages of transporting natural gas from suppliers to Turkey and Europe was a reflection of the Turkish foreign policy understanding, which believed that pipelines would increase Turkey's significance in the region and contribute to transforming Turkey into a central country. Despite the fact that the AKP's narrative included establishing a liberal natural gas market, the reluctance to make amendments to the Natural Gas Law, proceed towards volume release, decrease the market share of BOTAS and unbundle the company begged the question of the existence of political will towards a liberal market.

On the contrary, the private sector showed full support for a liberal market without making a distinction between the transit segment and other activities in the market. Although not much data was available on the transit issue in other market-oriented narratives, there were references to a dual case, which would include maintaining the current system of intergovernmental agreements for new pipelines and allocating capacity for third-party access in the current transmission system. These narrators insisted on the necessity of having a vertically integrated but legally unbundled company, which could be owned by the state alone or a joint venture of the state company and private sector, in some of the market-oriented narratives. The purchasing power of a big company, the geostrategic location of Turkey and the goal of establishing a liquid wholesale market necessitated the creation of a vertically integrated company, according to these narrators. For the private sector, such a vertically integrated but legally unbundled company was acceptable as long as it played fairly in a competitive market.

As for the state capitalist narrators, there was a clear opposition against any foreign involvement in the transit segment. The main division between the market-oriented and the state capitalist narrators was the latter's argument that the state should be the leading and decisive economic actor in the market. Therefore, there was an insistence on the necessity of having the state company operate the transit pipelines exclusively, showing the functioning of modern sovereignty as a primary institution. From a theoretical point of view, the agreement among the state capitalist and market-oriented narrators for the requirement of a legally unbundled and vertically integrated structure in the market demonstrates the functioning of balance of power in their narratives. The same primary institution functioned in the government's narrative on pipelines. Therefore, balance of power functioned in different narratives in different contexts.

A comparison of the EU and Turkish narratives can be seen in Table 6.1. The EU's goal of diversifying suppliers was in line with the goals of the Turkish actors. The benefits were reciprocal as these goals supported the EU's efforts at diversification, bearing in mind that the EU did not import natural gas via Turkey, except for Azeri gas (Shah Deniz I) to Greece. The Turkish actors' different approaches on the establishment of an energy hub and energy terminal and on its transit status did not make any difference for the EU's goal. This suggested a good basis for co-operation between the EU and Turkey. However, the positions of the EU and Turkish actors on the Eastern Mediterranean were in conflict with each other as the EU considered Turkey's drilling and exploration activities as a breach of the sovereignty of Cyprus. On the other hand, Turkey underlined the necessity of bilateral/multilateral agreements based on equity, which is the main principle in international law, on the determination of maritime jurisdiction zones and to find a solution to the Cyprus conflict in a way that allows the Turkish Cypriots to benefit from the hydrocarbons in the Eastern Mediterranean. Although the Turkish actors diverged on the methods of protecting its national interest in the region, there was support for Turkey's positions on both the maritime jurisdiction zones and the hydrocarbons around Cyprus within the scope of the state policy.

Table 6.2 compares the primary institutions constituting the EU and Turkish narratives and demonstrates the interrelationships among those primary institutions. The EU's diversification efforts to secure supplies supported Turkey's goal of securing supply on condition that this be realised via Turkey. Any European plans to transport Caspian and Middle Eastern energy sources to Europe via Turkey provided an opportunity for

Table 6.1 Comparison of the EU and Turkish narratives

Goal of EU narratives and narrators	*Goal of Turkish narratives*	*Turkish narrators*
Diversification (All actors in the EU)	Security of supply (all narratives)	All Turkish narrators
(*The EU goal was in line with the goals of the Turkish actors; however, the positions of the EU and Turkish actors on the Eastern Mediterranean were in conflict with each other*)	Establishment of an energy hub and being an energy corridor, protecting national interests in the Eastern Mediterranean (the name of the narrative: transit state and energy) hub	The government
	Establishment of an energy hub as a success story of liberalisation, protecting national interests in the Eastern Mediterranean (the name of the narrative: no transit, yes energy hub but as a success story of liberalisation)	Private sector, other market-oriented narrators such as the Competition Authority, Republican People's Party, some think-tanks
	Establishment of an energy terminal, protecting national interests in the Eastern Mediterranean (the name of the narrative: no transit, yes energy terminal)	The union of Petrol-Is, the Union of Chambers of Turkish Engineers and Architects, etc.
Extending market values via Energy Community (Directorate-General for Neighbourhood and Enlargement Negotiations of the European Commission, some Member States (e.g. the UK) in the European Council and Council of the European Union, some parties in the Parliament) (*This was in harmony only with the narrative of the private sector*)	Establishment of a competitive market, except transit (the name of the narrative: the market without liberalisation in transit)	The government

(*continued*)

Table 6.1 (continued)

Goal of EU narratives and narrators	*Goal of Turkish narratives*	*Turkish narrators*
Extending market values via the Energy Community and accession process (Some Member States (e.g. Cyprus) in the European Council and Council of the European Union, some parties in Parliament) (*This was in harmony only with the narrative of the private sector*)	Establishment of a competitive market (the name of the narrative: the market with liberalisation in transit)	Private sector
	Establishment of a competitive market, a dual policy in transit (the name of the narrative: the market with limited liberalisation in transit)	Other market-oriented narrators such as the Competition Authority, Republican People's Party, some think-tanks
	Low-cost energy (the name of the narrative: state capitalism)	The union of Petrol-Is, the Union of Chambers of Turkish Engineers and Architects etc.

Turkey to take into consideration its own security of supply. Accordingly, any Turkish plans to secure its supply and contact energy suppliers offered the potential for the EU to diversify its sources. Similarly, the EU's general goal to secure supply had the potential to support Turkey's diversification aim, and vice versa. The interrelationship between the EU's security of supply and balance of power in the Turkish narratives is one-sided since the EU's diversification goal was expected to create advantages for Turkey according to the AKP narrative. The interrelationship between great power management and security of supply in the EU's narrative was also apparent between the EU and Turkey. The existence of Russian great power and the necessity to diversify suppliers in the EU narratives do not contradict the Turkish narratives on securing supplies. Any EU efforts to obtain Caspian and the Middle Eastern energy sources and bypass Russia have the potential to contribute to Turkey's security of supply. The

Table 6.2 Comparison of primary institutions constituting the EU and Turkish narratives

EU narratives	*Primary institutions in EU narratives*	*Primary institutions in Turkish narratives*	*Turkish narratives*
EU narrative on diversification	Security of supply Great power management	Security of supply Balance of power Modern sovereignty	Turkish narratives on pipelines
EU narratives on extending market values	The market	The market State capitalism Security of supply Balance of power Great power management Modern sovereignty Contemporary sovereignty	Turkish narratives on restructuring the market

functioning of modern sovereignty in the Turkish narratives with regard to the Eastern Mediterranean did not match with any of the primary institutions in the EU narratives.

The co-operation regarding pipelines did not totally prevail in the narratives related to the market (Table 6.1). The EU actors' narratives on extending market values via the Energy Community or the Energy Community and the accession process were in harmony only with the Turkish private sector's narrative. Other market-oriented narrators were not entirely in line with the EU's narratives on extending market values. Their narratives and/or practices on the transit issue as well as the proposal of some narrators to keep the state monopoly in imports prevented full harmony with the EU legislation. According to the market-oriented narratives, the establishment of a competitive integrated market in the EU supported security of supply in Turkey as an integrated market with the same rules was assumed to contribute to secure supply. The EU's goal of extending its market values aimed to decrease the influence of the Russian great power in Turkey's securitisation process, although the liberalisation process increased the power of Russia in the downstream market with the help of transfer of BOTAS' contracts to the private companies in which Gazprom's subsidiaries were holding shares. There was an interrelation between the market institution and contemporary sovereignty, as harmonisation of legislation within the Energy Community paved the way for new regulative rules, such as legitimate intervention. As for the state capitalist narrative, their goal of ensuring low-cost energy was not in harmony with the EU's goal of extending market values owing to their opposition to competitiveness. Similarly, there was no relationship between either the market institution and state capitalism or the market institution and modern sovereignty, which functioned in the state capitalist and some of the market-oriented narratives with regard to the transit issue (Table 6.2).

Analysis shows that the type of integration changed according to the narrators. The positions of Turkish actors on energy security vis-à-vis relations with the EU both constrained and enabled integration (Fig. 6.1). Whereas the private sector's position enabled a converging energy security society as they aimed at full harmonisation with the EU including the transit segment, the AKP and other market-oriented narrators still favoured a co-operative energy security society. Although they were in favour of liberalisation, their different positions on the transit issue and restructuring of the market, some of which were flavoured with state capitalism, and concerns about modern sovereignty regarding the Energy Community prevented full convergence in these narratives. As mentioned in the theoretical framework, modern sovereignty cannot exist beyond co-operative energy security societies. However, with regard to the developments in the Eastern Mediterranean, the co-operative narrative of the market-oriented narrators became a conflictual one. Therefore, the positions of narrators changed according to the means in question. In the union narratives, the perception of low-cost energy did not derive from the assumption that competitive markets would serve to reduce prices, although the reference to security, low-cost energy and sustainability in the definition of energy security reflected some of the shared values/rules, which are signs for a co-operative energy security society. Their recommendation for the state to retain its position as the leading economic actor and to be decisive in the market as well as their opposition to any foreign involvement in the transit segment prevented them from being co-operative, thereby constraining any further integration. Their references to modern sovereignty confirmed their position. Accordingly, the state capitalist narrative entailed a less co-operative type of integration, which was the coexistent energy security society.

From a theoretical point of view, the analysis showed the decisive roles of the market institution, state capitalism and modern sovereignty in determining the integration types for the Turkish narrators. Given the pivotal role of the narratives on how to restructure the market in determining the type of integration, the decisive positions of the market institution and state capitalism were significant. However, the role of sovereignty was equally crucial despite being a supportive primary institution in the Turkish narratives. Similar to the discussion in the theoretical chapter, there were different understandings of sovereignty among the Turkish actors and the EU, especially with regard to the Eastern Mediterranean and the transit issue. Whereas the private sector was in line with the EU on contemporary sovereignty in the gas market, the AKP, the state capitalist narrators and other market-oriented actors referred to modern sovereignty in their arguments, along with contemporary sovereignty in the latter's case. Furthermore, whereas the EU had the market institution in its narratives, the state capitalist narrators discarded the market institution and some of the market-oriented narrators had some state capitalist elements in some of their narratives (e.g. transit). Therefore, the divergence of the preferred type of integration between the Turkish market-oriented narrators (except the private sector), the Turkish state capitalist narrators and the EU actors derived from the presence of state capitalism and/or modern sovereignty in the Turkish narratives. This also showed harmony between the primary institutions of state capitalism and modern sovereignty, and the market institution and contemporary sovereignty.

What does all this mean within the context of the European Commission's concept of pan-European energy community? As Fig. 6.2[1] shows, if we think of the pan-European energy community as a circle, the private sector's narrative was in line with the pan-European energy community, and thus stayed within that circle. The state capitalist narrative was outside the pan-European energy community's circle but bordered it. This represented the shared values of security and sustainability in their definitions of energy security. However, as mentioned previously, the harmony between the EU narratives on diversification and Turkish narrators on pipelines necessitated at best co-operation and produced no further results. Rather, the narratives on how to restructure the market played a decisive role in determining Turkey's place. Since the state capitalist narrative was not in line with the EU's market institution narrative, there was

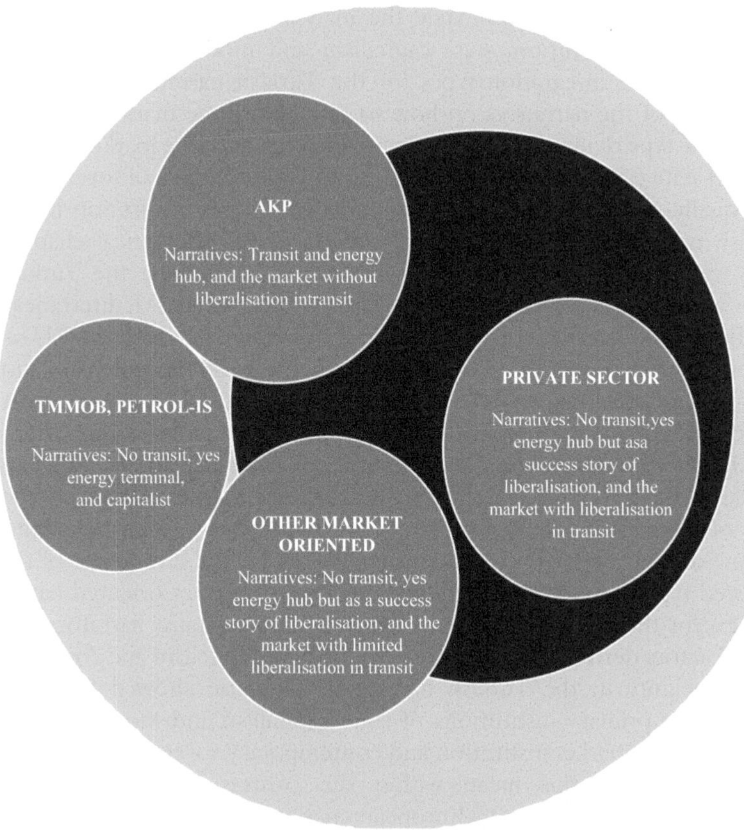

Fig. 6.2 Turkey in the European energy security society

no intersection. As for the other market-oriented narratives, they intersected with the pan-European energy community as the market institution was also present in their narratives. However, their positions on the Energy Community, marked by concerns about modern sovereignty and the transit issue, and some suggestions of some narrators with state capitalist features prevented their full inclusion in that circle.

Regarding the policy implications of the Turkish narratives, the AKP's consideration of transit pipeline projects as tools to contribute to Turkey's goal of being a central country influential in transforming the international system, necessitates co-operation with all actors including Russia and the EU. Although other Turkish narrators did not agree with this consideration, they also adopted a co-operative approach in transporting natural gas to Europe. Here, the EU's policy for diversification of suppliers and Turkey's goal of ensuring its security of supply suggest a good basis for co-operation in the sphere of natural gas. Regarding the relations with Russia, Turkey's dependency weakens its bargaining power and requires Turkey to support competing projects and seek a more balanced relationship, which requires continuous co-operation with other energy actors, including the EU. Therefore, the AKP's close relations with Russia would not prevent Turkey from being co-operative in competing projects. In light of the narratives, we may witness more efforts to reduce dependency in the event of political changes.

While Turkey's pipeline politics necessitate the continuation of co-operation with the EU, relations were incompatible regarding the Eastern Mediterranean. Since Turkey's position on the maritime jurisdiction zones is in line with the international jurisprudence, it is not likely that Turkey will change its position as long as there is no bilateral/multilateral agreement among the countries in the region on the delimitation of maritime jurisdiction zones. While the motivation on the problem of maritime jurisdiction zones derived from concerns on sovereignty, Turkey's aim in its reactions on the hydrocarbon activities of Cyprus and international energy companies in the region was to change the status quo on the Island, which it believes serves the interests of the Southern Cypriots. There was support from other energy actors who made declarations on the Eastern Mediterranean for Turkey's positions in the maritime jurisdiction zones and on the hydrocarbons around Cyprus, although their tools for pursuing foreign policy on this issue may differ. The Turkish Cypriot government's proposal to establish a joint committee for the benefiting from hydrocarbon resources in the region including revenue sharing can be considered a positive step for launching co-operation among related parties. Supporting such initiatives, rather than imposing sanctions, could contribute to the image of the EU as a "peace project".

Although establishment of a trading natural gas hub dominated the AKP's narrative, the limited progress in the liberalisation of the natural gas market hampers the achievement of this goal. Furthermore, the lack of initiation for the amendment of the Natural Gas Market Law since 2014, reluctance for volume release, lack of progress on the unbundling of BOTAS and the pricing policy urge us to question the presence of the political will to establish a framework for liberalisation in the market. The reluctance to a liberal regime on transit legislation is related to the AKP's foreign policy considerations on the utilisation of geopolitical location to increase the power of the country. In the event of a political change, alterations to the goal of establishing a competitive market would not be expected. Any re-structuring within BOTAS would not prevent the state from being the main shareholder. Efforts to transform the company into a national energy champion with a legally unbundled but vertically integrated structure can be witnessed, according to the narratives. The eventual termination of the long-term contracts in the 2020s provide an opportunity for any governing party(ies) to make progress in establishing a liberal market. Any political change would not make a difference in Turkey's reluctance to harmonise its transit legislation, since consideration of Turkey's geographical location as a leverage in pipeline negotiations is a common understanding among politicians. Therefore, continuation of intergovernmental agreements for transit projects would be expected. Examination of the Turkish narratives demonstrates that the significance of the transit issue for many actors has the potential to delay the harmonisation in this segment until accession while the analysis of the EU narratives shows that it makes no difference from the EU's point of view whether Turkey is a member of the EU or not, as long as it is a member of the Energy Community.

From an empirical point of view, analysis can be continued from where this book leaves off by inquiring into the driving forces in order to discuss the extent to which further integration is feasible in the Turkish actors' narratives. Furthermore, similar studies could be conducted using the same theoretical and methodological frameworks on different energy sources, such as renewables. A comparison of the positions of Turkish actors on different chapters in the accession process can also be made. This analysis showed that the English School theory and Buzan's structural interpretationist approach are indeed applicable to different regions and fields, such as the EU and energy. From a theoretical point of view, one can apply the same theoretical framework to different countries and regions. The framework can be developed by enlarging the unit, such as global energy affairs, and exploring the interrelationship between different primary institutions. Moreover, one can apply this kind of international society to different fields, such as agriculture or taxation. From a methodological point of view, generating a metanarrative and using that metanarrative to reframe the policy problem are possible further steps.

Note

1. Please note that the fact that the circles representing Turkish narratives are in different sizes does not matter. In addition, this figure illustrates the relationship between Turkey and the pan-European energy security society according to different Turkish narratives. The relationship among the Turkish narratives is not taken into consideration.

Bibliography

Aalto, P., & Korkmaz-Temel, D. (2014). European energy security: Natural gas and the integration process. *Journal of Common Market Studies, 52*(4), 758–774.

Alasuutari, P. (1995). *Researching culture qualitative method and cultural studies.* London, Thousand Oaks, New Delhi: SAGE Publications.

Buzan, B. (2004). *From international to world society.* Cambridge: Cambridge University Press.

Roe, E. (1994). *Narrative policy analysis theory and practice.* Durham and London: Duke University Press.

Index[1]

[1] Note: Page numbers followed by 'n' refer to notes.

D. Korkmaz, *Turkey and the EU in an Energy Security Society*,
https://doi.org/10.1007/978-3-030-45774-7

P

R

S

T

The manufacturer's authorised representative in the EU is Springer
Nature Customer Service Centre GmbH, Europaplatz 3, 69115 Heidelberg,
Germany. If you have any concerns regarding our products, please
contact ProductSafety@springernature.com

Printed and bound by CPI Group (UK) Ltd, Croydon, CR0 4YY
30/09/2026
02225645-0004